Upgrading & Fixing L...
For Dummies®

D1194997

My Laptop Info

Manufacturer's name*: _____

Model name*: _____

Model number*: _____

Serial number*: _____

Installed RAM: _____ MB

Hard drive capacity: _____ GB

Operating system and version:

_____

Operating system product key*:

_____

While the operating system is first starting,
my laptop's BIOS Setup is accessed by pressing
this key: _____

Modifications I made to the original hardware:

_____

_____

*Look on the underside of the machine for a sticker that
should have this information and more.*

Major Software Installed

Office suite product name and version number:

_____

Location of original discs and serial number:

_____

Support web site and phone number:

_____

Graphics software product name and version
number: _____

Location of original discs and serial number:

_____

Support web site and phone number:

_____

Video and audio editor/playback software and
version number: _____

Location of original discs and serial number:

_____

Support web site and phone number:

_____

Support and Warranty

Purchase date: _____

Store or online dealer name: _____

Order number or sales receipt number:

_____

Dealer's customer service phone number:

_____

Length of manufacturer's warranty: _____

Length of extended warranty: _____

Manufacturer's technical support phone number:

_____

Manufacturer's technical support web site:

_____

Internet and E-Mail

Internet service provider (ISP):

_____

Internet login/sign-on name*:

_____

ISP technical support phone:

_____

ISP technical support web site:

_____

My primary e-mail address*:

_____

My secondary e-mail address*:

*Do not write down your passwords in the same place as
your login name.*

For Dummies: Bestselling Book Series for Beginners

Upgrading & Fixing Laptops For Dummies®

Cheat Sheet

Things I Must Remember to Do

How Often	What to Do
Once a week (if used daily) or before trips	Install an antivirus program and keep it updated with new virus definitions.
Weekly	Install a Registry and system checker utility and examine if the laptop is in regular use. Conduct more frequent tests of the system if you experience problems using the computer.
At least once weekly	Check the hard disk for fragmentation if the laptop is in regular use. Defragment the drive any time the utility suggests that files are inefficiently stored.
Before major changes (like installations), after trips, after a full day's work on the road	Make backup copies of all essential data files on removable media (such as a CD-R, DVD-R, flash memory disk key, or external hard drive), or by transferring copies of files over a network to a hard drive on another machine.
Before major changes (like installations)	Check the Windows system settings to assure that important utilities such as System Restore are properly configured to maintain backup copies of settings, Registry entries, and other details for use in recovering from a failure.

Putting My Hands on the Controls

Control	Getting There
Control Panel	Start⇨Control Panel. Or from any folder window, at the right end of the address bar, ↓⇨Control Panel.
Device Manager	Start⇨My Computer⇨Properties⇨Hardware tab⇨Device Manager.
Display settings	Start⇨Control Panel⇨Display icon⇨Settings tab. From here you can adjust screen resolution and color quality or run Windows troubleshooting.
Date and time settings	Start⇨Control Panel⇨Date and Time. Adjust the date and time manually. Click the Time Zone tab to set the machine's geographic location. Click Internet Time to instruct the computer to synchronize with an Internet time server.
Hard disk drive capacity and utilities	Start⇨My Computer to show available hard disk drives; click to highlight a drive and then right-click to display the contextual menu. Click Properties. From the General tab you can see the drive's total capacity and amount in use. Click the Tools tab to display the built-in Windows error-checking, defragmentation, and backup utilities.
Security Center	Start⇨Control Panel⇨Security Center. Here you can check the status of the Windows firewall, automatic updates, and most antivirus software utilities.
System Restore	Start⇨All Programs⇨Accessories⇨System Tools⇨System Restore.

These suggestions are based on Windows XP; older versions of Windows operate in a similar but not identical manner.

For Dummies: Bestselling Book Series for Beginners

*Upgrading &
Fixing Laptops*
FOR
DUMMIES®

by Corey Sandler

WILEY

Wiley Publishing, Inc.

Upgrading & Fixing Laptops For Dummies®

Published by
Wiley Publishing, Inc.
111 River Street
Hoboken, NJ 07030-5774

WILEY

621.391
San

About the Author

Corey Sandler has written more than 150 books on personal computers, business topics, travel, and sports. A former Gannett Newspapers reporter and columnist, he also worked as an Associated Press correspondent covering business and political beats. One of the pioneers of personal computer journalism, he was an early writer for publications, including *Creative Computing*. He became the first executive editor of *PC Magazine* in 1982 at the start of that magazine's meteoric rise. He also was the founding editor of IDG's *Digital News*. He has appeared on the NBC's *Today Show,* CNN, ABC, National Public Radio's *Fresh Air,* dozens of local radio and television shows, and been the subject of many newspaper and magazine articles.

He lives with his family on Nantucket Island, off the coast of Massachusetts at the very end of the information superhighway. From his office window, when the fog clears, he can see the microwave tower that carries signals from his keyboard to the mainland 30 miles away.

He has lugged his laptop across the United States and around the world. Recent trips have seen him searching for and sometimes finding WiFi web connections and cell phone signals in Machu Picchu at 14,000 feet in the Peruvian Andes, in New Zealand, Australia, the Canadian Arctic, and in Svalbard, the northernmost inhabited territory of Europe, with the Arctic Circle at the edge of the North Pole ice pack.

He can be reached through his web site, www.econoguide.com.

Publisher's Acknowledgments

We're proud of this book; please send us your comments through our online registration form located at www.dummies.com/register.

Some of the people who helped bring this book to market include the following:

Acquisitions, Editorial, and Media Development

Project Editor: Tonya Maddox Cupp

Acquisitions Editor: Greg Croy

Technical Editor: Allen Wyatt

Editorial Manager: Jodi Jensen

Media Development Manager: Laura VanWinkle

Media Development Supervisor: Richard Graves

Editorial Assistant: Amanda M. Foxworth

Cartoons: Rich Tennant (www.the5thwave.com)

Production

Project Coordinator: Kathryn Shanks

Layout and Graphics: Carl Byers, Andrea Dahl, Mary J. Gillot, Barry Offringa, Lynsey Osborn, Heather Ryan

Proofreaders: Leeann Harney, Jessica Kramer, TECHBOOKS Production Services

Indexer: TECHBOOKS Production Services

Publishing and Editorial for Technology Dummies

Richard Swadley, Vice President and Executive Group Publisher

Andy Cummings, Vice President and Publisher

Mary Bednarek, Executive Acquisitions Director

Mary C. Corder, Editorial Director

Publishing for Consumer Dummies

Diane Graves Steele, Vice President and Publisher

Joyce Pepple, Acquisitions Director

Composition Services

Gerry Fahey, Vice President of Production Services

Debbie Stailey, Director of Composition Services

Contents at a Glance

Table of Contents

Introduction

We are not far from the time when a fully functional laptop computer will be a hair smaller and a gram lighter than the book you're holding in your hands. But we are still lifetimes away from the day when we no longer need a well-written and organized sheaf of printed pages to reveal how to get started and help us understand how to make the best use of high technology.

This book requires no power source other than the human mind. It will operate in any temperature and weather condition. And, I hope, it will help you fix things when they are broken and improve things when they are lagging.

I was present at the creation of the PC and I assisted at the birth of the first portable computer, which was about the size of a microwave and came with a long electrical extension cord. Since then I have worked my way through at least six generations and more than a dozen models of steadily lighter, smaller, faster, and better.

About This Book

First of all, this book sees the world through the eyes of a laptop owner. Laptops can do everything that a desktop PC can do, and in much the same way, but are built very differently.

The important difference is the construction. This book explores all sorts of ways to replace or upgrade components that slide into, connect to, or attach onto a modern laptop. You open hatches and compartments, too. But you will not open the sealed box that encases the motherboard and holds in place the LCD screen; that's not a job for Dummies. . .or even for most experts. It's too complex, too tight a working space, and usually not an economically sensible thing to do.

My goal is to give you news you can use, information that will help you fix problems, replace parts, and add external upgrades and workarounds. Laptop computers are not quite like the one-horse cart that Oliver Wendell Holmes memorialized in poetry; that wonderful one-hoss shay, built in such a logical way, ran 100 years to a day before all the pieces fell apart at the same time. Different components have differing life expectancies. Part of this book is a lesson in economics; does a broken machine stay or go?

Conventions Used in This Book

You're going to see some specific conventions regarding content. New words are italicized and explained. The right arrow in commands just separates the things you click. (For instance, "Choose Start⇨Control Panel" means you click Start, then click Control Panel.) Finally, and most specifically, *disk* refers to a floppy disk or hard drive; *disc* refers to a CD or DVD.

What You're Not to Read

You don't have to read the book from page one straight through to the end, although I'm sure you'll end up as a better person for the experience. If you know what you're looking for, you can dive right in at the section that deals with the problem you need to fix or the part you want to upgrade. You can also skip stuff accompanied by a Technical Stuff icon.

Foolish Assumptions

You're smart. You're smart enough to own and use a laptop, and you're smart enough to know you can use some expert advice on its care and feeding. And you're also smart enough to know that laptops are not the same as a desktop PC. If a video card fails on a full-sized personal computer, you or the tech-nosavvy teenage child of your Cousin Arthur can run down to the nearest computer store, buy a $29.95 replacement, remove a few screws on the PC case, and plug in the replacement. Not so with a laptop.

Windows in this book refers to Windows XP, which is at this moment Microsoft's latest and greatest operating system. If you are still using an older operating system — no older than Windows 98, Windows ME, or Windows 95 — you'll find that the commands and screens are similar enough that you can make adjustments to the text on your own.

How This Book Is Organized

This book is divided into six parts:

Part 1: Putting a Computer in Your Lap

Part I presents a field guide to the common laptop, telling you how to spot its important distinguishing characteristics and how to handle it with care.

Part II: Explaining What Could Possibly Go Wrong

Part II moves on to a meandering through the minefields. I offer some emergency fixes for common predicaments and some words of wisdom about how to decide whether a major repair makes economic sense or whether it is time to go shopping for a new laptop.

Part III: Laying Hands on the Major Parts

Part III delves deeper into the soul of the machine, with a tour of the memory, BIOS, and the motherboard and instructions on how to use facilities of Windows to check on their status, perform troubleshooting, and make critical adjustments. I also go inside peripherals, giving the information you need to know about disk drives (hard, floppy, and CD/DVD), the keyboard, pointing devices, and the LCD display.

Part IV: Failing to Communicate

Part IV presents the essentials of communication, an increasingly important part of the laptop experience. I'll show you how to break out of the box with wired and wireless networks, modems, and ports (including USB, FireWire, PC Card, and serial) that connect to external devices.

Part V: The Software Side of Life

Part V explores the software side of life, including the operating system and applications.

Part VI: The Part of Tens

Part VI is the world-renowned and endearing "Part of Tens" for Dummies. You'll find lists of problems, cures, and some of my favorite laptop things.

Icons Used in This Book

Here's the sort of guy I am: If you ask me for a cold beer, I might start in on an explanation of Bernoulli's Principle and how a refrigerator is related to the aerodynamics of a Boeing 757. I love this stuff; you can stop and learn all sorts of useless technical stuff or you can use your random access eyeballs to skip to the Tips, Remembers, and Warnings.

Here you'll find smart shortcuts, clever workarounds, and cool ideas that come from years of practice, experience, and gigantic blunders made by the author, his friends, and kind strangers.

This is, of course, something you shouldn't forget. It's important enough to get its own icon.

Be careful out there. Failure to read these warnings could invalidate the author's warranty.

Where to Go from Here

For some of you, the best advice is to go to where the problem is: This book is organized by component and subsystem. If the hard drive is not spinning, go to the section about hard drives; that's not so difficult, right?

If all is well and you're just the inquisitive type, good on you. Read the book in any order that interests you and remember the old Boy Scout promise: Be prepared. (Works for girls, men, and women, too.)

Part I
Putting a Computer in Your Lap

The 5th Wave   By Rich Tennant

JEEZ—YOU'D THINK THESE PEOPLE NEVER SAW A LAPTOP BEFORE!

GATE 9   ATE 8

In this part . . .

All laptops are computers, but not all computers are laptops. Size matters. Though the basic design of a PC applies to each, when it comes to laptop/notebook/portable devices, know the important differences: Don't drop them, don't let them get wet, and don't expect to easily plug in new internal parts.

This part of the book begins with an up-close tour of laptop design. By definition, a laptop is smaller, lighter, and tougher than a desktop machine. And it must be able to be unplugged from the wall and moved: to other desks, to cramped seatback trays on airliners, to factory floors, to classrooms, and all manner of places of convenience and peril. After the tour you explore ways and means to keep your machine in good working health.

Chapter 1

Fielding the Guide to the Common Laptop

In this chapter

▶ Taking the measure of a laptop computer

▶ Powering up for portable computing

▶ Viewing your work and pointing at words and icons

laptop is just like a desktop computer, except that it has to be

✔ Smaller

✔ Lighter

✔ Tougher

✔ Much less demanding of electrical power

It also has to include

✔ A high-capacity, relatively lightweight battery that can be recharged over and over again

✔ A built-in high-resolution flat LCD color display

✔ An easy-to-use but unobtrusive mouse, trackball, or other pointing device

That's not too much to ask, is it? Actually, it's quite a lot — quite a lot in a very small package.

Calling Them Anything but Late for Supper

Way, way back in the ancient history of personal computers, when I was the first executive editor of *PC Magazine,* the high-tech world was stunned at the arrival of a class of suitcase-sized computers that came with a small built-in CRT monitor, a handle on top, and a long electrical cord. They were called "portable" computers and they were portable — in the same way that you can move a television set from room to room. We preferred to call them "luggable" or "transportable" computers. Later on, the first battery-powered computers using monochrome and later color LCD screens arrived; they were called *laptop computers.* Some assumed that the user had a rather ample laptop and they (the computer, not the users) barely fit on an airplane's seatback table.

As internal components became smaller, lighter, and more tightly packed together, manufacturers coined the term *notebook computer* to indicate a machine with roughly the dimensions of a thick pad of letter-sized paper. Over time, the difference in size between laptops and notebooks became a matter of no more than an inch or two in length and width, and a fraction of an inch in thickness. Today, users can choose to pay more for a machine with a larger LCD display or one that weighs a pound or two less.

In this book I use the terms *laptop* and *notebook computer* interchangeably. As far as I'm concerned, it's a distinction without a difference.

Smaller but mighty

Why is smaller better than larger? Here's the most common reason: "The captain has illuminated the seatbelt sign as we prepare for landing. Please place your seatback and tray table in the upright position and stow all personal items beneath the seat in front of you." Or, you may want a notebook computer that you can bring with you to college classes or research libraries. And some users just like the compactness of an all-in-one PC that can be used in the den, the kitchen, and occasional excursions into the living room to show DVDs.

The length and width of a laptop may have reached its minimum size because of the need to offer a full-size keyboard and the desire of most users for a large display. The smallest of the small are just a bit larger than a sheet of office paper: about 11.5 inches wide by 8.5 inches deep. Laptops with the largest LCD screens are about 14 inches wide and 10 inches deep.

The thickness of the laptop may make a difference to some when it comes to slipping it into a handsome leather briefcase or a cushioned shoulder bag. The thinnest of the thin are as little as 1.3 inches thick.

Buy the numbers

IDC, which counts laptops and most everything else electronic and sells information back to the industry, ranks HP/Compaq and Dell Computers neck-and-neck in market share. In 2004, the two companies between them sold just under 50 percent of all notebook computers worldwide. In third place was Toshiba with about 12 percent of the market, followed by IBM with about 9 percent. Apple, which marches to its own drummer in technology and operating system, had about a 5-percent share; Sony also had about 5 percent of the market, and Gateway about 3 percent. Other companies held onto pieces of the remaining 20 percent of market share.

Lighter than a feather

Placed on a desk or on the floor, the weight of your computer is not much of an issue. A full-featured tower computer can weigh 30 to 40 pounds, and an accompanying monitor another 30 pounds . . . but once they are installed they just sit there.

But, of course, the whole reason behind a laptop or notebook computer is *portability*, whether it is a matter of moving the machine from one room to the next or running down the seemingly endless corridors of O'Hare Airport to catch the 4:55 flight to LA.

Over the years, makers of laptop computers have been engaged in a frenetic weight loss program, shedding pounds, then ounces, and now every possible gram. Just a few years ago, a 12-pound laptop was considered a lightweight champion; today's hottest svelte models can weigh in at as little as 4 pounds.

The more you travel with a laptop, the more your shoulders, arms, and back will appreciate the missing pounds. The biggest gains (or should I say losses) have come in slimmed-down hard drives, batteries, and the computer case itself.

Tougher than nails

A desktop or tower computer doesn't get moved from place to place very often, and when it does change location it is almost always turned off and carefully handled while in transit.

It's just the opposite for a laptop. By design, these devices are meant to be transported and are often powered up and running while they are moved. If my personal laptop had an odometer on it, I estimate it would show several hundred thousand miles by road, train, plane, cruise ship, and ferry boat to and from Europe, Asia, and every corner of the U.S. Truth be told, I've dropped the carrying case a few times and the computer itself has slid off several seat-back tables in its life. But it keeps on ticking. Why? Because it was designed for such a life.

A well-made laptop includes a sturdy case that shields the LCD and the internal motherboard from damage, and a hard disk drive with components that are capable of withstanding a reasonable amount of jolting and jostling.

Some makers protect the integrity of the notebook with internal braces, cushioning, and other design elements. And then there are the highest-tech solutions, including IBM's Active Protection System which includes a motion sensor that continuously monitors the movement of some of the company's ThinkPad notebooks; if the sensor detects a sudden change in direction—like the start of a tumble toward the floor—it can temporarily stop the motion of the hard drive and park its sensitive read-write heads within 500 milliseconds (which you and I might better understand as half a second.)

A well-made laptop also includes a carefully designed power supply and electrical components able to deal with a reasonable range of fluctuations in voltage. (Most modern laptops are able to automatically switch between wall current of about 110 volts as supplied in the United States, Canada, and a few other parts of the world, or 220 volts as you will find in Europe, Asia, and most everywhere else.)

Thinking like a Troubleshooter

When something doesn't seem quite right with your laptop, or if it flat-out refuses to compute, the first thing to do is to ask yourself this critical question: What has changed since the last time the machine worked properly?

Did you add a piece of software or make a change (an update, perhaps) to the operating system? Not all improvements leave the laptop in better shape than it was before you "fixed" it. Did you add new hardware, or a software *driver* to identify the component to the system? Computer techies invented a wonderfully dweebish word for this sort of situation: They'll suggest you *uninstall* something you installed and see if the machine works properly. Did you drop the machine, spill a gallon of lemonade on the keyboard, or run the laptop through an airport X-ray machine 877 times in a row? You may have some physical damage to repair.

I cover each of these situations, and many more, in the sections of this book.

Making a High-tech Power Play

Over the history of laptops, designers have been pulled in two directions:

- ✔ Machines with faster and faster processing speeds, more and more memory, higher-speed hard drives, CD and DVD drives, and bigger and brighter LCD screens. All of these require bits and pieces of the stored electricity in a laptop's battery.

- ✔ Requirements by users that their machines run for hours between recharges.

The solutions to this push-and-pull problem have included great advancements in the capacity of batteries and tremendous reductions in the consumption of electricity. On the battery side the solution did involve larger and heavier cells; modern batteries are lighter and smaller than ever.

Demanding less power

On the demand side, the newest class of processors including the Intel Pentium M are designed to take less energy to operate and to automatically step down their speed and power requirements whenever possible. Tight integration of chipsets on the motherboard also reduces power demand, and the chipsets themselves include sophisticated circuits that can reduce power consumption when possible and put the laptop into a sleep mode if nothing is going on at the moment.

Think about the life of a computer: Unless you are managing something extremely complex and doing it in real time — like controlling your personal space shuttle or calculating hundred-digit prime numbers, most of the time your machine is using just a small portion of its power. For example, while I'm writing this sentence, Microsoft Word is requiring only about 4 percent of the attention of my magnificent Pentium 4 processor. When I stop to admire the previous sentence, CPU usage drops to close to zero.

If you want to check the performance of your machine, go to the Windows Task Manager of Windows XP or Windows 98 by clicking the Ctrl+Alt+Del key combination and then selecting the Performance tab. CPU usage is displayed. See Figure 1-1 for a sample reading from a modern laptop; at the moment I took that screen shot, there was a streaming video image from a baseball game coming over the Internet, the laptop's WiFi adapter was searching for a connection, and the system's antivirus and system monitor utilities were active.

WiFi, about which you read a great deal more in Chapter 14, is the most common form of wireless communication used by laptops. WiFi, as well as wired networks, make a large demand on the system's microprocessor and other components. When they work well, everything is just peachy; when there's a problem with communication, it can spread like melted chocolate throughout your machine, slowing everything down to a sticky crawl.

Figure 1-1:
A perform-
ance report
from a
laptop under
a moderate
load. The
CPU is
lightly
loaded and
the system
has plenty
of working
room
available.

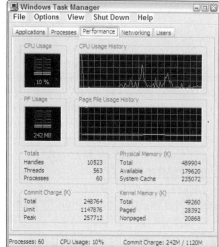

On a desktop machine, the difference between a hard-working processor and a more efficient system costs a few hundredths of a penny more per minute in operations, but the bucket of power is kept full by the plug that leads to the wall socket. On a laptop, though, every electron drawn from the battery is gone from the bucket until you get the chance to recharge.

Packing battery power

You don't have to be a molecular scientist to come up with the specifications for the ideal laptop battery: It should be as small and lightweight as possible, be able to accept and hold enough power to allow use for several hours or more (many business people define acceptable battery life as six hours or a coast-to-coast airline flight, whichever ends first), and be rechargeable dozens or hundreds of times before giving up the ghost.

The most common technology for laptop computers today uses a lithium ion solution; it replaced an earlier design based on nickel metal hydride (NiMH). Lithium batteries weigh less, which is good, and do not suffer from *memory effect* like NiMH units; that doesn't mean that the older batteries would know you by name — it means that they used to lose their ability to accept a full charge if they were recharged before they were fully drained.

Lithium ion batteries act more or less the same throughout their entire lives, and then just die. Running the display at its brightest, with no provisions for auto-dim or hibernation, depletes the battery much faster than other settings.

Many laptop manufacturers provide a power management utility that allows you to make settings that adjust screen brightness, hibernation times, and even the speed of certain classes of microprocessors to allow users to eke out every last drop of power from a battery. On most utilities you can also set audible or on-screen alarms for low power and instruct the system how you want it to act if the battery reaches a critically weak level. An example of a Toshiba utility is shown in Figure 1-2, along with a detailed report on the battery in use; a handful of laptops allow users to install a second battery in an internal bay.

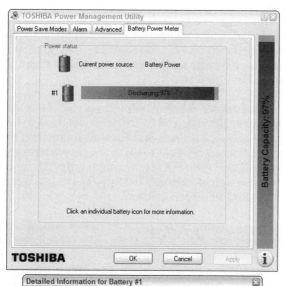

Figure 1-2: A power management utility permits adjustments in the way a laptop uses the battery.

Viewing with Clarity, Pointing with Precision

Okay, I admit it: I'm not just an author, I'm a technogeek. I bought one of the very first IBM PCs (paying nearly $4,000 for something that would not compare very well today to the processing power of my cell phone). And I also owned several of the very first luggable, then portable, computers. One of the first true laptops I worked with was an Epson PX-8, which was blessed with a very dim 8-line monochrome screen. It was capable of displaying text only, in one size and yes, all I could look at was eight lines of text at a time. But in 1983 this machine was the bee's knees; I wrote several books on my daily rail commute to work.

Consider now a high-end notebook of 2006. You could buy a machine with a 17-inch color display with resolution as high as $1,440 \times 900$ pixels, or a slightly smaller but sharper 15.4-inch display with $1,920 \times 1,200$ resolution. And you'd pay hundreds or even thousands of dollars *less* for the privilege.

I explain more about resolution a bit later in the book, but here's the bottom line: More is better. As far as screen size: Bigger is more beautiful and may be easier to read, but a laptop with an oversized screen can be very inconvenient to use on a seatback tray in airliner and in general is that much more difficult to move from place to place.

One of the breakthroughs of Microsoft Windows was the use of a mouse and a graphical user interface, allowing you to have the feeling of reaching into the screen to pick up and move objects and to issue commands by clicking. (Yes, I am aware Apple Computers beat them to the punch with the innovative but unlamented Lisa and then the Macintosh, but the idea actually goes back even further to research at Xerox Palo Alto Research Center and even before then to the Stanford Research Institute.)

And actually, my first experience with a pointing device was Miss Frank's three-foot-long varnished oak stick, which she used to specify pictures on the corkboard, show examples of cursive writing on the blackboard, and rap my knuckles when my head would droop forward. The only electrical presentation and educational tools in my ancient grade school were a record player, a filmstrip projector, and a creaky 16mm film projector. (And yes, I admit it: I was on the AV squad.)

We've progressed from mice to other devices, which are generically called *pointing devices:* trackballs, joysticks, tracking sticks, and touch pads among them. Laptop designers have done a good job of integrating a pointing device into the keyboard or beneath the thumbs in front of the spacebar. You can also purchase an add-on mini-mouse or use a full-size pointing device that connects to one of the laptop's ports.

Chapter 2

How to Treat a Laptop

In This Chapter

▶ Doing the right thing for your laptop's health

▶ Avoiding electrostatic shock

▶ Performing acts of kindness, care, and organization

A laptop computer is a bit like a baby: a very highly evolved, extremely intelligent, and almost infinitely capable infant, but a baby nevertheless.

✔ Though it has all, or nearly all, of the same parts as an adult. . .err, full-size PC, it's smaller.

✔ Its internal parts are very tightly packed together.

✔ Some of its components are made of materials much lighter and more delicate than those intended for PCs.

✔ The entire machine is encased within a plastic or other engineered material.

✔ It is small and portable, and though unlikely to wander off, it can be kidnapped or misplaced.

And so, like a baby, your laptop needs a bit of extra care and attention. I don't want to mislead you: Computer engineers have done a tremendous job of protecting your investment and data. Modern laptops include very durable cases, cushioned hard drives, and other security and defensive features.

Don't Try This at Home — or on the Road

Start out by considering some things you should *not* do to your laptop. Most of these are mere common sense, but everyone needs to be reminded from time to time that a laptop isn't immune to the laws of physics. They're pretty tough, but they still can be damaged by water, cracked by a fall, or erased by a strong magnetic field.

Obtain and maintain a good quality case that provides some cushioning for your laptop and protection against rain. If it's really pouring, find a strong plastic bag to wrap around your laptop within the case. Take it out of the bag as soon as you can, though. High humidity and large temperature swings are hard on things in plastic bags.

Don't do the following:

- **Don't drop a laptop off the desktop.** And don't let it tumble from an unzipped carrying case. Just don't. Although it is *possible* that the laptop and its components will survive, this is a chance not worth taking.

- **Don't place a heavy object on top of the case.** The cover of the laptop sits only a few millimeters from the delicate LCD screen and you could end up warping or breaking the display.

- **Don't allow the laptop to get wet.** Keep it away from cups of coffee, cans of soda, and glasses of water.

- **Don't turn off the computer while it's writing data to the hard drive, a recordable CD or DVD, or a floppy disk.** Information on the drive or disk could become corrupted or lost.

- **Don't expose your laptop to extremes of temperature.** Very cold temperature could make your case and LCD brittle and subject to cracking; the battery life will also be shortened by cold. Very hot temperatures could warp the case and LCD. Keep this in mind if you need to store your laptop in the trunk or passenger compartment of a car.

- **Don't let the laptop near strong magnetic fields.** They could corrupt or erase data on your hard drive or any floppy disks you may carry with you. Magnetic fields exist in and around large audio speakers, television sets, and some other electronic devices that aren't shielded to keep magnetism within their case.

- **Don't use your laptop in extremely dusty or dirty environments.** Dust or sand can get into the case through ventilation holes and cause damage to the hard drive, CD or DVD, and other internal mechanisms.

- **Don't open the cover to external ports on your laptop unless you are using one of the connections.** These ports include serial, parallel, and PS/2 connectors, all of which have been mostly supplanted by USB devices. Keep the cover closed to avoid damage to the pins and inadvertent electrical shorts from contact with metallic objects.

Ironically, among the most dangerous places to use a laptop is on the seatback table of an airliner — one of the most common locations people use them. To begin with, the table is small and somewhat flimsy. Then there's the nearby presence of cups of coffee and soda, cabin attendants pushing heavy carts through the aisle, and unexpected turbulence. You may secured by a seatbelt but your laptop isn't.

Aye aye, cap'n

A class of military and scientific-grade laptops are encased in aluminum or titanium packages and designed to tolerate abuse. These devices, sometimes called *mil-spec* (meaning that they meet military specifications) are capable of withstanding just about any insult: shock, heat, cold, and water among them. If they get dirty, they can be put through a dishwasher. They're quite expensive, and not what I'm talking about in this book.

But the greatest danger in using a laptop on an airliner is the possibility that the person in front of you will suddenly push back his or her seat. If your laptop becomes caught beneath the descending seat, it can snap your LCD screen like a stale breadstick.

You can employ several strategies:

- ✔ Politely ask the passenger seated in front of you to give advance warning before he or she lowers the seat.

- ✔ Position your laptop closer to your body and farther from the seat in front of you. Stay on guard for an unanticipated lowering of the seat.

- ✔ Attempt to wedge the seat in front of you so its movement is restricted or can't descend at all. Some travelers have figured ways to prop the seat up with a strategically placed book; you can also find plastic wedges for sale on the Internet.

Getting Electrostatic Shock Anti-therapy

Dutch scientist Pieter van Musschenbroek invented the Leyden Jar in 1745, and that wild and crazy man Ben Franklin flew his kite in a thunderstorm a few years later. It took quite some time before anyone could come up with a use for this crazy little thing they called electricity. In the Victorian era, no upper-class party was complete without a bit of social shock: a scuffle across a carpet and a kiss in the dark, or for the high-tech elite a hand-holding circle around a charged Leyden jar. Fast-forward to the 21st century. Little in our lives doesn't make use of electricity, including your favorite laptop and nearly all of its components. The screen is powered by a battery — a much-improved version of the Leyden jar — and the microprocessor, memory, and storage devices all depend on electricity to function. No power, no computer.

Ironically, though, the electricity that gives birth to a computer can also be the cause of its death. Other than a drop from the table to a concrete floor or a tub or water, the most significant threat to a laptop computer comes from *too much* electricity. The danger comes in two forms: a power surge that could fry the battery charger/AC adapter or a jolt of static electricity that could jump from your fingers to the keyboard or laptop's internal components.

You can protect your battery charger/AC adapter from unpleasant surprises by plugging it into a surge protector, an inexpensive accessory that should be part of every traveler's kit. Surge protectors can use a fast-acting circuit breaker, or a less-expensive fuse-like component that melts or breaks to cut the flow of power when appropriate, sacrificing its life for the device it's guarding. (In fact, you should consider using a surge protector for any valuable piece of electronics in your home or office. A $5 protector may save the life of a $2,000 HDTV, which is about as cheap as insurance gets.)

Now you come to static electricity, which is a lot more dangerous than you might imagine. Ponder this for a moment: Walking across the carpet in your socks in the winter can generate 35,000 volts of electricity. The biggest threat to your laptop comes if you open its case to install new memory or add other components. Get grounded before you open the bag and again before you touch the innards of the machine.

The generation of electrostatic voltage is affected by the relative humidity — the lower the moisture content in the air, the greater the voltage levels. The sock-stroll I just described could occur at a low 10 percent humidity, which is common in cold weather; at a moister 55 percent humidity, you might generate about 7,500 volts. You can generate a spark even without moving across the room. Breaking open plastic bubble wrap bag with a new stick of memory or other parts can produce 25,000 volts or more at 10 percent humidity and 7,000 volts at 55 percent wetness. Among the most treacherous devices in your home and office are plastic, vinyl, and sticky tape.

There's not a lot of amperage behind an electrostatic charge. Humans can usually feel a static spark at levels above 4,000 volts, but your sensitive little electronic device can be damaged by as few as 700 volts.

So, what are you to learn from this? Get yourself grounded.

If you've just walked across the room to your desk, get in the habit of touching something to discharge static electricity before laying hands on your computer. You can touch a metal desk chair or a desk lamp. In my office, I have an antistatic strip mounted on a corner of my desk; it's connected by a wire to a known ground — the center screw on a modern electrical outlet.

Committing Deliberate Acts of Kindness

In addition to preventing physical damage, you can take some steps to help maintain the health and longevity of your laptop.

When necessary, clean the LCD screen with a soft, lintless cloth barely moistened with water. Allow me to emphasize the high-tech cleaning solution involved: plain, clean water. After you have carefully cleaned the screen, dry it with another soft cloth. You can wipe down the external case with a gentle, non-abrasive cleaner and a soft, lintless cloth. But I'd rather see you stick to good old water.

Never use an abrasive cleanser or an ammonia-based window cleaner like Windex. Just water.

On a regular schedule, clean your hard disk drive. No, I am not talking about wiping it down with water. Rather, I am recommending that you use a suite of maintenance utilities such as Norton SystemWorks or individual components such as Norton AntiVirus or Executive Software's Diskeeper. Install these programs and keep them current to check such things as the Windows registry and the general state of health of your hard drive. In Figure 2-1 you can see the detailed report generated by Executive Software's Diskeeper 9, a third-party defragmentation utility that's faster and more comprehensive than the defrag program included as part of Windows XP. The program can be set to work in the background, to start when the machine is idle for a specified period of time (like lunch), or run at a scheduled time.

Schedule antivirus and maintenance scans of your system appropriate to the level of use of your laptop. If your machine is in daily use, it should be fully scanned once a week; if you only use your laptop when you travel, you can schedule a scan before the start of each trip.

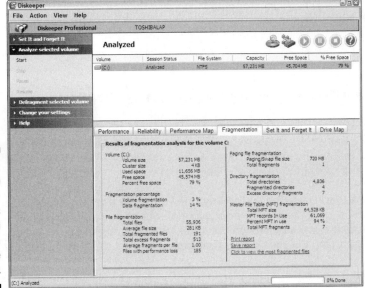

Figure 2-1: Diskeeper 9 Professional Edition gives your hard drive a complete checkup.

And the most important four-step program for protecting the data stored on your laptop is this:

1. **Make a complete backup of data on an external device or on removable media.**

2. **Keep the backup current. The more work you perform on your laptop the more often you should perform backups.**

3. **Leave your external backup device or removable media in a safe place at home or in your office when you travel.**

4. **See Steps 1 and 2.**

You can accomplish this sort of a backup program a number of ways. I use my laptop on the road and a PC in my office, so I have the original copy of my data in the PC's hard drive (and on an external hard drive attached to the network there). When I travel, I make backups to a CD-R using the CD recorder in my laptop, on a flash memory key, or on a lightweight external USB hard drive. I can also send completed in-progress files to myself by e-mail and leave them on my Internet provider's server until I am back in my office.

Quick definitions here: *CD-Rs* are compact discs that can be recorded to by the user; a *flash memory key* is a small stick of *nonvolatile* (doesn't need electrical current once written to) memory that can hold data, and *USB* is an all-purpose, high-speed communications port that has all but replaced older technologies including serial, parallel, mouse, keyboard, and other input and output connectors.

Now here's the most important part of the plan: I do not store my backups in the same case that carries the laptop. The reason should be obvious, but I'll explain anyway: If the laptop is lost or stolen, my data backup is in a different place.

Keeping it organized and safe

I've already compared your laptop to a living, breathing thing. It (your laptop, but a baby, too) needs to be cleaned and reorganized when things get messy; you can extend its life through a properly thought out and executed diagnostic and preventative maintenance program.

In my work, I use my laptop anytime I am away from the office. Although I travel a great deal — the equivalent of four or five months a year — that also means the machine sits on the shelf for weeks or even an occasional full month. Your use may differ. Your laptop may be the only machine you have, or you may carry it with regularly to interoffice meetings or college lectures. Or your laptop may only get up and go a few times a year. So adjust your cleaning and maintenance schedule to fit your particular calendar.

Whatever you do, begin by making a safe home for your laptop. Don't leave it perched on the corner of a desk or on the edge of a shelf; keep it out of direct sun and away from heating and cooling vents. Take care not to place anything heavy on top of the LCD cover. And spend the time to properly stow away or move out of tripping range any cables attached to the laptop.

Consult the instruction manual from the maker of your machine for advice on whether they recommend you keep an unused machine constantly plugged into an AC adapter to keep the battery fully charged. In some designs this *could* shorten the life of the battery; on the other hand, leaving the battery with an AC source for an extended period of time could result in its depletion, which could cause you to lose configuration settings in the system BIOS. (Your data and programs on the hard disk are safe, since they don't require power to retain information; see Chapter 6 for more on BIOS.) The other downside to leaving the machine unplugged is that may not be ready to go if you have an unexpected need for the machine. The fact is that a replacement battery isn't that expensive, especially for popular models from well-known manufacturers. If the original battery comes to the end of its life or doesn't hold a charge for a sufficient period of time, you should be able to get a new battery for $100 or less.

So, unless you travel as much as I do, your schedule *should* be different than mine. But for the record, here's how I care and feed my laptop:

- It has its own table, off to the side of my desk and secure from accidental tumbles.

- I keep the AC adapter plugged into the laptop at all times and attached to a wall current on the protected side of a heavy-duty power surge protector.

- The machine is attached by an Ethernet cable to a nearby router, allowing me to quickly download files before I set out on a trip. It also lets me update the antivirus and adware/spyware definitions through the broadband Internet connection on the router. I also connect to Microsoft's Windows Update for operating system patches and revisions. (Actually, I use Windows XP's facility to perform automatic updates to any machine that has a broadband connection.) See Chapter 13 for details about goodies like Ethernet and routers.

- When I return from a trip, the first thing I do is transfer any new files from the laptop to my desktop system and make sure that I keep my backup copies of files current. Depending on the project, I either maintain a second copy of all of my work on a separate, removable hard drive, burn new files to a CD, or do both.

You may prefer to use the automated facilities of Windows Briefcase or Synchronization Manager to automatically copy revised or newly created files from the laptop to your desk or the other way around. Personally, I prefer to manually manage the update in one direction or the other. At the start of each trip I create a new folder on the desktop with the travel dates and I take care to use the Save As feature of my word processor, image editor, and other programs to make sure that new work is stored in that easily locatable folder. The Synchronization Settings screen is shown in Figure 2-2.

✔ After uploading any work completed on the road, I manually instruct Norton SystemWorks to check for any anomalies with the Windows Registry, shortcuts, and other problems with file structures and indexes; because a laptop is often used intermittently, setting a utility to automatically run every Friday at 5:00 p.m. may not be the best practice–you may not have the machine on at that time or you may be using your battery on the road for work at that time . If I've been using the Internet while traveling or have connected in any way with an office network or loaded a file from a floppy disk or a CD or DVD, I run a full antivirus scan (which can take an hour or two) followed by an adware/spyware scan. If I haven't connected to another system in any way, I skip the scans.

Figure 2-2:
The settings screen of the Windows Synchronization Manager allows users to choose items to harmonize at log on, log off, when the machine is idle, or on a particular schedule.

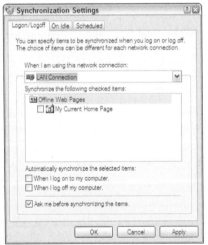

Other housekeeping tasks keep your laptop healthy, rapid, and wise:

✔ Empty the Recycle Bin once a week (or more often if you find that your disk is becoming fragmented too often).

✔ Unless you have a reason to keep this sort of information around, clear the Web browser history and any temporary Internet files.

✔ Use the Windows facilities or those of a cleanup utility to delete temporary files (including those that have a .tmp extension or ones that begin
with a tilde, like ~tempfile.dta).

You'll find tools to do these tasks as part of your system utility program,
or by right-clicking on the disk name under My Computer and going to
the Tools tab.

✔ If I've been using the system heavily — and especially if I've been working with large files such as digital images — I defragment the hard disk
drive. The more stuff I accumulate on the drive, the more frequently I
defrag the files.

Keeping it clean

To this point, I've been concentrating on setting straight the internal dirt of
your machine, from fragments of files to corrupted Registry items to fragmented drives. It's also important to keep a clean exterior.

Clean the LCD and case as needed. To clean the exterior of your laptop
system, use the following procedure:

1. **Lightly moisten a soft, lint-free cloth with either a 50-50 mixture of
   isopropyl alcohol and water, a non-ammoniated glass cleaner, or
   pure water. (Hot water works best.)**

   Never spray liquid cleaner directly on the system, especially the display
   or keyboard.

2. **Gently wipe the LCD display with the moistened cloth and follow with
   a dry cloth.**

   Be sure the cloth is not wet enough to drip and that the LCD is completely dry when you're finished. You can use a piece of an old, old
   undershirt that's been washed and cleaned so that it leaves no lint; if
   you prefer spending money, you can purchase an antistatic LCD-cleaning
   cloth from a computer supply store or an industrial lint-free tissue like
   Kimwipes.

3. **Gently vacuum the keyboard every few weeks or every few trips,
   whichever comes first.**

   Use a vacuum with a brush end to avoid scratching the case. You can
   vacuum from above or on an angle to get beneath the keys. As an alternative, you can use can of compressed air. Take great care to hold the
   can upright so the liquid propellant within does not come out with the
   air. Carefully hold your laptop at a sharp angle and work the jet of air
   down, from the top to the bottom.

You're going to be amazed, or disgusted, at the amount of junk that flies out from beneath the keys; I do hope you are not eating crumbly cookies at your desk, but there are many other sources of junk that can settle on the keyboard and slow down, gum up, or grind to a halt the workings. (If you need to know: hair, dandruff, pieces of skin, pet dander, pollen, spores, dust, oils, and all sorts of other stuff are all around you.)

If your vacuuming or puffing does not dislodge all of the gunk or if there is a sticky residue beneath the keys you may have to remove the keys and clean beneath. For more details, see Chapter 10.

Part II
Explaining What Could Possibly Go Wrong

In this part . . .

*O*h the things that can possibly go wrong within the svelte, sealed box that encases a laptop. Squeezed into an inch or two of depth and half a pizza box of length and width of a modern machine are a motherboard, microprocessor, memory, hard disk drive, CD or DVD drive, video adapter, wireless adapter, and half a dozen other high-speed ways to get information into or out of the box.

This part begins with a listing of common causes for failure and some relatively simple cures. And then I take a step away from technology and talk about economics: When does it pay to make an expensive repair and when does it make more sense to give yourself permission to buy a flashy, high-performance, new machine?

After that I focus on the essential Control Panel, Device Manager, and System Restore utilities of Windows, then jump over to the hardware side and explore memory, motherboards, and microprocessors.

Chapter 3

Things That Go Bump in the Night (or Day)

A laptop computer is a highly complex piece of electronics, more capable than any machine ever dreamed of when you were young. In fact, if it's a brand new model right out of the box, it's probably more capable than any machine you imagined a few weeks ago. But as complex as it is, unlike living, breathing, and conspiring humans, a laptop computer can fail only a few ways.

In this chapter I go over some of the ways a laptop can fail and explore emergency triage for treatable injuries. The good news is that relatively few paths lead to destruction or distraction; the bad news is that while some can be fixed and others worked around, the worst problems may not be worth fixing.

Big Troubles in Little Places

Laptops are not immune from the laws of gravity and physics. Someday a scientist may perfect an antigravity adapter. Until then, you've got to be careful to avoid dropping your laptop. And for those of us who don't have a $20,000 military-spec machine that is completely sealed from water — and especially soda or coffee spills — which are obvious and common causes of sticky keys and short circuits, I give you some suggestions on what to do when spills happen in the "Recovering from a Spill" section. Here are some of the ways a laptop can *come a cropper;* that's a great old English phrase that literally means to fall head-first from a horse but in today's lingo means to fail decisively:

- ✔ **Physical breakage.** Almost any laptop will be damaged by a fall from a few feet onto a hard surface. The case could split, the LCD screen could crack, connectors could break off, and the device could suffer internal injuries. Cables could become dislodged, the motherboard could crack, integrated circuits (you might call them chips) could come loose, and the hard disk drive could grind to a halt.

- ✔ **Water damage.** Spilling a bottle of water — or worse, a cup of coffee or a glass of soda — can literally gum up the works. The liquid can cause short circuits and sticky keys, or prevent fans, hard disk-, CD-, or DVD drives from spinning.

- ✔ **Power failure.** Electronic devices require electricity, either from a wall current or from a battery. Electrical points of failure on a laptop include the AC adapter, which reduces voltage from 110 or 220 volts to a lower level, usually in the range of 10 to 19 volts. The adapter can fail, or the computer attachment connection can break off. Within the laptop, a surge of electricity or a short circuit can damage circuits and components. Chapter 2 talks more about voltage and the reduction thereof.

- ✔ **Essential component breakdown.** The disparate parts of a laptop have a different expected lifetimes; some can be expected to work indefinitely, while others may only be reasonably expected to last a few years. There's no telling which part may fail first, but among the more likely are things like the LCD's backlight, another part of the display system called an inverter, exposed external connectors, and the AC adaptor or its associated charging and power components.

- ✔ **Microprocessor meltdown.** The computer's "mind" is a hybrid of a microprocessor (often a member of the Intel Pentium or Celeron families, or an AMD equivalent) and a block of RAM (random access memory). The microprocessor does the work, moving bits of information from one place to another and performing certain operations on them; the RAM is the machine's scratchpad, where it holds temporary notes on works in progress. Microprocessors rarely fail, although they can be damaged — along with much of the rest of the machine's electronics — by a power surge or a short circuit.

- ✔ **Memory loss.** Now here I'm *not* talking about RAM, but rather long-term storage. On most laptops information is semi-permanently stored on a hard disk drive. Some users may store information on a floppy disk drive, or on a recordable CD or DVD. I say *semi-permanently* because each of these three types of storage are mechanical in nature. A spinning disk or disc (CD and DVD makers betray their European lineage by using a "c" instead of a "k") holds digital bits of information recorded either as magnetic markings (on a hard disk or floppy disk) or as a dark spot or indentation (on an optically based CD or DVD). The hard disk drive's motor can grind to a halt, or the read/write head can crash into the surface, destroying both the mechanism and a chunk of stored information.

On a CD or DVD, the good news is that the failure of the mechanism doesn't mean that discs already recorded won't work in another drive; the bad news is that CDs or DVDs can be irreparably damaged with scratches, warps, or cracks, especially if exposed to extremes of heat or sunlight.

Identifying power adapter problems

The laptop is plugged into a wall socket. You press the On button but the lights don't flash, the screen doesn't change colors, and the earth doesn't move. The power doesn't be.

To identify the problem, let me break down the electrical system (before it breaks down by itself). Nearly every laptop uses *DC (direct current)* voltage, usually in the range of 5–20 volts; almost nowhere in the world outside a laboratory will that type and level of power come out of a wall outlet. Instead, when you connect a laptop to wall current, you are using a power cord that includes a small box that converts *AC (alternating current)* of 110 volts (in the United States, Canada, and a few other places around the world) or 220 volts (the standard AC voltage in most of the rest of the world.)

The electrical connector *rectifies* or *converts* alternating current to direct current (removing one of the cha-chas from the back-and-forth movement of AC to yield a steady cha) and also *transforms* the voltage from 110 or 220 down to the needs of your machine.

The adapter output can go straight to the motherboard or it can be diverted to pass through the laptop's battery to recharge it. (Actually, most laptops include a bit of electrical circuitry that allow you to use the machine at the same time as the battery is being recharged.)

Excluding a dead or uncharged battery — which I discuss in a moment — there are two likely sources of electrical problems.

The adapter may not be getting the AC juice it needs

Is the power outlet live? Check it by plugging in a lamp or a radio to the same outlet — not the one above or below it — to see if power is present. (Remember that some outlets are controlled by switches on the wall; Europe and Asia commonly have switches alongside most outlets.)

Is the charger properly connected? Some chargers use interchangeable power leads at the end that goes to the wall outlet; this allows for use of plugs with differing designs as required around the world. Make sure the lead is properly attached to the charger and that the charger is plugged into the laptop.

The adapter may have failed

Although commonly called a *battery charger,* on most laptops the equipment is actually a *voltage converter* that works with circuitry within the laptop to do two things: charge the battery and run the computer from wall current. The charger converts 110 or 220 volts of AC to DC voltage generally in the range of 5 to 20 volts; the conversion usually creates a bit of heat. The converter should not get hot enough to boil your morning coffee. If you see smoke or smell the distinctive acrid odor of burning electrical components, carefully unplug the converter and seek a replacement.

Adapter failure is a relatively rare occurrence, although it can be damaged by a power surge, hurt by a poorly regulated current, or suffer cut, crimped, or ripped plugs or wires.

Here's are some clues that can help you determine if the AC adapter is getting power from the wall, and if the laptop is getting voltage from the adapter. Look for a small pilot light on the AC adapter to indicate the presence of power; if the lamp is not lit, the charger may be dead. And many laptops display a little symbol or light to indicate the presence of an outside power source; if it's not there, something is wrong.

Assault and no battery

You're at 30,000 feet and the flight attendant announces that it's now permissible to use electronic devices. You carefully shift your feet, tuck in your elbows, remove your laptop from its case, and place it on the seatback table. But when you call for action, the laptop is as lifeless as an airline terminal tuna sandwich.

Electrical problems when you're not running on wall current could be related to the battery itself or the battery recharger. Or, the recharger might not have received proper current when it was plugged into a wall outlet. Here are some troubleshooting steps:

- **Is your battery installed properly in its slot and plugged into the electrical connectors?** On some laptops, the battery is held in place by a simple clip or sliding latch; it can become dislodged while you travel. On one trip, I arrived at my destination to find that the battery was completely missing — it was sitting home alone alongside my desk. On another trip, the battery came out of its attachment pins while going through the X-ray machine at an airport security check. Take the time to study your laptop's design and assess the chances of a battery incident.

✔ **Has the battery been recharged recently?** Batteries — especially older ones — may not be able to hold on to their charge for an extended period of time, even if they're not being used. When I plan a trip, I leave my laptop plugged into its charger for at least half a day before I depart; I keep it topped off in hotel rooms and airport lounges whenever possible.

✔ **Will the computer come to life when directly connected to an AC source?** If you're really at 30,000 feet, you're going to have to wait until you're changing planes at O'Hare or are happily ensconced in your hotel room, office, or home.

If the laptop does work when powered by an AC source but not when on its own, then your battery may have assaulted you for one of several reasons:

✔ **The battery reached the end of its life.** Although laptop batteries are rechargeable, they don't live forever. Sometimes they fail slowly, losing their ability to hold on to a charge over time. Or they may fail all at once, usually due to an internal electrical short.

✔ **The charger wasn't properly connected.** Some chargers use interchangeable power leads at the end that goes to the wall outlet; this allows for use of plugs with differing designs as required around the world. Make sure the lead is properly attached to the charger and that the charger is plugged into the laptop.

✔ **The charger wasn't getting the juice.** Are you sure you used a live power outlet? Check it by plugging in a lamp or a radio to the same outlet — not the one above or below it — to see if power is present. (Remember that some outlets are controlled by switches on the wall; in Europe and Asia, it's common to have a switch alongside most outlets.)

✔ **The battery charger failed.** Although this is a relatively rare occurrence, the charger may have been damaged by a power surge or poorly regulated current. The charger converts 110 or 220 volts of AC to DC voltage generally in the range of 5–20 volts; the conversion usually creates a bit of heat. The converter shouldn't get hot enough to boil your morning coffee. If you see smoke or smell the distinctive acrid odor of burning electrical components, *carefully unplug the converter* and seek a replacement.

When all is dead and done

You can check your AC adapter's or battery's health in several ways: The simplest is to find someone else who has the same make and model of laptop (in working condition) and swap first the adapter and then the battery.

If your machine had previously been dead to your adapter and the battery, but comes back to life with a known-good adapter, that tells you your adapter isn't working properly and needs to be replaced. If your machine had worked with your own AC adapter but not with your battery, and now it regains its will to live with a known-good battery, this is a pretty good indication that your battery has failed and should be replaced.

The other possibility — and it isn't good news — is that the power circuitry inside your laptop or the motherboard itself has failed. This could be the result of a short or break caused by a tumble, or electrically fried components. If you're semi-lucky, your laptop is still under warranty and the manufacturer will repair or replace the system; otherwise, this may be a situation where it would cost more to repair an older machine than buy a new one. Chapter 4 talks about where to go from here.

Recovering from a Spill

Water and coffee and soda are among your laptop's worst enemies. Just a little bit of a mix could damage or destroy your machine or cause you to lose data.

Some laptops are more vulnerable to damage from a spill on the keyboard than others, and it doesn't always have anything to do with the price tag. Some keyboards have a thin rubber membrane beneath the keys with electrical contacts molded right into little domes under each letter; that design may feel squishy and cheap to some users, but it stands up better to a splash or a flood than a more traditional design with springs and exposed contacts. How do you know which type of design you have? Take a look for yourself by prying off a keytop; if you're shopping, the information *may* be available from the manufacturer or a dealer.

The best way to deal with preventing damage from a mix of liquid and electronics is to keep them as far apart as possible. Keep your laptop as far away as possible from cups of coffee, glasses of water, and cans of soda. Having said this, I know all too well the joys of doing my work on the seatback table of a packed Boeing 737 with barely enough room to balance a paperback much less a laptop. I worry that the kid front of me is going to go for a joy ride and tilt his seat back, snapping the LCD screen in half. I keep a wary eye on the flight attendant in the aisle and the passenger alongside me, assuming that either one — or both — are capable of dumping a cup of soda on my machine.

All right, then: In the real world, stuff happens. If you have a choice of poisons, take the water spill. A hot cup of coffee, a cold glass of soda, or a glass of wine are each bad news; all of them are slightly acidic. Acidic liquids are nastier than nearly neutral water because they can corrode metal contacts. And both coffee and soda can become gummy and sticky as they dry.

Flying through the air with the greatest of ease

So where does a very cautious laptop traveler sit on an airplane? In my opinion, the best seat in the house is along the window in the emergency exit row; the second best seat is along the window in the row behind the bulkhead that separates one class or section of the plane from another.

I like the window seat because I don't have to worry about someone getting up and disturbing me or forcing me to move my portable office out of the way; I can do it to them, but not the other way around. The window also allows me to adjust the lighting for the screen.

The row of seats that aligns with one of the emergency exits offers at least one advantage:

The row of seats in front of you doesn't recline (because safety engineers don't want to block the door). On some planes, the exit row is a bit wider as well.

The seats that face the bulkhead also are safe from surprise reclines; on most planes, these chairs have a tray table that lifts up from a storage compartment between the seats. The principal disadvantage here is that you have no place in front of you to store your laptop during takeoff and landing; you have to find a place in the overhead compartment.

Here's the drill for an emergency recovery from a spill:

1. **If your machine is plugged into wall current, turn off the power at the circuit breaker in your home or office.**

   You don't want to touch a wet wire carrying 110 volts or so. If you're certain the spill is confined to the keyboard and hasn't reached the AC adapter, you are probably safe just unplugging the adapter from the wall; I'm not recommending you do that, though.

   If the machine is running on battery power, is still operating, and you don't see sparks, hear odd noises, or smell burnt electrical components, shut it down through the normal Windows process.

   If something is obviously wrong with the machine, turn it off immediately by depressing the Off switch or by removing the battery.

2. **Ground yourself by touching the center screw on the faceplate of a *dry* electrical outlet, or by touching some other metal object that reaches to ground.**

3. **If you haven't done so in emergency mode, remove the AC adapter and the battery and set them aside.**

4. **Disconnect any external devices such as a mouse, any devices attached to the USB, FireWire, serial, or other ports.**

5. **If any liquid is on the battery or AC adapter, wipe them carefully and set them aside.**

   If the AC adapter or the battery has been thoroughly soaked, your best bet is to consider one, the other, or both a loss. Replacement AC adapters and batteries are available from various sources, including the original equipment manufacturer, from laptop accessory companies like www.iGo.com, and on the used market through www.eBay.com.

6. **Remove any cards installed in the PC Card slot.**

   If they're wet, carefully dry them off. If any water has gotten into the narrow slot, dry out the area with a cotton swab, taking care not to leave any threads of cotton in the internal connector.

7. **Wipe off any liquid on the display.**

   Use a clean cloth dampened with water to remove any sticky residue.

8. **Remove the hard drive and the CD/DVD drives if they're installed in plug-in bays.**

   Dry them off if wet. Set them aside. Consult your laptop's instruction manual for specific instructions on removing a drive.

9. **Open the memory module container; remove and dry the memory modules.**

   Make notes on the placement of the modules. Set them aside.

   The most likely site to collect a puddle of pop or a cuppa java is the keyboard, and this may or may not be a serious problem. If your laptop has a plastic or rubber-like membrane beneath the keys this should protect against leakage to the motherboard beneath. If it has individual springs and switches beneath each key, the cleanup will be more laborious and, in the instance of a major spill, the prognosis is uncertain. It should be relatively easy to mop up a reasonable-sized mess.

10. **Hand-dry the keyboard surface with a lint-free cloth.**

    If you spilled soda or coffee, consult the instruction manual for your computer and learn how to carefully remove each of the keycaps for the affected area. If the instruction manual includes a picture of the keyboard, make sure you can see the names of all the keys and their locations; otherwise make a drawing of the board, paying special attention to the location of some of the specialized keys, including cursor keys, Page Up, Page Down, Scroll Lock, and the like. One other shortcut: Use a digital camera to take a picture of the keyboard.

11. **Clean the exposed membrane or switch cover and the keys themselves.**

    Leave the keys to dry before replacing them. By now you should have an open shell of a laptop.

12. **Leaving the display open, place the computer on a sturdy surface supported by two books or small boxes.**

This allows air to circulate all around the computer. Leave the computer and all of its separate parts to air dry for at least 24 hours. Do not use a fan or (horrors) a hair dryer to attempt to fast-forward the drying process. This is more likely to cause problems than solve them.

13. **Reassemble the pieces you have removed.**

Only do this a day or more later, after assuring that everything is dry and no dried puddles of sticky acid are anywhere on the machine. Remember to ground yourself before touching any circuitry or modules, and begin the power-up process with the battery first and the AC adapter second.

If in doubt about the safety of any part, you'd be better off replacing it instead of using it. Replacing a battery (perhaps $50–$100), an AC adapter (perhaps $30–75), or even a hard disk drive (about $200–$300) is always cheaper than replacing a motherboard.

When a CD or DVD Won't Go Round and Round

If a CD or DVD won't play well with your machine, two basic reasons are usually why: mechanical problems and computer resource issues. Remember that a CD or DVD drive is one of the few moving parts of a laptop (along with the hard disk drive, a floppy disk drive, and the internal fan), and machines usually have a finite life. Sooner or later the tiny motor that spins the disc or moves the tray in and out may fail. Or, the moveable rails and tray may become warped by heat or knocked out of kilter by bumping into another object or by being dropped. These causes are mechanical problems.

The other issue is that CD and DVD drives are among the most demanding of the computer's electronic resources: They require electrical power and a clean and generally uninterruptible channel for data (especially when the drive is being used to *write* a disc). Problems here are the causes of resource problems.

Suffering slipped discs

The most common mechanical problem is caused by an improperly inserted disc; in second place is a failure of the CD or DVD drive itself. Get in the habit of carefully inserting the disc into the tray. The hole in the disc should be seated perfectly centered on the spindle; if the disc isn't centered properly, or the disc itself is warped, the drive won't properly read it. Be gentle with the delicate CD tray. It isn't intended to bear much weight or pressure. If a disc doesn't easily center on the spindle, don't force it into place.

Sometimes a disc sticks and the tray won't open when you push the regular button. (Some laptops also allow software to open the tray, although this may not be the best feature. You don't want the fragile tray popping open in a situation where it could be damaged.) The procedure to open a stuck tray is decidedly low tech. Go find a paper clip and straighten it out. Look for a tiny hole on the front of the CD tray; darned if it isn't exactly the size of a straightened paper clip. Gently push in the probe to open the drive. If you've been good in this life or a previous one, the drawer opens and you can remove the offending disc. Try to determine if it was seated improperly or warped. Experiment with a fresh or known-good disc.

If you're unable to get the disc out using the standard release button or the emergency eject hole, you may have to remove the entire CD or DVD drive from the laptop and hope to gain access to the tray — or replace the mechanism if it has failed. Consult your laptop's instruction manual for specific instructions on removing a drive; on some systems it's as easy as unlatching the device from a plug-in bay, while on other systems you may have to remove several intervening pieces of equipment including the battery, floppy disc drive, or other devices.

While I'm on the subject of warped or otherwise inadequate discs, I want to pass along my recommendation against using one of those cute, oddly shaped CDs some companies or people insist on handing out at trade shows or other events. I've received star-shaped, Easter-egg shaped, and modern artsy mini-discs. Although in theory they work just as well as a full-sized CD (albeit with a smaller capacity), they're off balance because of their shape and more likely to warp. I don't use them myself and recommend you pass on them when offered.

Another possible mechanical problem that can shut down a CD or DVD is a failure of one of the drive's tiny motors or positioning devices. The primary motor spins the disc, varying its speed as required; though these devices represent great technological achievements, they nevertheless can seize or burn out. Some CD or DVD devices have a second, even tinier motor that opens and closes the drive tray; other designs are spring loaded. Finally, the little positioning motor rapidly moves the read/write head toward or away from the spinning disc's spindle to align with a particular location.

Yet one more point of failure is the tiny laser and its focusing lens. On a desktop PC, these parts are hidden within the drive; on a laptop, some designs put the laser and lens on the slideout tray, exposed to accidental damage. Don't touch the lens; you could move it out of alignment and the oils from your finger could distort its focus. Try to avoid allowing dirt to enter the drive. If the lens or tray does become dirty, try a gentle spray from a can of filtered, compressed air.

If you declare the drive DOA, it can be replaced — more or less easily, depending on the laptop. Or it can be supplanted by an external device that connects to a USB port. I discuss both options in Chapter 16.

Rescuing resourceless discs

The other likely cause for problems with a CD or DVD drive is a conflict in demand for system resources. I discuss how a modern computer manages interrupts (IRQs), DMA channels, and memory resources in Chapter 5.

All that's necessary to say here is this: When you first opened the box for your new laptop, it should have been set up so all the devices attached to the motherboard — memory, hard drive, CD or DVD drive, sound, network interface, modem, and the like — were properly configured. That's why the first thing you should do with a new computer is put it through its paces. Try each and every feature individually and run as many as possible at the same time.

If your new laptop doesn't work properly when brand new, it probably won't get better over time all by itself. Get on the phone or the Internet (if that's working) to the manufacturer's support desk and insist that they make your laptop work perfectly on Day One. If they can't help you, or if you don't like the way you're treated as a brand-new customer, take it back or send it back. There are plenty of other fishes in the sea.

I'm going to assume that the machine and the CD or DVD were working properly for a period of time and now have stopped. Before you do anything else, determine the following: Is the CD or DVD drive responding to electrical commands? Does the drawer open when you push the button? If you place a disc in the device, can you hear it spinning?

The other troubleshooting essential is to pay a visit to the Control Panel under Windows and see if it's reporting a hardware problem, a conflict of resources, or trouble with the device driver. For details on this important tool, see Chapter 5.

Hard Times for a Hard Drive

Death comes to us all; we just don't know exactly when or how. But that's another book. Let me get back to laptops and tell you this: Death comes to every hard disk drive. It's not a question of whether, just when. Before I even begin to discuss how to maintain, repair, or replace, let me get the most important rule of computing before your eyes: Make backups of your data.

Your programs can be replaced with new ones. Your laptop and its various components can be repaired or replaced. But if you have only one copy of your Great American Novel, your company's business plan, or your family photos, you're just one step away from a major loss. Make backups.

Here is the number one deadly signpost in the life cycle of a hard disk drive: **General failure reading drive C:**.

Just like the sign says, this is a message from your laptop from deep down below — from the system BIOS — that the computer is unable to read information from the hard disk. You might receive this message when booting up, before the operating system gets a chance to load; you may see the message while the machine is up and running.

If you're lucky, you've run into a momentary fault with the hard drive or its controller, a sort of a once-in-a-couple-dozen-million-nanosecond hiccup. The read-write heads might have ended up in an unusual location, or the hard drive motor may be stuck because of humidity, a tiny speck of dirt, or warping.

Try restarting the machine by pressing Ctrl+Alt+Del. If that doesn't work, turn off the power, wait a few seconds, and then turn the machine back on. You can even try a *very gentle* shock to the system. With the power turned off, carefully bang the bottom of the laptop case on a desktop. (If you're able to determine where the hard disk is on your laptop, concentrate your physical attention there.) I'm talking about a rap with about the force of a wrap of your knuckles on the table — hard enough to make a noise but not enough to cause pain. Then turn on your machine and hope for the best.

If you're lucky, the hard drive comes back to life and your system merrily proceeds as if nothing happened. You, however, are smart enough to immediately update your backups of all essential data to an external hard drive or a recordable CD or DVD. And you remember at all times that your hard drive is going to fail sooner or later; be prepared to replace it when it dies.

Checking electrical connections

If the hard drive is installed in a plug-in bay on the bottom side of your laptop, check to make sure it's properly connected to the system:

1. **Place the laptop on a sturdy, well-lit surface.**

2. **Disconnect the power adapter and remove the battery.**

3. **Remove the hard drive from its bay.**

   Consult the instructions for your laptop for specific instructions on unlatching the drive.

4. **Look for bent pins or other obvious signs of damage to the connector on the hard drive, or on its matching port on the laptop.**

   Some minor damage can be repaired by carefully moving pins back to their original position. Be sure you do not move pins back and forth repeatedly; this causes metal fatigue that could result in a break.

5. **Reinstall the hard drive in its bay, carefully following instructions in the laptop's manual.**

6. **Reinstall the battery and the power adapter and hope for the best.**

Hard luck stories

And if you're not lucky, and the hard drive never comes around, you've got a few other options:

- ✔ **If your laptop is still under warranty, send it back to the manufacturer or bring it into a service depot to have a new drive installed.** The computer maker should do you the courtesy of partitioning and formatting the drive and installing the operating system. (You do have backups of all of your important data, right? You need them to reinstall on the new drive. You also need to locate and use the original installation disks for applications.)

- ✔ **If your laptop is no longer under warranty, install your own replacement hard drive.** (I discuss hard drive replacement details in Chapter 7.) Once again, I'm hoping that you have all of your data on a backup hard drive or a set of CD-Rs or other media.

- ✔ **If you're so unlucky as to have a dead disk drive but not a full set of essential data backups, consider a disaster recovery service.** They don't work cheap — figure on a minimum charge somewhere in the range of $100–$250 and going up from there depending on the size of drive and the nature of the problem — but in most situations they can open a dead drive in a clean room and get it running long enough to transfer its contents to a new drive. The only miracle they cannot perform is the resurrection of data from a section of the disk that has severe physical damage. For example, if the read/write head crashes into the magnetized platter and gouges a hole, that section of the drive may be unreadable. (But then again, that portion of the drive just might hold something you don't need restored, such as the operating system, software, or a temporary Windows or Internet file.)

Closing the Operating Room

The machine's lights and LCD come to life and you hear the hard drive spinning, but the operating system doesn't load. Several possible reasons exist.

✔ **The hard drive's boot or "system" tracks have been corrupted.** This could be a harbinger of a failing disk drive, exposure to a magnetic field, or the result of an improper machine shutdown (such as a sudden cutoff of power).

You may be able to reinstall the system tracks or the entire operating system from an emergency recovery CD or disk. Such a disk may be provided by your laptop's manufacturer or created using a system utility program such as Norton SystemWorks.

✔ **You have a floppy disk in the drive, and the laptop's BIOS is set to attempt to boot from the floppy before trying the hard drive.** Unless you have a good reason to do otherwise, you should change the BIOS setting so it seeks to boot first from the hard drive. It should go to the floppy disk as its second or third choice, after also trying to boot from a CD.

One reason you don't want your laptop booting from the floppy disk drive is that floppies are easy carriers of computer viruses from one machine to another. Another is to prevent a dead start if the floppy disk drive contains data but not the operating system's boot tracks.

✔ **You ran out of space.** You should regularly check the dipstick on your hard drive, but in case you miss the approaching overstuffed disk, here's the most common on-screen warning sign: Insufficient disk space.

Bet you could figure this one out, right? First thing, deal with the immediate problem. If you're trying to save work in progress, try to store it somewhere else temporarily: on an external hard drive, across the network to another machine's hard drive, on a floppy disk, or to a CD-R.

Here's the way to use the facilities built into Windows to clear up space on your drive:

1. **Double-click My Computer and highlight the name of the internal disk drive of your laptop.**

2. **Under Windows XP, maximize the Details panel on the left side of the My Computer display.**

   There you see the drive's name, type of file system used on the drive, available free space, and total size. You can also see a graphical version of the same information, plus gain access to clean-up and defragmentation tools, by right-clicking the drive name and selecting Properties.

3. **Click the Disk Cleanup button to initiate an automatic utility that deletes temporary files, empties the Recycle Bin, and offers other compression and deletion tools.**

4. **Click the Tools tab and then the Defragment Now button to free up space by bringing together scattered file pieces.**

   For a quick fix, free up a bit of space by cleaning out the contents of the Recycle Bin. Go to the desktop, right-click the Bin's icon, and select Empty Recycle Bin.

5. **Remove old data you don't expect to require quick access to by copying to a CD or DVD.**

   To protect yourself, before removing anything from the hard drive, consider making two separate sets of copies that are stored in different places.

Give some thought about whether your hard drive contains some programs that you never use; use the Add/Remove Programs feature of the Control Panel in Windows to remove applications that are just taking up space. You can also look for unnecessary "sample" art and music files and superfluous tutorials for programs you already know how to use.

Never manually remove program files, drivers, or settings files. Always use an uninstall program supplied by the software maker or the Windows Uninstall Programs utility to do this properly. If you do end up making a mistake, your best bet is to reinstall the software from scratch instead of trying to put things back in the right places.

If after doing a bit of housekeeping you find that your hard drive is almost always near full, consider adding some storage space. Either swap out the existing hard drive with a new, larger one (which also requires reinstallation of an operating system and applications and some data transfer) or by adding a lightweight, portable hard drive to carry some of the excess.

Feeling the Fury of No Sound

Why has your laptop suddenly stopped singing to you? It's nothing personal: It's most likely an improper setting. You have at least four ways to adjust the audio levels on most laptops:

   ✔ **Use the small thumbwheel on the case that adjusts the volume of the *built-in* speaker or speakers on your laptop.** In most designs, if it's set to 0 or 1, you can do nothing on the software side to hear music or system sounds.

✔ **Adjust the volume (and in some cases the bass, treble, and balance settings) with advanced sound cards or audio chipsets that have specialized software controls.** It's called a *mixer,* and depending on the complexity of your machine, it can have half a dozen or more volume sliders for you to adjust.

As you can see in Figure 3-1, even a basic volume control for a modern laptop can be quite capable. In this instance, the Realtek AC97 Audio volume control panel used by many laptop makers includes a master volume and balance control at the left side, as well as individual controls for Wave (a standard sound format co-developed by IBM and Microsoft and available for use on most machines), SW Synth (an equivalent of the MIDI format used to synthesize musical instrument sounds; some sound cards fully support MIDI and call this control by that name), CD Player, Microphone, Phone Line, and PC Speaker. In addition to the master control, each can be individually adjusted and each can be muted.

- **If hearing no sound at all, look first at the master volume control.** This control is usually the first box on the screen. The slider should be set to a midway point or higher; if the mixer uses numbers, choose a value in the middle of the available range.

- **Make sure that the Mute All checkbox for the master volume control isn't selected.** If marked with an X, the mixer prevents the sound card from producing sound for any device it controls.

- **Look at the sound mixer's other output settings.** On a typical machine, these include CD or DVD, Wave, MIDI, Line, and Mic or Microphone. As with the master control, make sure that volume settings are at least the midway point, and ascertain whether the Mute box is selected.

✔ **Look for a volume control icon loaded in the Start menu.** On some systems the icon is a miniature version of the master volume control; on others it's a shortcut to the full control. Once again, look at the volume settings and for checkmarks in the master Mute box or in one of the other outputs.

✔ **If using external speakers, ensure they're plugged into the proper port on the laptop.** If they require a separate electrical current for amplification, check to see that the external speakers' batteries are in place or an AC adapter properly attached. The On switch or button should be in the proper position. And finally, look for a volume control on the speakers themselves.

The thumbwheel on the laptop case generally does *not* affect the volume level produced by external speakers or a headset attached to the audio output. The wheel only adjusts the internal speakers of the laptop.

Figure 3-1:
This Realtek AC97 Audio volume control lets you tweak many settings.

1 Can't See You in This Light

Can't see text or graphics on your LCD screen? Before you start considering the difficulty and expense of replacing the display (they're not often repaired), look for some simpler and easier solutions.

First of all, ask yourself that very important and most basic question: What has changed since the last time I used the computer? Then consider any or all of the following:

✔ Have you changed any settings for the LCD screen available directly from the keyboard?

✔ Have you changed the video settings available from the Control Panel?

✔ Have you added any software programs or device drivers?

✔ Has your antivirus program reported any problems? (You do have one up and running and are keeping it completely current, right? If you don't, stop right now, go get one, and install it. Or update the one you have. Do it right now; I'll wait.)

✔ Has your computer experienced any sudden crashes recently?

If the answer to any of these questions is Yes, consider whether you can undo the changes or change settings back to previous ones. As a last resort, use System Restore to undo changes to the System Registry.

Many laptop computers include facilities to adjust the brightness, and sometimes the contrast, of the LCD screen from the keyboard. Look for a sunburst or similar symbol on a key. You may have to hold down a special Fn or Function key to shift the key from its alphanumeric assignment to a command purpose; consult the instruction manual for details. Check also to see that you have not inadvertently directed the computer to ignore the LCD and instead output an image to an attached CRT (video monitor). If so, switch back to the LCD. Consult the instruction manual (or carefully examine the secondary labels on the keyboard) for details. For example, the key combination on one machine in my office uses the special Fn shift together with the F5 key.

If these suggestions don't solve the problem, then you have the seeming conundrum that goes something like this: How can I make adjustments to the video display when I can't see anything on the screen? These three ideas may shed some light.

Stop loading Windows and display the system BIOS screen

Here's idea number one.

1. **Consult the instruction manual for your laptop for directions to display the BIOS setup.**

   On some machines you see a brief notice on the screen as the machine first comes to life; you may be asked to press the F2 or Esc button.

2. **Look for a setting that changes the video output or selects an output standard or a display resolution. On most machines, it should read LCD for video output.**

   If you're uncertain about proper BIOS settings and can't get clear advice on help screens or the instruction manual, do the following: Write down all of the settings as they currently read.

3. **Once you are certain you have a record of the BIOS settings, look for a command on the BIOS screen that permits a reset to Setup Default.**

   Choosing the default should work fine if you haven't made any changes to your machine's hardware, such as installing a new hard drive or a different CD or DVD drive. The BIOS automatically recognizes the amount of memory installed and should determine the needs of drives, but sometimes the best plans go awry. That's why you made a complete and careful copy of the BIOS settings as they existed before resetting to the default.

4. **If you haven't made any changes to the BIOS settings, select Exit and Do Not Save Changes or a similar command.**

   If you have made changes, or reset the BIOS to the default setting, select Exit and Save Changes or a similar command.

If changes to the BIOS solve the problem, this is a good-news, bad-news situation. The good news is that the display is now usable. The bad news is that *something* caused the BIOS settings to corrupt or change without your intent. Possible causes include

- **A virus.** Make sure your antivirus program is active and updated. If you receive a warning of infection, be sure to follow all instructions to remove the virus. After the virus is removed and the system fully scanned, you should assign the BIOS to default settings or carefully make choices of your own.

- **A failing backup battery or capacitor.** Most laptops include either a tiny replaceable battery or a capacitor that draws power from the main battery when needed; these power sources keep alive the BIOS settings. Check the instruction manual for your laptop for information on locating this small coin-sized battery (if your computer uses one) and replace it if necessary. One clue to a failing backup battery is an occasional or regular loss of date and time when the laptop is turned off for a few days. Some laptops use a form of static memory to hold BIOS settings; this specialized memory doesn't require electrical power to keep recorded information.

  If you must replace the battery, check the BIOS settings. It may be necessary to assign the BIOS to default selections or carefully make choices of your own.

- **Exposure to a strong magnetic field.** Magnetism can be generated by metal detectors at security checkpoints, from medical equipment, and other electronic devices including large monitors, television sets, and audio speakers that are not electrically insulated *(shielded)* against leakage of electrical fields. Check the BIOS settings and go back to defaults or manually make selections.

- **A problem with the BIOS itself.** Within most modern laptops, the instructions that make up the BIOS are held in a specialized form of memory called an EPROM — an electrically programmable read-only memory. This form of static memory happily holds code for years, but can also be reprogrammed to refresh the BIOS or to update it with a new version that adds features to your laptop, supporting new elements of advanced operating systems or hardware.

  Consult with your laptop maker for information about available BIOS updates and instructions on how to download them. In most situations, you download an executable file to your laptop over the Internet and then click it to initiate an automatic installation.

With luck, problems with a system BIOS are a once-in-a-laptop's-lifetime event and can be fixed using one of the methods above. If you believe the BIOS isn't corrupted and its settings are correct, the next step is to look for problems with the operating system; I assume you're working with a version of Windows.

Reboot your laptop and select a Safe Boot

Under current versions of Windows, you can initiate a Safe Boot by restarting your machine and holding down the F8 function key as soon as the BIOS test information begins to appear on the screen. The Safe Boot options, listed in Table 3-1, vary slightly based on the version of Microsoft Windows you're using.

Table 3-1:	Safe Boot Options for Windows XP Pro with Service Pack 2
Safe Boot	*What It Does*
Safe Mode	Starts Windows with the basic set of device drivers and services. Safe Mode uses the generic vga.sys driver at 640×480 resolution with 16 colors in the palette. In most cases you can get the machine running and then go to the Control Panel to change settings or to add, remove, or update troublesome device drivers. If you have added software, see if the program includes any adjustable video settings. Or, Add/Remove Programs from Windows (or a specialized removal program associated with the new application to uninstall the software). Reboot the system and restart.
Safe Mode with Networking	Works in the same manner as basic Safe Mode, adding just those necessary drivers and services needed to connect your laptop to a wired or wireless network.
Safe Mode with Command Prompt	Starts your machine and goes to the hidden operating system prompt, a facility that reaches back to DOS and the original PC. From the command prompt you can examine the file structure, erase or add files, and run certain utilities (including virus removal tools). Use this choice only if you have specific instructions from a technician or a software program.
Enable Boot Logging	Turns on a utility that records each step taken by the computer and the operating system in getting ready to run Windows. The results are recorded in a text file called Ntblog.txt. You can search for the file from within Windows or go directly to it by navigating to the %SystemRoot% folder.

Safe Boot	What It Does
Enable VGA Mode	Uses the existing video device driver but chooses a basic setting of 640×480 pixels. This is another way to get out of a bind that results if you choose a video mode or other setting beyond the capabilities of your video adapter, your monitor, or both. Once Windows is loaded you can go to the Control Panel and make adjustments before rebooting.
Last Known Good Configuration	Can be a lifesaver if a new problem crops up suddenly. Windows reboots using the settings it employed the last time the machine ran properly. Once the machine is running, you can go to Control Panel or applications to make adjustments.
Directory Service Restore Mode	A facility that some technicians may ask you to invoke. Using this mode repairs directory services for Windows-based domain controllers; if you don't know what that means I'd recommend you not experiment with this option without a qualified technician on the phone or by your side.
Debugging Mode	Another technical tool that shouldn't be undertaken without assistance. If you go down this route you can read and make changes to some specific memory computer and hard drive locations; data can also be sent from your computer on a serial cable to another computer running a debugging program (and is presumably in better shape) than the one you're having problems with. Be careful in there.
Disable Automatic Restart	On system failure, forces the machine to shut down instead of restarting under certain conditions. This allows you to perform a "cold" boot that resets the hardware and the software from a power-off condition.
Start Windows Normally	Instructs the machine to ignore the Safe Boot choices and instead start Windows in its normal mode.
Reboot	Goes around the Safe Boot process. The only difference between this and Start Windows Normally is that the hardware is reset.
Return to OS Choices Menu	Of use if you set up your computer to be capable of choosing from various operating systems: different versions of Windows, for example, or Windows and a flavor of Linux.

Many laptops include a feature — selectable from the BIOS or from the Video Display menu of the Control Panel — that allows you to set the LCD brightness when running on AC power at a higher level than when the laptop's running on batteries. This can extend the usable life of the battery by a significant percentage.

Hardware failure

This is the worst possible scenario: most likely either the LCD display or the video controller display. Neither is a happy circumstance, unless your machine is still under warranty. (But then again, why has a relatively young machine suffered a catastrophic failure?) Make sure you don't have a high-tech lemon; make sure any repairs come with a proper guarantee and keep a close eye on your machine's performance as it approaches the end of the warranty period.

Under Windows, go to the Control Panel and check the Device Manager under System Properties. Look for one of two things: a red X indicating that a device has been disabled or has failed, or a yellow exclamation point indicating a resource conflict or a problem with the associated driver.

Resource conflicts don't arise out of the air; if the display (or any other piece of hardware) was working properly yesterday but not today, stop and consider what has changed. Have you added any new hardware? Have you changed settings? Have you updated or changed device drivers? Consider going back in time by using System Restore. You can find the key to this simple but essential tool in the Cheat Sheet.

If you suspect a hardware failure, you can take a few steps to identify which part is causing the problem. The first is to try to determine whether the LCD or the video display adapter is at fault.

1. **Check your instruction manual and locate the port — usually a nine-pin female connector called a DB9 — on the machine.**

   Most laptops include the ability to output a video signal to a standard computer monitor.

2. **Bring your laptop to a desktop (or bring a monitor to the vicinity of your portable computer) and attach the standard computer display to the DB9 connector.**

3. **Turn on the monitor and use your laptop's keyboard commands to toggle the output from the built-in LCD display to the attached monitor.**

   On some machines you press and hold the Fn or Function key together with one of F keys at the top; other machines may require you to go into the BIOS to enable the output to a monitor. Yet another method requires selection from an on-screen utility, which could be problematic if you can't see the LCD display.

A properly working monitor is a good indicator that the video display circuitry on the motherboard or a small video display adapter on a separate card is functioning properly. (You may have to adjust the monitor's resolution from the Control Panel if, as is likely, its specifications are different from the built-in LCD panel.)

Another way to check the health of the video display circuitry on some machines is to attempt to output a signal to a standard composite television set; many laptops offer a direct video output for such purposes. The connector is usually a yellow female RCA connector — the same design used to connect components of a stereo audio receiver or VCR. As with output to a computer monitor, the laptop includes a toggle to enable use of a TV. (If you receive a signal, you likely need to adjust resolution to a relatively coarse 640×480 setting to see the full screen.)

Black, white, and striped screens

A completely dead LCD tells you very little except that the display isn't getting power, isn't getting a video signal, or isn't getting either. But if the LCD shows something — vertical or horizontal lines, a blush of color, or a weak or washed-out image — you can make an educated guess. Thanks to my friends at www.portablecomputer.com, here are a few common LCD conditions to watch for:

DIY FYI

Here's a checklist (in a typical order of steps) for the removal of an existing LCD and the installation of a new one on a typical laptop:

✔ Save all work in progress, exit all applications, and shut down the notebook.

✔ Disconnect all external devices.

✔ Disconnect the battery pack.

✔ Remove the battery pack.

✔ Removal of the hard drive and CD or DVD drive (some laptops).

✔ Remove screws from the bottom of the case that hold the keyboard in place.

✔ Turn the laptop right-side up and slide the keyboard out from its holding clips.

✔ Lift the rear edge of the keyboard.

✔ Release the connector that holds the keyboard cable and slide the unit away from the laptop.

✔ Install a new LCD into the connector and then reverse all of the steps to reassemble the laptop.

Depending on your comfort level, this may sound like an easy job or an impossible one. The fact is that this is by no means heavy lifting — any replacement of a component within a laptop requires only basic skills with a screwdriver and sometimes tweezers or jeweler's pliers. But it is close work and requires great attention to detail and care. I've done it a few times and can't say I found it enjoyable or especially rewarding.

✔ **Cracked, torn, or slashed LCD.** Sorry, but physical damage to the LCD itself cannot be repaired; the only option is to replace the display. Depending on the laptop, this could cost between $150–$300 for parts, plus labor. The first question to ask: Is this laptop worth the expense? The second question: Can I do this repair myself?

Doing the repair by yourself certainly saves you the cost of someone else's labor, but don't underestimate the amount of time it will take you. And remember that if you have a professional do the job, his or her work (and usually the parts) have a guarantee.

✔ **Black screen.** A totally unresponsive, black screen like the one in Figure 3-2 can be the result of a failure of the LCD or the LCD inverter, a specialized piece of electronics that energizes the screen. The LCD may be repairable by a competent specialist; a failed inverter can be replaced with a new unit.

Figure 3-2:
A black
LCD screen.

Black LCD screen

To rule out failure of the video display adapter or circuitry, try an *external monitor* — a standard computer monitor attached to the laptop, just like a display connects to a desktop machine. If it works, the motherboard and video display adapter of the laptop are likely performing properly and the LCD is at fault.

✔ **White or washed-out screen.** A totally white or washed-out screen, like the one in Figure 3-3, is indicative of a problem with the LCD that can generally be repaired by a specialist.

✔ **Horizontal or vertical block.** Like rolling or static interference on a home television set, an off-color, bright, or dark band that extends horizontally or vertically across a portion of the screen is generally a problem with the LCD that can be repaired by a specialist. You can see an example in Figure 3-4.

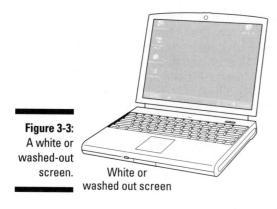

Figure 3-3:
A white or washed-out screen.

White or
washed out screen

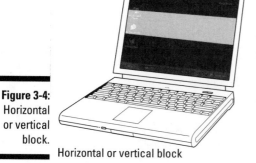

Figure 3-4:
Horizontal or vertical block.

Horizontal or vertical block

✔ **Crossed lines.** White or black lines that cross the screen, meeting at 90-degree or nearly 90-degree angles like the one in Figure 3-5, usually mean a problem with the LCD that can generally be repaired by a specialist.

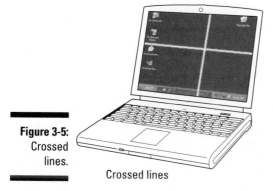

Figure 3-5:
Crossed lines.

Crossed lines

✔ **Horizontal lines.** One or more horizontal white or black lines that extend across the width of the screen, like those seen in Figure 3-6, are a problem with the LCD that can generally be repaired. As a matter of fact, if the lines are very distinct, a repair shop may be able to follow them directly to a broken connection that's causing a loss of information on screen along the edge of the LCD; in a small percentage of jobs the connectors can be repaired rather than having the expense of a new LCD.

✔ **Vertical lines.** One or more vertical white or black lines that extend across the width of the screen like those in Figure 3-7 is a problem that can generally be repaired.

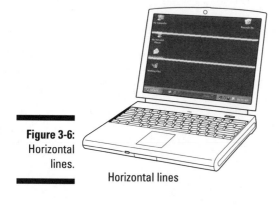

Figure 3-6:
Horizontal
lines.

Horizontal lines

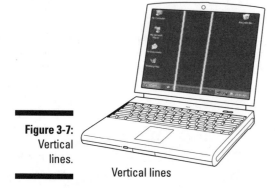

Figure 3-7:
Vertical
lines.

Vertical lines

✔ **Discoloration.** Off colors, faded colors, or a color wash across a portion of the screen is generally a problem with the LCD that can be repaired by a specialist. See Figure 3-8 for an example.

✔ **Dim display or faded image.** A weak display of text or graphics as seen in Figure 3-9 may be caused by a repairable problem with the LCD, or a failed LCD converter that must be replaced.

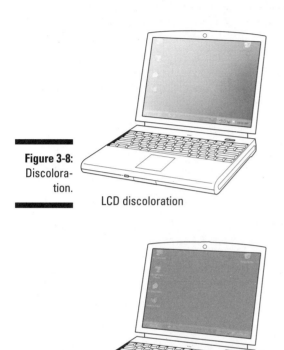

Figure 3-8:
Discolora-
tion.

LCD discoloration

Figure 3-9:
Dim display.

Dim or faded image

Chapter 4

When to Repair and When to Recycle

*W*hen your laptop breaks, you face a question that's more financial than technical, sometimes more emotional than rational, and always more complex than simple.

The cause of the problem is the nature of a laptop. Although it is, at heart, just a miniaturized desktop computer, a laptop is much more difficult and expensive to repair and its internal parts tougher to replace. Changing a video card or even upgrading an entire motherboard on a desktop is a job well within the financial and technical means of many computer owners; doing the same on a laptop may not make sense on any level but emotional.

Staying Put or Getting Gone

Let me start with the fact that repairs for laptops are expensive. They almost always use proprietary parts and highly integrated, tiny components including a built-in LCD screen and internal video, audio, modem, network, WiFi wireless, and other features. (*WiFi* is the most common design for wireless communication; see Chapter 13 for details.)

I'm just talking through my hat here, but I think the numbers are probably not far from reality: If you were to buy a brand new laptop today for a typical price of about $1,250 and then seek to build a clone from new and unused individual parts, you'd probably spend at least twice as much for the components, and spend 6 or 8 or 10 hours putting the pieces together. If you were to assign that cloning job to a professional repair shop, the cost of that computer — parts and a day's labor — would be something like $3,000.

Now, obviously, you're not going to waste money in that way. However, it's a much less obvious decision when it comes to determining whether to repair a malfunctioning screen on a three-year-old laptop. Is it worth putting a few hundred dollars into a machine that would resell on eBay for $150? The answer, as you see later, is *maybe*.

Speaking very roughly, a basic repair for a laptop usually runs in the range of $150–$250. For that amount of money you should be able to get an LCD *component* (not the LCD itself) or a broken connector repaired. If the motherboard itself is fried, or damaged be repair, the cost to bring the laptop back to near original specs could be several hundred dollars.

So, does your laptop stay or does it go. . .to the shop?

I suggest you answer these questions before making the ultimate decision:

- ✔ **What's the approximate worth of the laptop when it's in working condition?** One relatively easy way to gauge the value of a used laptop or almost anything else is to check the listings on eBay. Start by looking for your exact make and model; if you can't come that close, look for an equivalent machine using the same processor (Pentium, Celeron, AMD, or other) running at the same speed, a similar amount of RAM, and a similar-sized hard drive.

- ✔ **What's the approximate cost to purchase a new machine of equivalent or greater technical specs?**

  The fact is that laptops keep getting better and better, with prices going down or value going up. If your original machine cost $1,000, after a year or more the same amount of money buys a much more capable machine. As this book goes to press, the low end of laptop computing sits at about $650 for a quite-capable machine most likely built around a Celeron or equivalent AMD processor. The screen size at that price level is likely to be an adequate 13 inches in diagonal measure, there will be a relatively small hard drive, and basic audio and video capabilities.

  The high end stands at about $2,500, and for that you get an ultra-slim, ultra-light, ultra-fast machine with a large, bright screen. Expect to also receive CD-RW and DVD capabilities and built-in modem, networking, and WiFi facilities. In between lies the largest segment of the market: fine machines priced from about $1,000–$1,500. These machines have all of the latest features, but aren't quite as light, thin, or fast as the top of the line.

The economics of repairs and upgrades on a laptop underlie one of the basic money-saving rules for electronics: Buy one step behind the newest models. Remember that the machine that looked like the most fantastic model yesterday is just as good today, and even sweeter with a sharp markdown in price.

🖊 **Is there something particularly special about the laptop you currently have that makes repairing it worthwhile?**

Does it possess a particular feature you can't find in a new machine? Is it particularly well suited to your needs? And now you can do the math. Say you're otherwise satisfied with the laptop you have; you have no need to upgrade to a $1,500 replacement. If you can repair your machine for $200 (and receive a warranty from the shop that promises the original failure will stay fixed for a reasonable period of time; 90 days is a minimum, and 6 months typical) sending it to the shop is probably worthwhile.

But say the cost of the repair is $300, the model you have is only worth about $150 on the market, and the old machine is barely adequate for your needs: It's too slow, the screen is too small, and it lacks modern built-in facilities such as a large hard drive, CD-R, network interface, and WiFi. In this case you would spend $300 and end up with a machine that inadequately meets your needs.

Asking an Expert

One of the experts I consulted for this book was Wesley Forrester, who owns and operates www.portablecomputer.com, a laptop repair service. Forrester was quick to acknowledge that some machines *could* be repaired but probably shouldn't be.

"Is there something about this specific model that is special?" he asked. "If you can't part with it, that may be the answer." Older notebooks have some features that newer ones lack. One is an internal floppy disk drive, which can be useful in quickly transporting files from one machine to another without setting up a network or direct wire connection between them.

Another feature quickly becoming obsolete on laptops is an old-style serial port. On many modern machines, the emphasis is on use of the USB port. And, Forrester pointed out, even though a USB port can be made to mimic a standard serial port — something I discuss in Chapter 16 — some older software and hardware may be incompatible with that sort of workaround. As one example, some otherwise perfectly capable credit card processing equipment works on a DOS level (outside of Microsoft Windows) and the machine may not recognize the existence of a USB port or a substitute serial port that uses the USB facility.

The other class of machines that may be worth paying for repair are those at the high end of the market, laptops that may be just past a one-year warranty and for which the cost of a replacement might be more than $1,000 or even close to $2,000. If it costs you $250 to get back a machine worth $1,500, that's a good deal; if it costs you $250 to repair a machine that has a value of just a few hundred dollars, you're probably better off biting the bullet and buying a new or refurbished machine.

Experiencing a breakdown

I came across Forrester and his company as I was beginning research for this book. One of the laptops in my office — a trusted Gateway Solo 2500 SE — gave up the ghost soon after I began writing about repairs. One morning the LCD screen was bright and sharp; a few hours later I turned the machine on again and the screen was a sickeningly pale white with just a ghost of an image that would appear for a moment and then recede back into the ether.

The first thing I did was try to isolate the problem. That laptop, like many others, has an alternate video output: It could be connected to a desktop computer monitor or to a standard television set (a valuable facility for showing pictures or presentations at a meeting). And so I connected a cable from the Gateway to a TV and turned on the laptop. There was Windows and my desktop; I quickly checked a few applications and the health of the hard disk drive and then turned off the machine.

I knew that my motherboard was functioning properly and my hard drive was okay. It was most likely that the video adapter on the motherboard was undamaged as well; the chances that the internal LCD output would be dead while the television output working was slim. The likely culprit: something to do with the LCD itself. At worst, the LCD had died; with luck it was something less, like a failed inverter or backlight.

On a laptop, the *inverter* is a piece of electronics that sits between the motherboard and the LCD. Its purpose is to invert the video output. Remember that in some ways, an LCD works in the opposite manner of a monitor. A monitor makes a white character on the screen by illuminating a particular set of phosphor dots *(pixels)* on the screen. An LCD's natural color is white (as enhanced by its backlight). It makes a black character or a colored image by changing the electrical state of one or more layers of filters. The inverter regulates the power to the LCD; the inverter has to be exactly matched to the machine or it could easily blow out the backlight and the LCD.

And so I sent the machine off to Forrester and www.portablecomputers.com. About a week later I had my surprisingly pleasant answer: After hundreds of thousands of miles of travel all around the world by plane, train, automobile, and ship, my Gateway was still in very good condition. Somehow, though, the tiny cable that connected the LCD to the inverter and the motherboard had worked its way out of the socket. Plugged back in firmly, the laptop was now as good as ever. That will be $200, please.

Could I have found the problem by myself? Probably. I've never been afraid to take equipment — cars to televisions to computers — apart. But I know how difficult it is to work within the tiny confines of a laptop, and I also know that replacement parts aren't something that can be found at the nearest SuperCompAmericaCity Store.

Basic repair news from the shop

With my repaired Gateway back in service — I use it as an extra Internet display, monitoring the news or a baseball game when not on the road — I called Forrester to discuss the work his company had done on my machine.

A basic repair costs about $200. Most of that expense involves labor. The same approximate charge likely applies to reseating a disconnected internal cable or replacing a basic component like an inverter or LCD backlight (more about those in a moment). The worst case for most laptops — or at least the most expensive repair worth considering — is replacement of a fried, cracked, or otherwise damaged motherboard, a project usually priced at about $300.

After determining the motherboard problem, the shop tries to fix it. Failing that, they replace the board with a refurbished motherboard of the same design and maker. Apparently upgrading a laptop's motherboard is tough because each computer and maker are so proprietary about products.

With my machine, Forrester said, the problem was relatively rare but an easily fixed one. The work and expense in reattaching a loose cable or restoring a loose connection comes with the time it takes to properly disassemble and reassemble the laptop.

More common causes of problems with laptops are actual component failures. About 50–60 percent of all laptop breakdowns are related to the LCD, Forrester said, and the most common point of failure on modern laptops are the LCD's backlight or inverter. The *backlight* is a specialized lightbulb, usually fluorescent and located along the bottom of the LCD; Forrester described it as very fragile and tricky to work, a 10–12-inch long pencil-like bulb with metal connectors at each end.

His company stocks four types of backlights, which work with something like 90 percent of all LCDs. If he has to repair a machine that uses one of the rare 10 percent of other lamps, he has to special-order a new bulb or find a recycled replacement scavenged from a similar machine. More tricky to keep in stock are inverters, which are mostly proprietary to each maker's combination of motherboard and LCD; it's very rare to find one inverter that works with two different notebook models, even similar series from the same manufacturer, according to Forrester.

After the LCD and its associated components, the next most common type of laptop problem is failure to boot up. This problem is most often with the motherboard. Perhaps the most common source of failure here comes when power connectors or ports break off the computer itself, a problem more common with some brands of laptops than with others.

The most vulnerable laptops are those where the power connector (which attaches to the external power supply) or the ports are actually part of the motherboard itself. A misattached cable or an unfortunate bounce or movement of the laptop can cause them to crack the motherboard or snap off. In some cases, a professional laptop repair shop can reattach or resolder a damaged connector; if you're not lucky, the sort of problem demands a new or refurbished motherboard.

The failure of a laptop's hard drive or CD or DVD drive no longer automatically demands the services of a repair shop, Forrester said. Modern laptops mount their drives in removable, plug-in carriers that attach to connectors in bays. Consumers can easily do this sort of repair.

The Good, the Bad, and the Cheaply Made

I live in a tourist town, and it's interesting to watch the comings and goings of restaurants. The places that offer the best food or the best prices have been in business for years and years, and are easy to recommend. Word spreads very quickly about any place not worth visiting and by summer's end there's a For Rent sign in the window.

To some extent, it's the same story with computer makers. (Were you wondering where I was going with the restaurant business analogy?) The companies that have been around for a decade or so are still selling machines because they've built a base of customers who respect the products or the support and service they receive. Over the years a few companies have come and gone, along with their products.

I'm absolutely not going to say that a new company won't come along and offer a great product at a great price with excellent support. All I can say is that as I write these words, here are the top five sellers of PC-compatible laptops:

- ✔ Hewlett Packard, including subsidiary Compaq
- ✔ Dell
- ✔ Toshiba
- ✔ IBM
- ✔ Fujitsu/Siemens

Add to that list the top seller of Apple iBook machines:

- ✔ Apple

Now here's a deep dark secret well known within the industry but less so among the general public: Many laptop sellers don't manufacture their products, instead farming them out to independent Asian sources and sometimes changing from one factory to another for different models. And even companies that actually assemble machines usually buy most of their components from other sources. Finally, a big maker may maintain full control over the production and assembly of its machines but do so in third-party factories.

So, Brand D may have many of the same parts as Brand C, but be put together in two different factories. Or brand I may be assembled by the some company that assembles Brand H, but using unrelated components. Or Brand T may make or design all of its own components, but assemble its product in a third-world factory.

And then all of this alphabet soup is likely to be scrambled into different combinations the next time I sit down to think about it. Just as one example, at the end of 2004 IBM sold its entire consumer PC business (including its well-regarded ThinkPad laptop product line) to Lenovo, the largest Chinese computer *assembly* company. Lenovo has made many IBM products for years as well as those of other suppliers. With the sale, Lenovo is likely to take the number-three position in worldwide sales after HP and Dell.

The fact is, when you buy a Dell or Toshiba or IBM made by Lenovo, you're trusting in the *design* and *specification* capabilities of the distributor (the brand name), hoping that the factory or supplier they choose does a good job of assembly and testing, and that either the seller or the distributor stands behind its product with first-class support and service.

I asked Forrester about the models he sees most often in his shop. His mixed report: Sony and Dell products have the highest occurrence of LCD problems, which isn't unexpected since most of their machines use screens from the same manufacturer. The maker of the problematic screens? Neither Dell nor Sony but rather Samsung, the Korean conglomerate.

Compaqs and corporate cousin HP laptops, Gateway machines, as well as many OEM products (sold under brand names of retailers that have no factories) often fail because of problems with their DC power jacks, the connector where the AC adapter attaches. (An *OEM* is an Original Equipment Manufacturer, a company that make components that other companies incorporate into their brand-name machines.) Forrester said that Toshiba and Dell have avoided this problem through more robust engineering, while IBM and Sony put a cable between their DC connectors and the motherboard, which protects the expensive board.

Toshiba is overall the best-engineered laptop, according to Forrester; for what it's worth, as a user that's my opinion as well. That's not to say that Toshiba's technical support is the best, and it's also true that other makers may offer faster or flashier machines. But Toshiba makes a solid, durable machine. Actually, the Japanese company uses factories in China and elsewhere in Asia to make its machines.

Some of the larger OEM manufacturers include Acer, Compal, Quantex, and Twinhead; you may find machines with these names or private label machines at retail stores. The machines may be just fine, but finding replacement parts may be problematic.

Chapter 5

Surviving Basic Training

*I*t's not possible to write a book about troubleshooting hardware without dealing with software and settings, nor the other way around. Things hard and soft are tightly interlinked; each requires the other to work properly.

The design of Microsoft Windows and other modern operating systems places a set of more-or-less interchangeable, compatible pieces of hardware on one side of the equation; on the other are the management and control of the hardware through applications and utilities. In between lie two critical, changeable elements that bring the two together: a set of device drivers that interpret generic commands from the operating system (so that they meet the needs of the particular pieces of hardware in your system) and a System Registry (which holds settings, configurations, and customizations).

Unbuttoning the Essential Windows Control Panel

The Windows Control Panel is the relatively user-friendly place where the hardware meets the operating system. Here you can confirm that Windows can communicate with pieces of hardware; look at the device driver and repair, replace, or remove it; and search for pesky conflicts between machine resources.

The contents of your Control Panel vary depending on the hardware components of your laptop, plus special software and utilities installed by the maker. Think of the panel as if it were a wall full of dials and sliders that establish and tweak your machine's personality.

The Control Panel varies from machine to machine, depending on the hardware installed within the case or plugged into a port or connector. Various pieces of software also add management utilities. An example of the Control Panel from one of my laptops, a modern Toshiba model, is shown in Figure 5-1.

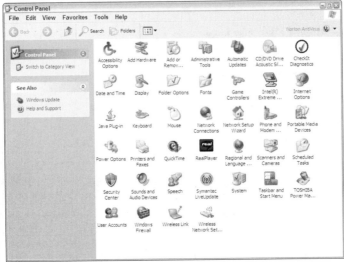

Figure 5-1:
A typical
Control
Panel on a
current
laptop.

Double-click any of the icons to open a subpanel that includes at least one page of settings; most devices offer several tabbed pages of other customization options. Here are the most important of the several dozen:

- ✔ **Accessibility Options.** The controls here are principally aimed at making the computer easier to use for people with special needs, including typing, hearing, and vision difficulties. Even people without these accessibility needs may find options here of benefit to them.

- ✔ **Add Hardware.** This option opens a wizard to help install software to support new hardware added to your system and to troubleshoot problems you may be having with installed equipment.

  If a new piece of hardware comes with an installation CD, as most now do, you should use that CD and its own installation process instead of using the Add Hardware Wizard. In addition to convenience, this ensures that device drivers and other utilities are put in exactly the proper order and location and that settings match the manufacturer's recommendations.

- ✔ **Add or Remove Programs.** This utility can install or uninstall software on your system. Use the down arrow or the mouse to click individual pieces of software and learn important information, including the amount of space taken up by the program, when it was last used, and whether the software is used rarely or occasionally.

Just as with the Add Hardware Wizard, if a piece of software comes with its own installation and removal utility, you're always better off using those facilities instead of asking Windows to figure out the process by itself. Most customized installation programs from software manufacturers record all steps taken when they first put on the machine; they can operate in reverse to pick up all the widely spread pieces placed on the drive.

✔ **Administrative Tools.** If Microsoft or another manufacturer asks you to make adjustments to some of the security policies or internal services that run when your computer is started, or if you're advised to check the performance of your computer's services, this is the place to go. For more details, check the Microsoft Knowledge Base. You can get there from the company's home page, at www.microsoft.com. Among the elements of the tool panel are

- **Data Sources (ODBC).** This is a programming interface for applications that use Structured Query Language (SQL) to access data.

- **Event Viewer.** Here you can view or manage logs of system, program, and security events as a troubleshooting and fine-tuning tool.

- **Local Security policy.** This facility allows you to adjust password policy, user rights, and other security options on most computers; settings here can be overridden by users with administrative privileges.

- **Performance.** Here you can view or collect data about the activities of your computer's memory, processor, disk drives, network, and other important facilities.

- **Services.** This portal manages basic computer services and sets and controls recovery actions.

✔ **Date and Time.** Here you can adjust the laptop's internal clock and date and acknowledge the machine's home base in a particular time zone; knowing the time zone allows the computer to automatically make adjustments for Daylight Savings Time. On current versions of Windows, you can also assign the computer to regularly update its clock based on an Internet time server so all of your machines can be synchronized to an official clock.

✔ **Display.** Depending on the make and capability of your display adapter (or the built-in features of your motherboard), you can visit this panel to choose screen resolution and color quality, and manage multiple monitors if you have an external device attached to your laptop in addition to the LCD. You can also choose a theme for colors and appearance of Windows, make adjustments to your desktop's look, and turn on or off a screen saver that shuts down the LCD or puts a power-saving and privacy-maintaining image on the display after a period of inactivity.

✔ **Keyboard.** Here you can check the operation of your built-in keyboard and set some preferences, including character repeat rate and cursor blink rate.

✔ **Mouse.** The maker of your laptop or some of its components can customize a panel here to control many of the features of the built-in mouse, pointing stick, or touch pad. You can also adjust the button configuration (switching primary and secondary buttons if you choose) and set the double-click speed for selection of options.

✔ **Power Management Utility.** Especially important to the operations of a laptop computer, this utility — usually customized by the system manufacturer — allows users to customize the processor speed and the screen brightness under AC power and battery power. You can also set alarms to warn of the approaching depletion of power.

✔ **Security Center.** Microsoft added a central control panel in Service Pack 2 of Windows XP to help oversee and manage important security features including firewall, virus protection, and automatic updates. The maker of your antivirus software may place a customized control panel here or adapt Microsoft's options.

Microsoft's Security Center may not recognize some third-party antivirus and security programs and must be controlled by their own panel. That doesn't mean they're not fully capable, just that in some way they diverge from the definitions laid down by the masters of your machine's world at Microsoft.

✔ **Sound and Audio Devices.** The maker of your sound card likely placed a panel to control some of its hardware features, including recording and playback settings. Some makers rename the panel with custom titles such as AudioHQ (used by Creative Labs).

Other features, unrelated to repairing and upgrading a laptop, include panels to control Internet options and special-purpose programs related to Web image display or streaming audio or sound stored on your machine. These features include Internet Options, Java Plug-In, QuickTime, RealPlayer, and Speech controls.

For the first few generations of PCs, users had to be very aware of which *IRQs* are used by the system (IRQs are system interrupts, which are the equivalent of the hardware waving its hand back and forth asking for the processor's attention) and which *DMA* channels are in used (direct memory access channels allow data to be transferred between peripherals and internal memory without involving the microprocessor). Today, though, the facilities of current Windows versions — including self-configuring plug-and-play devices and the magically expandable USB system — make these kinds of problems almost a nonissue. Almost. If the Control Panel's Device Manager tells you that a piece of hardware isn't working because of an IRQ or DMA conflict, you have to either disable that component or seek the assistance of its manufacturer in forcing it to use a different set of resources. (*Plug-and-play* devices are designed to be automatically recognized by the hardware and the operating system when installed; all USB devices are supposed to be of this design, and many components that attach to other ports can identify themselves to the system.)

Getting there

Depending how your machine has been set up, several routes take you where you want to go. The most common is to click Start and then choose Control Panel; on some machines you may have to click Start, then Settings, and finally choose Control Panel. Next, double-click the System icon to display the System Properties panel. A generic laptop has a generic panel; some major manufacturers have special dispensation from the Creators at Microsoft to customize the panel slightly. If the panel has been customized by the maker of the hardware you will often see the model name, information on the microprocessor in use, and the total amount of installed RAM. The General tab of a System Properties panel on a modern Toshiba laptop is shown in Figure 5-2.

Figure 5-2:
The General tab includes information about the operating system version, including any major Service Pack updates, plus the name of the registered owner and the serial number for the Windows version.

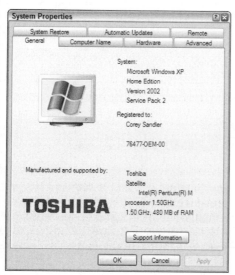

Your goal here, though, is to burrow a few levels deeper into the Control Panel. Choose the Hardware tab and then click the Device Manager button. Get in the habit of coming here first anytime your machine is feeling poorly or making you sick. The Device Manager gives you an instant check on the status of all major pieces of hardware and is the gateway to deeper probes and troubleshooting guides.

Your first assignment is to eyeball the page. In the best of all possible worlds, you see the names of all the devices and nothing more; if Windows has detected a problem, it raises a flag. Three possible conditions exist, one of which is good, one of which is troubling, and one of which is officially bad news. The initial display of a typical Device Manager is shown in Figure 5-3.

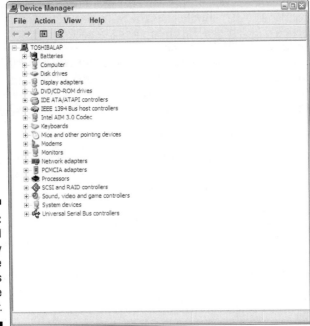

Figure 5-3:
The initial
display
of the
Windows
Device
Manager.

✔ **Good News:** If you see nothing other than the name of a device, the system is aware of its presence and has detected no problems. This is a good thing. You can, though, double-click and open the device to read about the details of the device driver software it employs, the resources it uses, and (for some elements) some of the hardware settings.

✔ **Troubling News:** If you see an exclamation point (!) in a yellow circle, Windows is warning you of its concern about a potential conflict. Well, I guess the machine doesn't really care, but it's programmed to raise a flag if it finds two or more devices that just might ask for the same resource at the same time or if it has found that two or more devices have, in fact, conflicted recently (although not right at this moment). The exclamation point can also mean that Windows has found a problem with the device driver for this piece of hardware and suggests that you pay attention to the matter.

✔ **Officially Bad News:** If you see an X in a red circle, you've got a problem right here, right now. In fact, the problem is so bad that this particular piece of hardware has been disabled by Windows or cannot be recognized at all by the operating system.

No news is good news, so don't make unnecessary changes to settings that aren't reporting problems. However, if you see an X in a red circle you need to troubleshoot the problem, make changes, or disable the hardware. If disabling the hardware, you can attempt to reinstall its drivers and associated software to rehabilitate it or use an external workaround. For example, a failed internal touch pad can be replaced by clip-on trackball that attaches to the system using the USB port.

If you see an exclamation point in a yellow circle you may or may not have to do anything. Sometimes Windows finds conflicts between devices that don't affect the ability to perform intended assignments. You can use the Device Manager's troubleshooting function to isolate the source of the problem or you can uninstall and reinstall drivers; placing a fresh copy of a driver or an updated version often resolves conflicts because the system is smart enough to seek conflict-free locations for devices and utilities.

Donning your managerial hat

Note that alongside each group of similar devices is a + or − sign. Click the + to open the details contained in each class. An opened Device Manager is shown in Figure 5-4. On a laptop, the typical devices follow.

Click the Driver Tab of the System Properties panel for any device in the Device Manager and on most machines learn the name of the provider of the driver, its date of creation and version number, and other details. You can click buttons to view details of the driver files, update the driver for the device with a new version from the Internet or CD, roll back the driver to a previous version if the device fails after an update, or completely uninstall the driver. (Here's how to get there: Open the Windows Control Panel, then choose System icon⇨Hardware tab⇨Device Manager tab. Finally, double-click an individual piece of hardware and choose the Driver tab.)

Figure 5-4:
The Device
Manager
screen with
several of
its hardware
classes
opened.

Batteries

Here you find information about the hardware side of the battery charger. You also learn about the software side, including device drivers that manage power use and monitor the available charge.

Computer

This is a general checkup on the motherboard; most modern laptops use a Microsoft specification and device driver called ACPI Uniprocessor PC. If the motherboard has a problem, you're going to have to deal with a repair shop or the manufacturer; if the device driver has a problem, you may be able to reinstall the driver from the original system disc supplied by the laptop manufacturer. In a best case scenario, the driver is easily found and installed by the system; in a worst case you have to reinstall the operating system, which may result in the loss of data and program files.

Disk drives

Most laptops have just a single internal hard drive; you should see either the name of the manufacturer and a model number or a code that represents the same (although it may not make immediate sense to you). You may be able to decipher the code name by plugging it in as the object of your search engine, or you may have to call the disk drive or laptop manufacturer. On one of my laptops, the code is an otherwise opaque IC25N060ATMR04-0; using Google, I determined with a few keystrokes that this is an IBM Hitachi 9.5mm 60GB hard drive with a 4,200 RPM spindle speed and a 2-MB buffer. (You read more about what those specs mean in Chapter 7.)

Depending on the maker of your laptop, the other tabs on the Properties panel may be filled out with additional information, or they may be blank. (Customized machines are more likely to have detailed descriptions; if your machine is one of 100,000 of a particular model, you may not get that information.)

Display adapters

Built into the motherboard of your laptop or plugged into a tiny *daughterboard* that attaches to the main board, the display adapter manages the conversion of a "picture" made up of 0s and 1s in memory into an image viewable on the laptop's LCD (and in most cases on an external standard video display). Like other elements of the computer shown in the Device Manager, you can check on the health of the hardware, look for conflicts of resources, and remove, reinstall, or update the device driver.

Depending on the type of hardware in your laptop, you can choose tabs on the Display Properties page that do the following:

- ✔ Use a predesigned **Theme** or create your own. A theme consists of a background plus sounds, icons, and artistic elements.

- ✔ Make a **Desktop** layout using one of the pictures or designs provided by Microsoft as a background for your desktop or use one of your own photos for this purpose. Any image you store in the My Pictures folder of your desktop is considered available for use as a background image. You can also browse elsewhere on any attached drive for other images.

- ✔ Choose a **Screen Saver** and make settings that determine how long the system must remain idle before it comes on. If a video monitor (not an LCD) is attached, you can adjust monitor power settings that include the ability to shut down the monitor (leaving the computer running) or go into a hibernation state. On a laptop, most computer makers have a spe-cialized set of power settings for the LCD, including the ability to run the screen at full brightness when powered by AC wall current and make less power demands when the battery is in charge. Most laptops can also display a Power Meter that reports on remaining battery charge, and sound an alarm, shut down, or put the machine into hibernation at a particular voltage level.

✔ The **Appearance** tab allows users to customize the appearance of Windows including colors, effects (such as fading or scrolling type in or out), point size, and font style.

✔ Of great importance is the **Settings** tab, where you can choose the screen resolution. (A modern laptop can usually pack as much as 1280×800 pixels or 1400×1050 and even more.) The trick is to get as much resolution and as much information onscreen as you can see and use; there's no point to using a resolution that results in images, icons, and type too small to see. You can also choose the *color quality,* the number of colors used by the adapter in creating images; the highest setting on most laptops is 32 bits. High resolution and high color settings are both dependent on sufficient video memory.

✔ **DVD/CD-ROM drives.** Most current laptops include a CD or CD-R and many feature a combination drive that will also read data from a DVD and show videos. You can check the properties of the hardware and make changes or adjustments to the device driver.

Controllers

IDE ATA/ATAPI **controllers** report on the hard disk drive controller, with both hardware and device driver tabs. IEEE 1394 Bus host controllers are the component of the motherboard in charge of managing FireWire input and output, using the IEEE 1394 specification.

A laptop's built-in **keyboard** is monitored here. If you add a second external keyboard, it may be assigned to this category or managed by the USB controller. A laptop's built-in **pointing device** — which can be a touch pad, a pointing stick, or a tiny trackball — is monitored here. If you add a second external pointing device it may be assigned to this category or managed by the USB controller.

An internal **modem** built into the motherboard, attached to it on a tiny daughterboard, or (in some designs) attached to the laptop through the serial or USB port is managed here. A fourth design, one in increasing use especially as dial-up modems become less common because of the growth of wireless and wired broadband connections, is a software modem which uses the facilities of the computer's microprocessor and its memory to emulate the hardware of a modem when needed.

The laptop's display adapter considers the built-in LCD as a **monitor** and usually will also work with an external standard video display. Some machines can operate both at the same time, and others can also send an image to a standard television set.

Adapters

A state-of-the-art laptop may include several network **adapters**, including a standard wired *NIC (network interface card),* a 1394 (FireWire) network adapter, and a wireless network adapter. The PCMCIA adapters section of the laptop manages the functions and drivers for a PC Card, a quick and relatively easy way to add new features using a credit-card-sized device. The PC Card is rapidly giving way to the USB port as a means to enhance and adapt a laptop.

Processors

This section monitors the microprocessor on the motherboard. You can learn some of the details of the model of microprocessor in your machine and can repair, update, or reinstall the driver if needed. A failure of the microprocessor generally requires a visit to a repair shop and possibly a replacement of the motherboard as well as the processor.

SCSI and RAID controllers

SCSI (Small Computer System Interface) is a specialized interface that was originally used for high-speed disk drives and other devices. They were on what we once considered small computers but today are refrigerator-sized electronic dinosaurs; *RAID* is an acronym for Redundant Array of Inexpensive (or Independent) Disks, a system used in some large offices to maintain backup copies of data on banks of identical but independent drives. Neither of those original uses are common on laptops, but SCSI and RAID technology is used on some of the most current machines to work with advanced technologies including memory sticks, Secure Digital Cards, and xD Cards used as storage for digital cameras and portable audio devices.

Sound, video, and game controllers

Modern laptops have incorporated all of the functionality of their desktop cousins in circuitry built into the motherboard.

System devices

These motherboard components are generally not adjustable or replaceable by the user.

Universal Serial Bus controllers

Also a part of the motherboard, you generally find between one and three such circuits to manage the nearly infinitely variable USB port.

Coming Back from the Future: System Restore

One of the advanced features of Windows XP (Home and Professional) and Windows ME is the ability to use a utility called System Restore. System Restore, shown in Figure 5-5, allows you to go back in time — at least when it comes to system settings and device drivers. You can instruct the system to revert to the settings it was using the last time it worked properly. Depending on how you configured your machine, System Restore makes a record of settings every day, as well as anytime a new piece of software is installed or a system setting is changed.

Depending on how many changes you've made lately, and the instructions you've given the System Restore utility, you may be able to go back at least a week — more if the laptop isn't used daily — which should be more than sufficient for finding a moment before drivers or settings were altered. Even if your machine is running an earlier version of Windows, you can purchase a third-party utility like Symantec's Norton GoBack that accomplishes the same task.

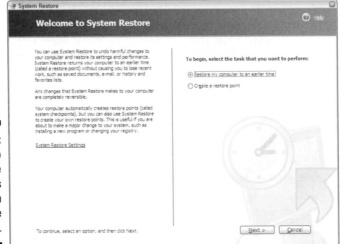

Figure 5-5:
The setup page for the Windows System Restore utility.

These utilities only undo changes to settings and drivers; if you go back in time, you do *not* lose any data — text, e-mail, photos, music, and the like.

You need to do three things to make the most of System Restore:

- ✔ Make sure it's configured to make regular copies of system settings.

- ✔ Manually instruct it to copy the current setting before making a major change to the system (including hardware installations and software updates).

- ✔ Experiment with restoring your system settings to an earlier condition if your computer develops problems immediately after installation or first use of new hardware or software.

To load System Restore, click Start⇨Accessories⇨System Tools⇨
System Restore. On the left side of the panel you see an option for System
Restore Settings. You can turn off the utility. This isn't something I ordinarily
recommend unless you suspect the System Restore utility itself is causing
problems.

Set a reasonable amount of space for use for System Restore storage points;
I'd recommend leaving at least 5 percent of your disk available for this purpose. You're not likely to use anything near that amount of space but it's
better to have more possible space than less. On the right side of the panel
you can instruct the laptop to create a restore point right now. Choose this
option before making major changes like I just identified. And here is also the
place you can restore your computer to an earlier time; if you select that
option you see a calendar that lists all available restore points. Some are
listed as System Checkpoints, which are those automatically made by the
computer based on the schedule you established. If you go to the trouble
(as you should) of manually instructing the system to make a restore point
when changes are made, you see whatever notes you attached.

Some installation programs initiate a System Restore for you and make a note
as a precautionary step. This is a good thing.

Chapter 6

Brain Matters: Memory, Microprocessors, and BIOS

*H*umans are not machines, and machines are not humans. But since humans created machines, we have some similarities and parallels. To understand a bit about how your laptop works, you should use your memory, brain, and mind.

In this chapter I discuss replacement and upgrade of computer memory, control of the system BIOS, and a bit about the microprocessor on your laptop's motherboard. As you prepare to consider upgrading or replacing these essential elements of your laptop, begin with an exploration of memory, brain, and mind.

Doing Some Computing

A human being's memory is the storage place for things learned. The brain is the management center where decisions are made and systems (the heart, the lungs, the digestive system) are controlled. And the mind is the home to feelings, emotions, creativity, and consciousness. Now consider the highly advanced electromechanical computer, in the instance of this book, in its miniaturized laptop form.

The computer equivalent of human memory is its *storage system,* which can consist of a hard drive, a floppy disk drive, a CD or DVD drive, and a few other forms of electronic filing cabinets. Here is where the machine may have a bit of advantage over humans. A computer's storage capacity is essentially limitless; you can keep adding more and more disk drives, or creating more and more CDs or DVDs, or connecting to the Internet, which is expanding almost without limit. I discuss storage systems in Chapters 7, 8, and 9. Your computer's brain is its *microprocessor.* This electronic circuit manipulates data based on rules and instructions. Though not all that smart, it is very fast, and that makes a great deal of difference.

Now just to make things confusing to humans, sitting in between the computer's storage system and the microprocessor is its *computer memory,* more properly referred to as *random access memory (RAM).* The computer gets its work done here: Think of it as the scratchpad, the building block, the assembly place for your words, numbers, pictures, and sounds before they are displayed, printed, or put in the file for future reference. The most important thing to remember about RAM is that it's *volatile,* or temporary, memory — quick, capacious, and relatively inexpensive but requires a near-continuous source of electrical power and regular refreshing of its contents. Put another way: Turn off the laptop, and RAM loses its memory.

It's also important to understand exactly what *random access* is and see how it differs from *storage.* Think of RAM as if all of the information your computer is working on is spread out on a large tabletop — a very, very large tabletop, perhaps more like an aircraft carrier. This type of memory is called *random access* because the computer's brain — the microprocessor — is capable of reaching directly into RAM to retrieve a specific piece of information or instruction. Your computer's very smart processor has an index that tells what's on the table and its exact location; that's random access. Compare that to data stored on a rotating hard drive. On that sort of system, the drive's read/write head has to wait until the block bearing the information moves into position beneath the head.

Even slower is data stored on a *sequential* media like a tape cartridge; here the system has to wait until the tape physically moves from one reel to another to a particular spot. If one section of a piece of data is at the beginning of the tape and the other is at the end, there can be a significant lag in retrieval. Why, then, use sequential media? The only good reason for modern systems is to store backups of huge files or make ongoing backups of real-time transactions like those from a bank or a stock exchange.

You may have noticed that no computer really duplicates a *mind . . .* except that some deep (human) thinkers believe we're approaching the point at which a machine can begin making independent decisions. Today a machine can "remember" information, make decisions based on very complex sets of

Mind over matter

Among the most creative minds to ever consider the nature of a computer's "mind" were Alan Turing and Arthur C. Clarke. Turing was a British mathematician who helped crack the German Enigma code during World War II. In 1950 he put forth the Turing Test as a way to judge computer intelligence. One way to conduct the test: If a subject at a monitor (it was a teletype in the first proposition) cannot tell if he or she was communicating with a machine or a fellow human being, then the machine had reached independent intelligence and consciousness.

Coincidentally — or perhaps not — in that same year novelist Clarke wrote a short story called "The Sentinel," which became the source material for Stanley Kubrick's classic science fiction movie *2001: A Space Odyssey.* In that film — released in 1968 at the dawn of era of the personal computer — the central computer of the spaceship, a machine by the name of Hal, seemed to lose its (his?) mind when confronted with conflicting instructions. More than half a century later, there's yet to be a computer like Hal that can say (and mean), "I'm afraid, Dave."

rules designed by programmers, and some advanced designs can even "learn" new rules and adapt existing ones based on experience gained over time. But what's missing (thus far) are consciousness and creativity. Machines don't know they're metal, plastic, and silicon, and though a computer can be taught to recognize the setting sun or a winsome smile, it doesn't feel awe or love or fear.

Improving Your Memory

A zippy processor and a fantastically capable operating system and software are great to have. So is a bottomless checking account and a body that doesn't quit, but we can't all be that lucky.

In the best of all possible worlds, your laptop would have

- The fastest microprocessor on the market
- More than enough of the fastest RAM available

In the real world, though, you may have to make some compromises. So, here's my rule: Assume a choice between the fastest processor on the market and not enough memory, or a merely adequate processor and an abundance of RAM. Go for the memory.

For the record, according to Microsoft and Intel, today's operating systems and processors demand at least 64MB of RAM; the machine will work, but you'll probably be unhappy with its performance. (Windows XP works with 64MB, but Microsoft recommends 128MB or more.) Earlier versions of Windows work with as little as 32MB. Either way, running a modern machine with insufficient memory is kind of like saying you can drive a car that has four flat tires; it moves, but not very fast or very well.

You know the somewhat unrealistic minimums. Does that mean you should go crazy and install gigabyte upon gigabyte in a laptop? In a word, no. Remember three things about memory:

- ✔ In general, more memory is better than less memory.

- ✔ The amount of memory that seemed unrealistically large two years ago will appear ridiculously insufficient a year from now.

- ✔ There is a tipping point that varies based on the microprocessor and the motherboard. That tipping point is where you have enough memory for your needs. Adding more would be a waste of money, a drain on battery power, and could even slow down the machine.

In my opinion, the tipping point for an older machine for most users (based on a Pentium III or older equivalent microprocessor) is in the range of 192–320MB. Current machines (working with a Pentium 4, Pentium M, Intel Celeron, or AMD equivalent) would be happiest with somewhere around 512MB; if you do a great deal of graphics or audio work, you can boost RAM to 1GB.

If you're buying a new laptop, the lower-priced models typically come with 256MB of RAM, which is merely an adequate level of memory. (And some of those machines use motherboards that steal away some of that RAM for workspace for the video adapter; that's called *shared RAM.* Nothing is inherently wrong with shared RAM except that you have that much less working space; there may be 256MB within the case of the laptop but only 192MB is available to the microprocessor.)

If you're running Windows XP and advanced software (including graphics programs like Adobe Photoshop, Web design software, or audio editors), I suggest you purchase a machine with 512MB of RAM.

Modern machines are capable of working with several gigabytes of RAM, although that may be unnecessary; older machines using earlier microprocessors had maximum capacities ranging from 256MB to 384MB. And if you're looking for a way to boost the speed of a laptop you already own, you can do little that's more cost effective than increase the amount of memory. The best news of all is that adding more memory (or swapping smaller memory modules for larger ones) is very easy to do. I show you how in this chapter.

The very first IBM PC, like the one that holds down the floor in the back closet of my office, was introduced with a base memory of 16K. That's 16 kilobytes; a *kilobyte* is roughly ⅟₁,₀₀₀ of a megabyte depending how you do the counting. A modern laptop with 256MB of RAM has about 16,384 times as much memory.

Handling memory

How much memory can your laptop handle? In two words . . . it depends. Older machines may have been built around motherboards and chipsets that can work with only 256MB, while modern machines use designs every bit as capable as a desktop PC, with capacities for 1GB or more of RAM.

When all else fails you should read the instruction manual that came with your machine. You can also give the manufacturer a call; be prepared with the model name, model number, and serial number.

You also find some valuable online tools at the Web site of your manufacturer and at the sites of several third-party memory sellers. You can research the capacity and type of memory used in your machine at model sites such as www.dell.com and www.gateway.com. Belarc Advisor is a free utility that explores your machine and produces a full report on installed software and hardware. The company promises that information is maintained on your machine and not transmitted to persons unknown. You can find it at www.belarc.com/free_download.html.

You also find that many laptop makers include a diagnostic program on your machine. A report examining the configuration may be included. For example, Figure 6-1 shows a report generated by the Toshiba PC Diagnostic Tool on one of my machines.

I also visited a database of information at the Crucial memory site to learn about an older machine in my office, a Gateway Solo 2500SE. I was advised that the maximum capacity for the Gateway 2500SE is 288MB. I also learned that the machine had two memory slots, organized as two banks of one. That's a nice simple statement, right? Right.

Here's what that means: In addition to any memory permanently installed on the motherboard, two slots allow for expansion, and they are (in this machine) electrically separated into individual banks. This allows me to add one or two expansion modules; I can install both at the same time, or one at a time, and they can be of the same capacity or different from one another. (As I already discussed, though, they must be of the same physical design to fit in the available slots, and use the same memory technology, although they can differ in refresh speeds and how often the system writes and rewrites data to individual memory locations.)

Figure 6-1:
The basic
screen of
the Toshiba
diagnostic
tool gives
you model
name, part
number,
serial
number, and
current
installed
hardware.
The Diag-
nostic Tool
tab allows
testing of
most
machine
components.

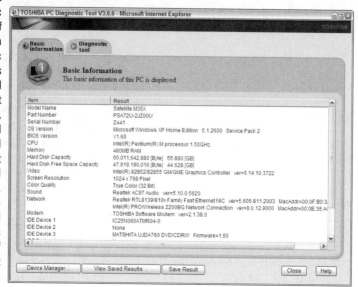

Your machine might instead be designed to require memory expansion as
one bank of two; that means two available slots are organized as a single
bank. Therefore, you need to buy and installed *matched pairs* of memory and
install them at the same time in the available slots. Other possible designs
include banks of four, which require installation of four modules at a time.

What do you do if your available expansion slots are already populated with
modules? Alas, the only solution for expansion is to remove the older, smaller
modules and replace them with new, larger ones. (Don't throw away the old
memory, though: You may be able to donate them to a school or charity, or
you may be able to resell them on eBay or other electronic flea markets.)

When you do buy memory, keep the limits in mind: It is less expensive to buy
larger-capacity memory now rather than buy a smaller module now and then
replace it with a larger unit later.

Multitasking, multiprocessing, and multimedia

Laptops don't really run more than one program at a time. Instead, the microprocessor is capable of rapidly switching its attention from one application to another, giving the *illusion* that more than one program is churning away at the same moment.

Remember, too, that many programs don't require the active attention of the microprocessor all the time. For example, a word processor spends most of its time just sitting there on your screen, dumbly displaying whatever you have most recently written or loaded from the hard drive.

Programs more demanding of the processor include multimedia — display of video from DVDs or the Internet, graphics manipulation applications, and graphics-intensive games. If you have more than one of these programs open at a time, you may see an occasional slowdown or pause in activity as the microprocessor shifts its attention from one to the other.

Having too much of a good thing

Can you have too much memory? Ah, another one of those trick questions. Here are some untricky answers:

- ✔ **In general, more memory is better than less memory.** The operating system loads faster, applications run better, and you find it easier to *multitask* (have several programs open and available at the same time).

- ✔ **Almost every laptop limits the amount of memory with which it can work.** In most cases, you can install more memory than the system will recognize, but the laptop only recognizes and makes use of RAM up to its limit. In other words, if the machine has a limit of 512MB and you install 640MB, the computer should still perform properly but not make use of memory locations above 512MB. (A few machines, though, may completely refuse to work or may crash or act unpredictably if the motherboard finds more RAM than it expects. Check with the maker of your machine for advice.)

- ✔ **Memory requires electrical current to initialize; RAM contents must be regularly refreshed.** This keeps data in place and accessible. The more memory you have, the higher the demand on your laptop's battery. I'm not talking huge amounts here; the hard drive, CD or DVD, and the LCD screen draw much more power than memory. But there is a cost to the use of RAM.

Doing the very least you can do

Nearly all modern laptops have an easily accessible hatch on their bottom that can be opened to reveal slots that accept industry standard memory modules. If a slot is open, you can just insert a new module, close the door, and turn the machine back on. (I guess I forgot to remind you once more to always turn off your laptop, remove its battery, and unplug the AC adapter before performing *any* work under the covers. *There:* You have been reminded.) Check the specifications for your laptop or examine the actual memory modules in place to determine the type and speed you need for an upgrade. The major memory makers or distributors have Web sites you can visit that help you look up your particular machine.

In 2006, nearly all new laptops use tiny 200-pin SODIMM modules. The next issue is the bus speed; most common is PC-2700, followed by slightly slower PC-2100 RAM. And finally, most memory modules for laptops are *Non-ECC,* meaning they don't include extra circuitry for error correction; a dwindling percentage of laptops insist on the slightly more expensive ECC memory. Older laptops used slightly larger sticks of memory, including 144-pin SODIMMs. A *module* is a small circuit board that holds one or more pieces of memory and installs into a slot connected to the motherboard. Each computer also has a *bus speed,* which is the speed limit for data moving between the memory and microprocessor, and the microprocessor to internal devices.

Your assignment is to match what you already have in place. You cannot mix Non-ECC with ECC memory, and you cannot put anything other than a 200-pin SODIMM module in a slot built for that size circuit.

The only gray area involves speed. If your machine's motherboard is built to use PC-2700 RAM, you get the best performance by using memory of that speed; if you install slower PC-2100 RAM, the laptop should work, but all memory operates at the slower rate. Conversely, if the motherboard is built for PC-2100, buying PC-2700 RAM is a waste of money and *might* cause operational problems.

Here are some Web sites for memory manufacturers and distributors for research or purchase. You also find memory configuration information at the Web sites of major computer retailers, including CompUSA, PC Connection, and others.

- ✔ **Crucial Technologies** at www.crucial.com
- ✔ **Kingston Technology** at www.kingston.com
- ✔ **PNY Technologies** at www.pny.com
- ✔ **SimpleTech** at www.simpletech.com
- ✔ **Smart Modular Technologies** at www.smartm.com

Populating poorly

One unpleasant practice of some laptop makers is *populating* their systems with a minimum amount of RAM and using up all available slots in the process. For example, one model may offer 128MB of RAM and do so by placing a 64MB module in each of the only two slots under the hatch. Why would they do something that mean and nasty? The answer, not surprisingly, involves money. Like most everything else in high technology, newer, faster, larger devices cost more than older, slower, smaller versions. The maker might save a few dollars by using two 64MB SODIMM instead of a single 128MB module.

And some laptops come with one memory module soldered in place or otherwise permanently installed, leaving only one slot for you to use in the pursuit of enhancement. Your only choice: Buy as large a second module as you can justify, up to the tipping point for your machine.

You'll have to know the configuration of your machine for yourself. You may be able to find out how many slots are available and what is installed in each by running a diagnostic program, or you may have to open the hatch and see for yourself. (Remember: power off, battery out, sturdy work surface, and so on.)

And although it pains me to do so, it's not such a big deal anymore to remove a too-small memory module and replace it with a larger one: The price of memory has plummeted so far and so fast. As this book goes to press, a 256MB 200-pin SODIMM sold for about $50, and a 512MB version for about $95.

When you go shopping, pay attention to the price, the price differential, and warranty. I explain each in a moment, but notice that nowhere did I mention "brand." That's because — with the exception of the cutting edge of technology where cost is not as important as performance — RAM has become a commodity. One company's 256MB PC2700 200-pin SODIMM is all but identical to another company's product of the same specifications.

The not-so-deep secret is that few manufacturers make memory; many companies that sell modules are repackaging or relabeling RAM made by third parties. That is certainly the situation if you buy memory directly from the maker of your laptop: Dell, just as an example, does not make RAM. And that company may change sources based on supply and prices. It doesn't matter to you as a user.

The three other elements I suggested you look at:

> ✔ **Price.** Pay as little as you have to, and include in your calculations shipping, handling, and tax. Some companies that sell on the Internet appear to have great prices but tack on ridiculous charges to mail a two-ounce

module. Other Web sites may seem to be a bit more expensive, but don't charge sales tax and ship for free. Do the math.

- ✔ **Price differential.** Conditions change because of supply and demand. In a perfect world, a 256MB module should cost a bit less than two 128MB modules. (Why less? Although the chip capacity is larger, the manufacturer has only the expense of one piece of circuit board and pins.) But sometimes the price differential or ratio goes out of balance. Look for bargains.

- ✔ **Warranty.** RAM is a very stable product; it undergoes testing before it leaves the factory, and in most situations it lasts longer than the computer in which it is installed. A small percentage arrive dead or pass away shortly after first installed; if the memory works for a few weeks without problem you can probably stop worrying about it failing. For that reason, many sellers offer multiyear and even lifetime warranties. You should look for a good warranty. Buy from a company you can reasonably expect to remain in business for a while. Good choices include the five I've listed in this chapter as well as OEM manufacturers including Hitachi, NEC, Samsung, and Toshiba.

What do you do with extra memory modules removed from your system? Well, in addition to selling them on eBay, you might want to consider donating them to a school or charity that can use them to upgrade their own machines.

Checking memory level without removing the covers

You can figure out how much memory is inside your machine at least five ways:

- ✔ **Read the specifications from the manufacturer.** In theory, with a brand new machine what you get is what you see in the original papers for the computer. However, I'd rather be absolutely certain that I've gotten what I paid for. And I'd like to be sure that all the memory has made it from wherever it was first installed without coming unseated from its connectors.

  And, of course, if you are purchasing a used computer, it doesn't matter what the specifications say: See if the previous owner has added any memory and if the machine recognizes all of the installed modules.

  I recommend you perform at least one of the following four tests:

- ✔ **Watch the RAM counter spin as the laptop boots up.** Most system BIOS test memory when the machine is first turned on, displaying a count onscreen. The problem here is that the information may go by too quickly for you to read.

✔ **Consult the report available under Windows in the Control Panel.**

1. Click Start➪Settings➪Control Panel.

2. Double-click the System icon.

3. Under Windows XP, go to the General tab. There you see information that includes the operating system version, the registered owner, OS registration number, microprocessor type and speed, and the total amount of installed RAM. Under older versions of Windows (including 98SE, 98, and 95) go to either the General or the Performance tab to obtain the same information.

✔ **Go to the System Information report.** The report is part of Windows 98 and later, including Windows XP.

1. Go to Programs➪Accessories➪System Tools and select System Information. You find a similar screen available as part of the Microsoft Office applications Help screen.

2. Open one of the programs such as Microsoft Word or Microsoft Excel.

3. Click the Help menu.

4. Click About Microsoft Word➪System Info.

✔ **Use the facilities of a system-optimizing or diagnostic program.** Norton SystemWorks or Norton Utilities are examples. The manufacturer of your laptop may provide a diagnostic program as part of the basic suite of software installed on the machine.

TECHNICAL STUFF

Zeros and ones, ones and zeros

Like it or not, in the world of personal computing some of the rules of math do not apply. Where else can 64K mean 64,000 or 65,536 or somewhere else in that neighborhood? It all comes down to whether the counting is being done in decimal, binary, or marketing numbers. The decimal system is the one you use when you buy apples at Super Shop and Nosh. Ten Red Delicious at $1.25 apiece cost $12.50, with no ifs, ands, or buts. In the decimal world, 1,000 is the number that comes after 999.

But computers live in a binary world where counting is based on powers of 2. Data — whether it is a letter of the alphabet in Word, a number in Excel, or part of a picture in a graphics program — is represented as a stream of computer words made up of just 0s and 1s. For example, the word 1 0 1 0 1 0 1 0 in binary is equivalent to the decimal value 170. (You read from right to left: no 1s, one 2, no 4s, one 8, no 16s, one 32, no 64s, and one 128.)

Individual *binary digits* are called *bits*. When they are brought together in an 8-bit computer word they constitute a *byte*. Although it is possible to come to a nice, even 1,000 in binary math (1111101000), technical types seem to prefer the simplicity of 10000000000, which converts to 1,024 in the decimal world. And so,

(continued)

(continued)

when computer designers talk about a 16K chip they mean a circuit capable of dealing with 16×1,204 bits of information, or 16,384 bits.

In large numbers like those on a hard disk drive, the math starts to get fuzzy. Consider the giga-byte: In technical terms a *gigabyte* is 1,024 megabytes or 1,024×1,024×1,024. A designer may come up with a 40GB hard drive, and that's what it is called in the lab because it contains 40 giga-bytes. But if you convert the binary to decimal, the capacity totes up to 43,980,465,111,040 bytes. When the marketing department gets hold of that new drive, they start printing up labels that say: "44GB."

Staying current with modern memory

The good news is that memory makers keep coming up with ways to boost the speed and capacity of RAM. And even better, they have generally managed to keep the relative prices of memory on a steep downward spiral: you almost certainly pay the same or less today for a memory module that is significantly larger than last year's (or last month's) latest and greatest. The not-quite-so-good news is that there is a dizzying array of available memory types, and you've got to match your module to the laptop you are upgrading. Start with the memory type and then find it in the proper physical module size.

Here's a quick tour of the most modern RAM designs used in laptops.

DDR

Double Data Rate (DDR) is an advanced form of SDRAM (about which you read more in a moment). The most common means of identifying DDR is like this: PC1600, PC2100, PC2700, and PC3200.

In that usage, the numbers refer to the total bandwidth of the entire module, whether there is one, two, four, or however many memory chips soldered to the little SODIMM. *The higher the number, the greater the bandwidth and therefore the faster the memory can work with your system.*

Less commonly, DDR can also be rated in this way: DDR333, DDR400, and so on. In this usage, the designer identifies the data transfer rate of the compo-nents. PC1600 was originally designed for systems with a 100 MHz front-side bus. Since these modules are DDR — Double Data Rate, you recall — that means they are capable of 200 mega-transfers per second (MT/s). You're deal-ing with computer words of eight bits, so you've got 200 MT/s times eight, or 1,600. A PC1600 module has a total bandwidth of 1.6GB of data per second, which is where the 1600 number comes from.

The *front-side bus* is another name for the system bus; on modern machines there's also a *back-side bus,* which connects the microprocessor to a second-level *cache* — specialized memory that holds recently used or anticipated commands and data. The back-side bus is very fast, but extremely limited in its capacity and its purpose.

But now that we've got that down, you should also be aware that you may not be able to find new PC1600 modules; this design has been supplanted by PC2100 modules — which work in a system looking for PC1600. In techie talk, an advanced technology that also works with older designs is declared to be *backward compatible.*

Since I've brought up the subject of PC2100, here's the skinny on these little chips: They are meant to work with systems with a 133-MHz front-side bus, and with DDR that yields a 266 MT/s data transfer rate and a 2.1GB total bandwidth, which gives the module its PC2100 name. (PC2100 arrived with the first Pentium III and AMD Athlon microprocessors. If you install a PC2100 module in a machine that is looking for PC1600, it operates at the lower bandwidth.)

Next up were PC2700 and PC3200 DDR RAM. They follow the same math. PC2700 was designed for systems with a 166-MHz front-side bus yielding 333 MT/s data transfer rate and a 2.7GB bandwidth; it is sometimes called DDR333. PC3200 was designed for systems with a 200-MHz front-side bus yielding 400 MT/s data transfer rate and a 3.2GB bandwidth; it is sometimes called DDR400.

The high-end for DDR memory, not yet that common in laptops, uses a 266-MHz front-side bus. Do the math backwards: That means a 533 MT/s data transfer rate and a 4.2GB bandwidth. So, its name is PC4200 or DDR533.

SDRAM

Synchronous Dynamic Random Access Memory (SDRAM) is the industry's basic form of memory. The most modern version of SDRAM, which you already explored, uses a technology called *DDR* or *Double Data Rate.* The naming convention for SDRAM is straightforward; names begin with *PC* and are followed by the speed of the front-side bus.

For example, PC66 works with systems based on a 66-MHz front-side bus; this older scheme was introduced with early Pentium and Macintosh G3 systems. PC100, for computers using a 100-MHz front-side bus, is more common and employed on motherboards based on Pentium II, Pentium III, AMD Athlon, AMD Duron, and Macintosh G4 microprocessors. The next step up is PC133 for 133-MHz bus systems.

Refreshing speeds

Another specification for memory is its *refresh speed,* which tells you how often the system writes and rewrites bits of data to individual memory locations. Think of it as a rejuvenation process.

Remember that dynamic memory only holds data when it is receiving power; over time — or when the power is turned off — the contents of dynamic memory are lost forever. This doesn't mean you are going to lose the manuscript for your Great American Novel or the design for your personal intergalactic space probe when you turn off your laptop — just be sure to save any work you want to keep on your machine's hard drive. The storage on a hard drive is more or less permanent once data has been written with an electrical pulse to a metallic surface that can hold a magnetic charge. You explore hard disks, and what I mean by "more or less permanent," in Chapter 7.

Memory's refresh speed is just one element of a computer's overall speed. Refresh rates are measures in *nanoseconds (ns);* the lower the number, the more often the memory is rewritten per second. But a memory chip or module with a fast refresh rate can be hamstrung by a slow bus speed or a limited bandwidth. If you think of bus speed as the speed limit and bandwidth as the number of lanes on a superhighway, you can see how you need both speed and bandwidth in order to move vast quantities of data rapidly.

Feeling special with ECC memory

A special class of RAM is called *ECC (Error Checking and Correcting)* memory. This type of circuitry continually checks the data in search of garbled or lost data; in some circumstances it can repair the error by itself or at least report the problem to the user.

Who might need ECC memory? If your computer is controlling a life-support system in a hospital or managing the New York Stock Exchange, in few or no situations is an "Oops" acceptable. For the rest of us, the very rare instance where a computer hangs up or corrupts memory is not such a big deal, and very few consumer laptops use ECC memory.

Although ECC offers some significant advantages to certain users and applications, unless the PC is properly designed, the use of error-correcting memory may actually slow down the computer's operations somewhere between a tiny bit and a whole bunch.

Yotta, yotta, zetta

It may seem all Greek to you, and much of it is; computer designers use various suffixes and symbols as shorthand to distinguish thousands, millions, billions, and higher numbers. The lowest of these is *kilo,* which means 1,000; when applied to bits or bytes, though, think 1,024. Next up is *mega* for million, and *giga* for billion. Here's the binary shorthand table for bits or bytes:

Term	Meaning	Value in a Binary Number
Kb	Kilobit	1,024 bits
KB	Kilobyte	1,024 bytes
Mb	Megabit	1,048,576 bits
MB	Megabyte	1,048,576 bytes
Gb	Gigabit	1,073,741,824 bits
GB	Gigabyte	1,073,741,824 bytes
Tb	Terabit	1,099,511,627,776 bits
TB	Terabyte	1,099,511,627,776 bytes
Pb	Petabit	1,125,899,906,842,624 bits
PB	Petabyte	1,125,899,906,842,624 bytes
Eb	Exabit	1,152,921,504,606,846,976 bits
EB	Exabyte	1,152,921,504,606,846,976 bytes
Zb	Zettabit	1,177,132,856,203,590,762,496 bits
ZB	Zettabyte	1,177,132,856,203,590,762,496 bytes
Yb	Yottabit	1,205,384,044,752,476,940,795,904 bits
YB	Yottabyte	1,205,384,044,752,476,940,795,904 bytes

Much as I would like to take credit making it up, the last two suffixes are for real and not some inside reference to an old *Seinfeld* episode. A yottabyte, which is equal to 2 to the 80th power if you're counting bytes or about 10 to the 24th power, or 1 septillion in the decimal world, gets its name from the next-to-last letter of the Latin alphabet.

All you need to know is this: If your laptop requires ECC memory, you may not be able to use non-ECC modules. And if your PC is not designed to work with ECC, you can't just plug in error-correcting memory and gain its advantages. (In the best case, the memory works without ECC functions; in the worst case, the system crashes or functions erratically with the wrong memory installed.) And just for the record, ECC memory is more expensive and sometimes harder to find than standard memory. Don't buy it unless you need it.

Laptop memory module design

Leaving aside the specifications for the memory itself, you also must match the type of module to the available slot on the laptop. Among modern laptops you find three forms of modules.

Proprietary cards

A *proprietary card* works only with a particular model or brand of laptop. This may mean you have to buy replacement or upgrade modules from the manufacturer at whatever price the company sets (that's what I call a *monopoly*), or you may have to search for supplies from specialized suppliers.

You might want to shop for used proprietary memory modules from sources on the Internet, including eBay auctions and from direct sellers. Be sure to protect yourself against fraud by using a credit card or a guarantee offered by an auction sight.

SODIMM

The most common current design is the *Small Outline Dual In-line Memory Module,* better known to technodweebs (present company excepted) as *SODIMMS.* A SODIMM is a SODIMM is a SODIMM, at least when it comes to physical dimensions. The tiny cards are 5cm long by 2.5cm tall, or about 2×1 inch. Where SODIMMS can differ is in the number of pins that connect to the computer's bus; the more pins, the wider the pathway for data, and higher the potential speed.

You find modern SODIMMS with 144 or 200 pins; an older class of SODIMM has just 72 pins. This is a situation where you need to exactly match the needs of the computer — if the socket has 144 connectors, the SODIMM must have 144 pins. Several modules are shown in Figure 6-2: An older-sized 72-pin SODIMM is on the left; then there's a higher bandwidth 144-pin SODIMM in the middle. And finally, I've got a picture of a tiny, modern 144-pin MicroDIMM on the right.

SODIMMs have identifying notches along the pin end of the module that prevent installation of the wrong type of memory in a slot. Don't ever try to force a module into a slot that doesn't readily accept the memory carrier; if it seems like you have to force a module into place, you are probably trying to use the wrong type of module.

Figure 6-2:
A 72-pin
SODIMM is
top left, a
144-pin
SODIMM
is top
right, and
a 144-pin
MicroDIMM
is on the
bottom.

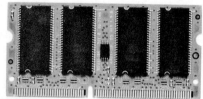

Some techie-types get all exorcised over whether the memory modules you purchase have connector pins that are plated with gold, tin, or aluminum. Their concern has a kernel of truth: Gold is the most stable and least likely to corrode or otherwise cause problems with the electrical connection between memory and the motherboard. But tin (and less commonly, aluminum) also works for many years without problem. In theory, the worst case is a mix-and-match of gold-plated connectors in the slot and tin on the module or the other way around; over time, the lesser metal (tin) may pass some of its molecules over to the gold, causing oxidation. To avoid the problem, use gold-plated modules with gold-plated connectors, and tin plate with tin plate. To my way of thinking, this is a problem that — if it happens at all — takes many years to occur, and laptops are much more likely to die of other causes or just become outmoded before this becomes an issue.

MicroDIMM

The smallest of notebook computers may use a tiny memory module called a MicroDIMM, which is 3.92×2.54cm, or about 1.5×1 inches. Like SODIMMs, MicroDIMMs are available with either 144 or 172 pins. The pins on each side of the MicroDIMM are not electrically connected, permitting two independent data paths between the module and system. The modules do not have notches along the pin end, but they do have a top and bottom. On most machines the module is installed so that the memory chip labeling faces toward you as installed in the slot. MicroDIMMs provide a 64-bit data path, and in modern machines they can be installed one at a time — they do not need to be installed in pairs.

Installing New Memory: Safety First

Memory is subject to damage from electrostatic sparks and from power surges. Once in place within your machine, it's mostly protected by the circuitry of the AC adapter, charger, and the battery; the moments of highest risk come in the installation of memory. Here is the best procedure to follow when installing new memory in a machine:

1. **Place the laptop on a sturdy work surface that has good lighting.**

2. **Completely discharge the power in the laptop before opening it.**

   Start by unplugging the power cord from the wall. Then remove the battery pack.

3. **Make sure you have the proper tools to open the memory compartment.**

   On most machines you need a small Phillips-head screwdriver. A handful of manufacturers are less friendly to do-it-yourselfers and close the compartment with Torx or other fasteners that require use of special tools; you may have to visit a hardware store or computer retailer to obtain proper tools in that situation. In Figure 6-3, I'm opening the panel on the bottom of a modern laptop.

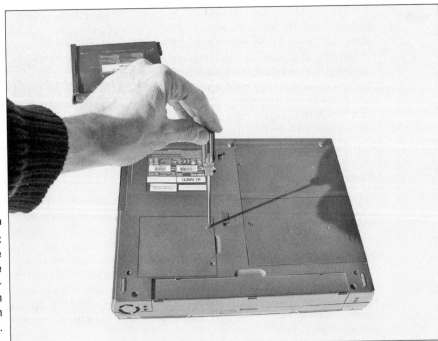

Figure 6-3: Opening the door to the RAM compartment on the bottom of a laptop.

4. **Ground yourself before touching any internal part of the computer.**

   Sit still in a chair and touch a metal pipe or the center screw of an electrical outlet to remove any charge you may have built up walking across the room.

5. **Install new memory modules or remove and reinstall problematic ones.**

   The modules are designed to fit in place in only the proper orientation, and once connected are held in place by small clips. In Figure 6-4, I'm preparing to lower a SODIMM into place as the second bank of memory.

6. **Put the battery pack back in place and attach the AC cord.**

Figure 6-4:
Placing a
128MB
SODIMM
into the
available
slot on an
older laptop.

When memories go bad

As I've already noted, memory modules don't often fail all by themselves. That doesn't mean never, though. Your laptop can lose its memory a few ways.

You recently changed the computer configuration

Remember the first question to ask yourself when you attempt to troubleshoot a problem: What has changed since the last time the laptop worked properly? Have I just added new memory? Have I made any changes to the operating system? Did I drop the laptop from the top of the stairs? Did it land in a barrel of water?

Backing up just a bit: If you just added new memory modules and the system doesn't recognize them (or doesn't work at all), check the new memory. See if you can determine if you have a problem with the modules, with your the new memory installation, or with your computer.

1. **Turn off the power, remove the battery, and ground yourself.**

2. **Take the cover off the memory container.**

3. **Remove the newly installed modules, leaving the original ones in place.**

4. **Make sure the original module or modules are properly connected and latched in place.**

5. **Replace the cover and return power to the system.**

Does the system boot up and run? If not, the problem is probably unrelated to the new memory you're trying to put in the system. On the other hand, if the system comes back to life with its original memory modules, suspect the new modules: Do you have the correct size, speed, and memory type? Are you correctly installing the memory?

I was upgrading the memory in an older laptop (a Gateway Solo 2500SE). The new module I put into the connector was working, but the system only recognized half of its 256MB. To make a technical support story short, I was advised to try swapping the position of the original smaller module and the new larger one. Voila! Both were recognized.

If you cannot get the system to work with the new memory and are sure the specifications, latch, and installation are correct, the memory may be dead on arrival. If you have access to another laptop that uses the same memory, try the suspect module in that machine; otherwise, get in touch with the seller and exchange or return the module.

Abuse

By design, laptops are intended to be moved from place to place. They're expected to be placed in overhead compartments of airplanes and in trunks of cars, and suffer various minor jouncing and bouncing. A laptop's memory can fail because of accidental or intentional abuse:

✔ **Getting fried.** If the laptop's AC adapter or other internal electrical components fails, a voltage spike may pass through the motherboard, reaching the RAM modules in their connectors. If this rare occurrence happens, your memory modules will probably be the least of your problems — most everything else along the way is likely to be damaged beyond repair.

Components can also bet *baked* by overheating. All electrical components generate heat, especially high-speed microprocessors and memory. Laptops include small fans that are supposed to exhaust some of the heat; in most designs the fans are to turn on when heat builds and shut off to save power when not needed. If the fan fails or if the laptop's vents are blocked, internal parts can be damaged. Get in the habit of checking the fan's operation regularly, and quickly turn off any machine that produces a burning odor. An overheating laptop is a machine due for a service visit to a technician.

If concerned that your machine's internal cooling system is insufficient for your needs (or if you work in a particularly hot environment), purchase an external fan system that sits beneath the computer and increases airflow. One such product is the Vantec LapCool, which attaches to the computer's USB port for power (and adds a four-port USB hub in compensation). This sort of external cooling should help most laptops, although the extra fan draws precious battery power and adds another piece of hardware to your traveling bag.

✔ **Getting shocked.** Any electronic component can be damaged or destroyed by electrostatic shock. The memory modules should be properly protected inside their closed container on the bottom of case. They are at risk any time you remove the cover and any time you handle them. Make sure you ground yourself before touching any memory module.

✔ **Getting disconnected.** It *shouldn't happen* but a memory module can work its way out of its connector. Make sure you ground yourself before touching the modules and reseating them.

Dying of natural causes

All things come to an end, and though I've already stated that a memory module — if it works when you first plug it in — is likely to outlast the rest of the laptop, that doesn't mean it might not die of natural causes. A typical claim for *MTBF (mean time between failures)* for RAM is about seven years, which takes into account (sorry for the insensitivity but here's what they call it) infant mortality.

If a machine's RAM was working one day and suddenly stops working the next, ask yourself the questions under "You recently changed the computer configuration." If nothing untoward has occurred since the laptop last worked properly, perform the checks suggested. Look to see if the modules are properly seated and perform a smell test for the odor of burnt electronics (kind of a combination of burning leaves with a bit of old tires thrown in).

If you cannot get the RAM to work, try to find a compatible machine at a friend's home or in your office and substitute your RAM into a working machine. If that second machine fails, you can assume your laptop's memory has died; contact the module maker to see if it is under warranty. If the second machine works and you're certain you have checked the original machine to assure proper installation, an injury to the motherboard or other circuitry may have happened. You have to decide if the laptop is worth repairing.

Hanging on half-dead

One of the most annoying situations is an intermittent problem: Sometimes it works and sometimes it doesn't. This is often the result of bad connections between the memory and the motherboard — corrosion, cracks, or improper seating of the module in the connectors.

1. **Turn off the power, remove the battery, ground yourself.**

   You know the drill by now.

2. **Open the memory container on the laptop.**

3. **Carefully remove the modules and look for corrosion, cracks, or improper seating of the module in the connectors.**

   - **Corrosion or gunk:** You can carefully clean them with a weak solution of water and isopropyl alcohol or purchase a specialized electrical contact cleaner; use a clean cloth to gently clean the connectors. Some users prefer a clean rubber pencil eraser; be sure to remove all pieces of rubber from the module before you reinstall it. If you can see gunk inside the memory container, carefully vacuum out the dirt.

   - **Cracks:** It's not worth attempting to repair the memory; replace it with a new module. If there are cracks with the attachment point inside the memory container, you'll have to decide whether the laptop is worth repairing.

   - **Improper seating:** Sometimes all it takes to reestablish a good electrical contact is removing and reseating the module.

4. **Latch it in place, following the computer manufacturer's instructions.**

Another possible cause of intermittent failure is overheating. If your laptop works when first started and then fails after running for a while, check for proper operation of the fan and that none of the ventilation ports are blocked. Heat can cause the holder for the memory contacts to expand, resulting in a bad connection, or it can cause the memory module itself to break contact.

Getting a headache

Your laptop uses all available memory, but it starts from the bottom of the barrel and works its way up. If you have just barely enough memory in your system, chances are that every last available bit has been exercised. But if you have memory to spare, only certain programs — graphics editors, audio editors, and some web sites — may reach deep into the closet for the upper reaches of memory.

If your laptop's memory failure is intermittent, see if you can trace it to the use of a particular piece of software or a particular action taken while using that program. Or see if the problem only occurs when you have multiple programs open at the same time. Here is a good place to use a diagnostic program that goes into the RAM and works every memory location. If the diagnostic tells you that some portion of your memory module is not working properly, replace the module. (Contact the module maker to see if it's under warranty.)

Troubleshooting more memory

Consider these things when troubleshooting memory problems.

Installation

Use the proper type of memory. Make sure it's mounted on the correct module design. On a new installation, be aware of any special demands from the motherboard manufacturer. For example, some systems insist on modules being installed in matched pairs. Other designs may work better with faster or larger modules in the first slots and slower or smaller modules in secondary slots. As said earlier, some systems have relatively low ceilings on the maximum amount of memory. Some older machines don't automatically recognize the presence of new RAM, instead requiring you to go to the BIOS setup screen to specify the amount installed. Check your instruction manual or consult the support desk or Web site for information.

Make certain the module is properly installed. Some designs have key slots that must mate with pins on the connector; others have asymmetrical shapes that determine whether they are right side up or upside down. Most designs require the module to be locked into place with holding clips and these should only engage if the memory is correctly mounted.

Have you recently been inside the case of the laptop to install or remove other pieces of hardware? You may have inadvertently disconnected a cable. Go back over your recent steps and double-check your work. Have you just installed a new operating system, a major update to the operating system, or significant new software that demands more? Check with the support desks for the software and the memory maker to see if patches or changes should be made. You should also run a capable system diagnostic program and a Windows Registry checker such as Norton SystemWorks.

Demands and settings

Read onscreen messages that reveal memory failures of a particular type or at a specific location. Consult with the support desk for your laptop or memory maker for advice on resolving this sort of problem. It may indicate a problem with the memory itself, with the motherboard (more difficult, if not impossible, to economically repair), or with the system BIOS.

Have you made manual settings under Windows for managing virtual memory? In general, you're better off leaving it up to Windows to control memory use in place; that is the operating system's default setting. If you've made manual settings, try disabling them and going back to Windows control to see if (at least this once) Microsoft is smarter than you are.

Check your BIOS. If expanding the memory beyond its previous limits, you may be exceeding the previous capabilities of the system BIOS. Consult your laptop maker to see if an updated BIOS is available for your motherboard; following the instructions very carefully, download and install the new BIOS.

Does the problem occur in other specific situations such as when the computer is picked up and moved from one location to another while running? This could indicate a problem caused by electrostatic discharge or a flaky connection.

Dirt, grime, and odor

Remove and ensure the pins are clean and the connector isn't blocked by dirt or debris. Don't use a chemical solvent on the pins unless *oxidation* (rust or discoloration caused by exposure to air) or dirt is evident; if you must clean the module, use a special-purpose electronics solution such as Flux Off, available at electronics or computer equipment stores. Reinstall the modules.

Ensure a good power supply. A failing supply is a bit less likely with a laptop computer than with a desktop model, but still possible. Try to determine whether the problem occurs when the machine is running on battery power without an AC adapter attached (this may indicate a failing battery or internal electrical system) or whether it only happens when the AC power is attached (which might indicate a problem with the adapter or with the charger circuitry). The charger and battery can be easily and relatively inexpensively replaced; the circuitry within the laptop case is a more complex and expensive repair ordinarily addressed by a professional repair service.

Getting a Boost from BIOS

If you stop and think about it, one of the great mysteries of computer life is this: How does a stone-cold, unpowered, piece of plastic and silicon become a functioning computer with the push of the On button? Put another way, how does a laptop know how to load and act on instructions before it's already at work?

The answer lies in the interaction between something called the *basic input/output system* or *BIOS,* the lowest-level set of instructions for your computer and an equivalent set of basic code put in place on the hard disk drive when the system first received power. The process is called *booting* the computer, as in the old (and physically impossible) assignment of "pulling yourself up by your bootstraps."

The BIOS in a modern laptop is a single chip that establishes your machine's basic personality; a whole industry of companies writes this sort of code, selling it to laptop makers. Thus, a modern Toshiba may use a BIOS made by Phoenix; Dell and IBM have offered machines with BIOS code written in-house as well as by a third party. (Phoenix and Award merged in 1998; the other big player in the field is American Megatrends, Inc. or AMI. Smaller companies, often supplying generic BIOS code to generic laptop makers, include ABIT and MR BIOS.)

As a laptop owner, here's what you need to know about BIOS code:

✔ Every machine has to have one.

✔ Some are slightly better than others.

✔ It is somewhere between extremely difficult and impossible to change one brand of BIOS to another in a machine you already own.

✔ A modern BIOS rarely fails, although electrostatic shock or virus could result in damage or changes to its code.

✔ BIOS chips in current laptop models use a technology called *Electrically Erasable Programmable Read-Only Memory (E-PROM).* If you stop and think about it, this is somewhat contradictory title: a chip that's both read-only (meaning it cannot be written to) and electrically erasable and programmable (meaning its contents can be expunged and replaced with new information). What this really means is that the user or a repair facility can restore the BIOS programming or update it to a newly defined version of the BIOS.

The BIOS serves three functions: bootstrapping the system to life; conducting a quick diagnostic check of the motherboard, memory, and input/output devices and ports; and then overseeing the most basic system functions that operate outside the operating system. The BIOS, for example, is in charge of managing the incoming signals from the keyboard and the in-and-out pulses from the mouse or other pointing device.

In both logical and physical terms, the BIOS sits between the hardware on and attached to the motherboard and the operating system, which is first resident on the hard drive and later is loaded into memory. Many advanced motherboard and adapters features — in a laptop this includes devices plugged in to a daughterboard or attached to a USB port or a PC Card connection — come with small pieces of software called *device drivers*. These drivers help the basic system work with the specialized functions they offer. In logical terms, device drivers sit between the BIOS and the operating system.

Why are there differentiated "layers" of control? This is one of the reasons modern PCs are nearly infinitely adjustable to purposes known now or developed tomorrow. The BIOS handles basic housekeeping, the drivers adapt the machine to any specialized hardware, and the operating system is free to respond to the user without being concerned whether you have a Belkin-, Keyspan-, or Microsoft-brand *network interface card (NIC)* or other piece of hardware.

Turning a BIOS inside out

As the machine comes to life, watch very carefully to see the machine go through a quick diagnostic check of its major components. It usually speeds by too quickly; try keeping a finger near the Pause/Break key (usually in the upper-right corner of the keyboard) and press it to freeze the screen and read. Press Esc (on some machines, Pause/Break again) to resume the zippy test.

Here is some of the information contained in the boot-up diagnostic, in this case from Phoenix NoteBIOS 4.0 on a Toshiba Satellite laptop:

```
CPU = Intel(r) Pentium(r) M Processor 1.50 GHz
479M System RAM Passed
2048 Cache SRAM Passed
System BIOS shadowed
Video BIOS shadowed
Fixed Disk 0: IC25N060ATMR04-0
ATAPI CD-ROM: UJDA760 DVD/CDRW
Mouse initialized
```

When you first turn on your laptop, the options in the BIOS screen are already set to their default settings, but you are given the opportunity to make changes and set the clock and date the first time you run the machine. A number of laptops I've worked with come ready to go — although the time and date may have been set in China and need to be adjusted for my office on the East Coast of the United States.

Figure 6-5 shows some selected sections of a Phoenix BIOS, revealing the option, the setting (with any defaults shown in boldface), and some explanation.

MainScreen Option	Setting	Explanation
System Time:	[14:22:25]	Set the clock for the computer; the internal rechargeable battery will take over from there and modern versions of Windows will automatically adjust for Daylight Savings Time and Standard Time. The clock is pretty accurate but can sometimes run a few seconds slower or faster than another machine. Under Windows you can also enable a utility to synchronize your laptop's time with another computer or with a time server out on the Internet such as Microsoft's **time.windows.com** or the federal government's **time.nist.gov.**
System Date:	[08/31/2005]	Today's date, as tracked and maintained by the internal rechargeable battery.
Hard Disk:	XXXXXXXX-XXX	The BIOS of a modern machine will automatically identify the make, model number, and serial number of the internal hard disk drive.
Quiet Boot:	**[Enabled]** [Disabled]	In this particular BIOS, if Quiet Boot is enabled (the **default** setting) the machine will go from power-on to Windows as quickly as possible and not bother to go through pre-boot diagnostics. If Quiet Boot is disabled you'll see the diagnostics zip by.
Power on display:	**[Auto-Selected]** [Simultaneous]	In the default setting of Auto-Selected, if the laptop detects a *powered-on* external display connected to a CRT port, it will send the display signal only to the CRT; otherwise it will use only the LCD. If Simultaneous is selected, the video display adapter will send a signal to both the LCD and any attached CRT.

Figure 6-5:
Sections of
a Phoenix
BIOS.

(continued)

(continued)

Option	Setting	Explanation
LCD Display stretch:	[Enabled] [Disabled]	This setting applies only to lower resolutions for the LCD. When stretch is Enabled, the video image is electronically stretched to cover the entire screen.
System Memory:	640 KB	System Memory is the laptop's "lower" memory where most of the operating system and some programs reside; this is a holdover design that harkens all the way back to the original IBM PC, a time when 640K was more than anyone could possibly imagine requiring. This is not a user-changeable setting, although if you see a number lower than 640K you most likely have a problem with the machine's memory or its motherboard
Extended Memory:	478 MB	Extended memory is the block of memory above the first megabyte of RAM; modern machines play tricks to recover the space between the 640K of system memory and extended memory. Depending on the design of your laptop, this number may seem lower than you expect; on many devices the video adapter grabs a piece of installed RAM for its own use. In the instance of this Toshiba laptop, the built-in Intel Extreme Graphics circuitry on the motherboard can "share" from 16 to 64MB of RAM for its purposes.
BIOS Ver.:	V1.60	A report on which version of BIOS is installed; most modern machines can update their BIOS to later versions if they become available by downloading a file that "flashes" the reprogrammable read-only memory chip.
Language:	[English(US)]	On this machine, I could change the language for BIOS screen settings from English to Japanese.

Security is another available screen that's part of Phoenix BIOS and most others. Here you can set a User and Supervisor password, and require the use of a password each time the computer is booted. This is a matter of personal preference and security; if you leave your machine unattended, you may want to enable various levels of passwords. On the other hand, if you forget your password, it can become a major project to get it reset.

Passing on the word

On most modern laptops running Windows passwords come in three types and levels:

- **BIOS or User Password.** If enabled, this request for password appears onscreen every time the laptop is started, restarted, or brought back from standby mode.

- **Supervisor Password.** Similar to the User password in its time of appearance, the intention is to allow a supervisor or IT department to prevent changes to system settings without permission. The Supervisor can change anything and everything, including the User password.

- **Windows Logon Password.** This level of password controls the opening of Microsoft Windows. Under older versions of Windows (including Windows 95, 98, 98SE, and ME), the password only protects customization of the Windows environment; you can get around the password request by clicking Cancel or pressing the Esc key.

If using a more current operating system (including Windows XP, 2000, and NT), the Windows Logon password is intended to protect against unauthorized access to the computer contents. You cannot skip past the password request, although you can set up the system with a blank, or *null,* password, which means that you need only to press Enter to get into the hard disk.

Finally, if your laptop is set up to use a network, it may have one more level of password protection: a request that you type in the magic word to get on the network. If you skip over this request, in most systems you can use your computer locally but not in connection to others.

The case of the lost password

The good news is that a password can provide a reasonable level of protection against unauthorized use of your computer (at the User and Supervisor level) and access to its contents (at the Windows logon level). That's a really good thing for laptop users since the whole idea of a portable computer is that it is, well, portable. If someone steals your computer from an overhead compartment or from a hotel room, you can at least hope that your private data is secure.

The bad news is that if you forget a password, it can be very difficult and sometimes expensive to fix the problem. Most manufacturers require you to send the laptop to an authorized repair facility — along with proof that you're the device owner — to have the passwords reset or removed. Another bit of bad news: Most password schemes present a pretty weak wall against a thief removing the hard drive from your laptop and installing it in another machine to retrieve its contents. Some laptops truly lock away the contents of a hard drive, including some of the IBM ThinkPad line.

If I were talking about a desktop computer here, I could give some advice about trying to locate the BIOS reset button or jumper on the motherboard; the same sort of reset exists on most laptops, but access isn't very easy.

You might want to try a few of these things before shipping the machine to an authorized repair facility because of a lost password:

- **Ask the laptop maker if it will provide a back-door password to access the BIOS.** These codes exist, and some manufacturers of laptops or the BIOS are freer with revealing them than others. You may be (in fact, you should be) asked to prove you are the owner by providing a customer or invoice number from the original seller.

- **If the laptop has a CMOS backup battery (accessible through a compartment on the bottom of the case), remove the battery for at least an hour.** This should result in the BIOS returning to its default settings. Most modern laptops, alas, no longer have a user-accessible CMOS battery. Check the instruction manual or consult the maker to find out if your machine has a CMOS battery or instead uses flash memory (which does not require a continuous source of electrical power to hold information).

- **Troll the Internet in search of published lists of backdoor passwords.** Be aware, though, that some systems shut down after repeated attempts to use the wrong password. You are no worse off than you were at the start, except that now you definitely have to get the machine to a repair facility to have the BIOS reset.

  Believe it or not, some of the backdoor passwords are very obvious: Toshiba for Toshiba machines, Dell for Dell machines, AMI or A.M.I. for laptops using AMI BIOS chips, and PHOENIX or phoenix for Phoenix-based machines, and so on. There's no guarantee these will work, but they're worth a try. Note that these workarounds are aimed at the User or BIOS passwords; the Supervisor password may be more deeply locked away.

- **Consider using password-cracking services or software.** This may or may not solve the problem. Some of the companies are on the up-and-up while other companies or programs exist in or near the netherworld of hackers and virus writers. Be careful out there. By my way of thinking, if the company is *very demanding* of you to prove your proper ownership of a laptop, a hard drive, or an individual locked file, they're probably legitimate; if they're very casual about the whole matter, be concerned.

One software solution that seems to work is a freeware program called KILLCMOS which, when loaded from a bootable floppy disk, resets the contents of the BIOS to the default configuration. Of course, if your machine doesn't have a floppy disk, you have to figure a way to get the program onto a bootable CD and get your laptop to boot from the CD, which it may not do unless you've enabled this in the BIOS in the first place. Find KILLCMOS by searching on the Internet. Be sure to run your antivirus scanning program after you use this or any other freeware.

Customizing alarms

Current versions of the PhoenixBIOS has an Others screen that allows you to enable or disable an audible alarm when battery power is low — a good thing in most cases. Another alarm can be set to beep anytime the LCD cover is closed while the system is running, which may or may not be of value to you.

Finally, you can turn on or off the System Beep, which announces that the computer's diagnostics have been successfully completed before the operating system is loaded. If you suspect that your motherboard or other components are not functioning properly, enable this beep. Its absence can help you diagnose a blank screen — all you'll know is that the motherboard and memory seem to be working properly. You won't know whether there's a problem with the Windows installation or the LCD without further testing.

For many users, the most important set of options on a BIOS screen for troubleshooting purposes is the Boot or Boot Order option. Be default, most machines are set to attempt to load the operating system from the internal hard drive. If that drive fails, or if the system tracks on that drive are somehow damaged, find some other way to bring the computer to life and either repair the hard drive by reinstalling the system tracks or extract the data files to another machine or removable media.

Depending on your machine's configuration, you may be able to select the hard drive, the CD-ROM/DVD drive, a floppy disk drive (if present — many new machines no longer off a built-in floppy), other removable devices attached to the USB port, or by booting over the network from a remote computer.

Flashing for fun and profit

If that headline grabbed your attention too directly, you may have other things on your mind. *Flashing* is the process of erasing the contents of an existing

BIOS within your laptop and replacing it with an updated version (or, rarely, removing a corrupted version of the BIOS and replacing it with a clean copy).

This operation is very simple, but be very careful to follow the instructions of the laptop maker or BIOS provider. If you go astray, you could end up in a situation where the BIOS is erased or corrupted and not getting far enough into the system to load its replacement.

For most machines, the process involves downloading a new set of instructions and then copying them to a *bootable* floppy disk drive. Then you shut off the machine and boot from the floppy and install the new BIOS. In doing so you run the machine at a very basic level, without Microsoft Windows or other operating systems loaded. The fly in the ointment for many owners of new laptops is that most no longer come equipped with a floppy disk drive. Therefore, the process becomes a bit more complex. You may have to create a *bootable* CD and include the BIOS update there, or you may be able boot from an external device like a USB memory key.

I'm being purposely vague here because I want to make sure that you follow the instructions for your particular machine and BIOS. Any author who claims to tell you that there is one, single, all-purpose method to update the BIOS on any laptop out in the field is . . . wrong.

Before you update any BIOS chips, make a copy of all of the entries on your system's CMOS Setup screen; in most cases, you have to resort to a pen and notepad, although a handful of BIOS designs allow you to print their settings or save them to a file.

Upgrading Motherboards and CPU

Tread carefully all ye who enter here. No law says you cannot upgrade a microprocessor or even change the entire motherboard; if this were a book about desktop computers, you would be ready right now to dive into a discussion of opening the box, unscrewing hard drives and power supplies that are in the way, and laying static-free hands on the motherboard or the microprocessor.

But . . . this book is about laptops. Though you can open the case, remove drives, fans, and other components that are in the way, I don't recommend doing this yourself for several reasons:

- ✔ Working within the close quarters of a laptop is a difficult task, requiring above-average technical skills and at times the use of special tools.

- ✔ Although laptops within a certain manufacturer's family of devices may use similar motherboards, there is no such thing as a generic laptop board that fits into any case. You have to purchase an exact replacement from the manufacturer or a third party; you may be able to buy a used motherboard from a repair shop. (Desktop computers generally use one of several common form factors, allowing you to put a Brand X motherboard into a name-brand case or the other way around.)

✔ Because laptop motherboards are almost all custom made or customized, it may not be feasible (or smart) to install a faster microprocessor. Some processors are soldered into place, which ends the discussion. In other situations the laptop's design may not accept a plug-in replacement that draws more voltage, generates more heat, or is otherwise different from the original CPU.

✔ Even if the deeds can be done, that doesn't mean it makes economic sense. Weigh the cost of a new motherboard, a new microprocessor, or both against the price for a new machine. If you farm out the work to a professional repair shop, add $200 or so for just the labor involved.

✔ Oh, and one more thing: Dollar for dollar and electron for electron, if you're trying to eke out more speed from your laptop, boosting the amount of RAM is the smartest thing you can do. Doubling RAM from 256MB to 512MB and keeping the same microprocessor gives much more power than keeping the memory and spending several hundred dollars for a few hundred more megahertz of processor speed.

On most laptop motherboards, the microprocessor is held in a *ZIF (zero insertion force)* socket. This means that once the locking mechanism is released, the chip just slips into place. On a desktop machine, the socket usually uses a lever to lock the processor; specialized laptop motherboards may use a lever or a small screw.

Part III
Laying Hands on the Major Parts

The 5th Wave   By Rich Tennant

"He saw your laptop and wants to know if he can check his Hotmail."

In this part . . .

*I*t's sometimes easy to think of a computer as only electronics: chips and circuits and wires. In fact, though, moving and spinning mechanisms do much of the real work — or at least the functions.

I explain how hard drives, floppy disk drives (in the midst of their disappearing act), CD/DVDs, keyboards, mice, and trackballs work . . . and how to deal with their inevitable failure. That's right. It's only a matter of time before mechanical devices grind to a halt; with luck that comes shortly after you've moved on to a new laptop. If not, see how some of these parts can be replaced and others worked around with external fixes. (I also squeeze in LCDs, which are an interesting electromechanical hybrid.)

Chapter 7

Easing In to Hard Disks

Most of the glamour goes to the body, and sometimes there's some credit for having a brain. What I mean is that though a laptop's physical design and microprocessor are essential components, not an awful lot of work is going to be accomplished without a capable hard drive. Like comedian George Carlin once famously observed about the real reason we have houses and apartments: We need a place to keep our stuff.

The hard drive is the home of your booty, your treasure. It holds the operating system that brings the laptop to life, the applications that give it a purpose, and the words, pictures, and music you have created.

Diving in to a Hard Drive

A *hard drive* is, at its heart, a very large, very fast revolving storage closet. Information is recorded in the form of electrical marks inscribed by one or more electromagnets that move in and out to reach the magnetically marked tracks of the spinning disk.

Although a hard drive (aka *hard disk drive*) is in many ways similar to a floppy disk drive in concept, it has several major differences:

✔ Many drives have several rigid platters rather than a single floppy disk.

✔ To go along with the multiple platters, the drive has an equivalent number of read/write heads — one for each side of the platter.

✔ The drives spin at a very high rate of speed; a typical laptop hard drive rotates at least 4,200 times per second, compared to 300 times per second for a floppy disk drive.

✔ Hard drives are sealed units, with their platters and read/write heads protected from damage by dirt, dust, and sticky substances that could make it literally grind to a halt.

✔ Motherboards and hard drive controllers have advanced to the point where they are capable of very high transfer rates for the data recorded to or unloaded from a drive.

Desirable downsizing

A hard drive in a laptop is just like a hard drive in a desktop or tower computer *except* that it is usually much smaller, much lighter, much less demanding of electrical power, and considerably more resistant to damage or problems related to the fact that a laptop is specifically intended to move from place to place.

The drives have to be smaller, of course, because they need to fit in the tight confines of a notebook case. In a modern notebook computer, the hard drive is about the size and weight of a pack of playing cards. Most notebooks use drives that are two-and-a-half inches wide and a bit more than one-third inch thick (9.5mm); today's tiniest are just 8.5mm thick, which is almost exactly one-third inch.

Hard drive manufacturers are already offering even smaller drives; the next step down is a 1.8-inch-wide device that can be installed in a PC Card or as an embedded drive within the case. The tiniest commercially available drives

---

When hard drives hit the big time

The first hard drives for personal computers were nearly the size of a shoebox and about as heavy as a brick, and offered a storage capacity of 5 or 10 megabytes — the capacity of just a handful of today's floppy disks or CDs. (But at the time, they were considered modern marvels of miniaturization; before the advent of the PC, hard drives were the size of a small refrigerator.)

The IBM PC-XT, the great-great-grandfather of nearly every desktop, notebook, and laptop computer, came with a five-and-a-quarter-inch wide, three-inch-tall hard drive that weighed several pounds. These first units drew as much as 30 watts of power and with an access speed of 80 ns — unacceptably demanding and painfully slow by modern standards.

today are half again as wide, at 0.85 inches; the first such devices have capacities of as much as 4GB. Stop and think: That's less than an inch square and smaller than a postage stamp. The first uses of this sort of tiny drive are expected to be in cell phones, digital audio players, PDAs, and digital cameras.

Designers (and buyers) are continually clamoring for drives to be lighter for a real reason: Their shoulders and backs hurt from dragging around 10 pounds of laptop, power adapter, and other accessories. Every ounce that can be trimmed from a laptop gives the marketing department something else to brag about.

Current 2.5-inch notebook hard drives weigh somewhere near 100 grams, or about 3.5 ounces, an amazing feat of productive shrinkage. As this book goes to press, makers including Toshiba offer 1.8-inch-wide drives with a capacity of as much as 60GB and weighing just 62 grams, or just over two ounces. And the same company's 0.85-inch 4GB device weighs 10 grams, or about a third of an ounce. (You would have to stack about 45 of these drives atop each other to come up with a pound's worth of electronics.)

Because laptops are intended to be powered at least part of the time by a rechargeable battery rather than from AC wall current, another important specification for a hard drive is its power consumption. The less power required by the hard drive, the longer the battery will last, or designers can try to get away with a battery of a smaller capacity. And the more wattage a hard drive demands, the more heat it generates within the case, and that must be exhausted by a fan, which itself draws power.

A modern 3.5-inch hard drive for desktop and tower computer usage spins at 7,200 or 9,600 rpm and requires a 5-volt power source; at startup it draws as much as 10 to 11 watts. A typical 2.5-inch internal laptop model, with 100GB storage, spins at 4,200 rpm and requires 5 volts. At startup, the power draw is typically about 4.5 watts, dropping to about 2 watts for reading and writing.

Toshiba's 1.8-inch 60GB drive, which spins at 4,200 rpm, requires only 3.3 volts and demands as little as 1.2 watts to start up and 1.4 watts for reading and writing. And the tiny 0.85 drive has about the same miniscule power demands, although it spins at only 3,600 rpm and currently has not gone past 4GB in capacity.

Other than size, weight, and power demands, a laptop hard drive is very similar in design to a desktop drive. The fact that they are small does require some tradeoffs, though. For example, a typical 3.5-inch drive may have as many as four platters, a laptop drive may have only one or two; coupled with the smaller size of the platter itself, this reduces the portable drive's maximum capacity.

Another effect of downsizing is a reduction in the data transfer rate. First of all, most laptop hard drives spin at a slower rate than those in a desktop machine, which slows down the pickup or putdown of data. Secondly, the data transfer is fastest at the outer tracks of a drive — tracks with the largest circumference. Here size does matter — the tracks on a tiny drive are, well, tinier than a bigger one.

Remember, class, that you calculate the circumference of a circle by multiplying its diameter by Π. The diameter of the platters for a 3.5-inch drive, once you subtract the center spindle and leave a bit of space at the inside and outside as a buffer, is roughly 3 inches; say that the diameter of the platter for a 2.5-inch drive is about 2 inches. And, of course, you all can recite the value of π to 20 places: 3.14159265358979323846. You did know that, right?

Obviously, then, a 3-inch circle has a circumference of about 9.4 inches while a 2-inch circle a mere 6.3 inches. So, even if you leave aside the difference in rotational speed between a 9,600 rpm 3.5-inch drive and a 4,200 rpm 2.5-inch device, there's also the fact that the larger drive has a circumference about 50 percent larger. More circumference means the capacity for more data in a particular track. At the same rotational speed, more data in a track means faster throughput.

Having a flash of memory

Although it is always dangerous to announce that a technology has reached its zenith or nadir, it does appear that hard drives are not likely to get much smaller than the current miniature champions of 0.85 inches in diameter. The problem is that even though engineers continue to increase the density of the data squeezed onto a disk, the shrinking physical size of the platter keeps chipping away at capacity.

Tiny hard drives are expected to double in capacity to about 8–10GB by 2006, using new technologies like perpendicular recording, which places sectors on a more efficient slant instead of at a right angle to the core (outer) circumference.

At the same time, makers of _flash memory_ — like the tiny cards used to store images on a digital camera and in cell phones — are finding ways to make their nonmechanical RAM chips tinier and tinier and more capacious. And flash memory offers faster access to data since it is a random access medium — the controller can go directly to a particular memory location without having to wait for a spinning platter to come into position under a read/write head that has to make its own repositioning.

At the moment, high-capacity flash memory devices are still considerably more expensive than a mini hard drive of equivalent size. But over time, that differential is expected to become less and less, and at some point a miniature flash memory card may cost the same as a hard drive, and that may mark the end of the road for mechanical disks in portable devices including laptops, digital cameras, and video cameras.

Hunkering down for a mobile life

The good news about a laptop is that it can move from place to place, allowing users to bring work home from the office or on an airplane or commuter train. They can be used on a hotel table, atop a bar, or on a lanai at the beach.

The bad news is that moving a laptop exposes it to the possibility of being dropped, falling off a table or bar, or getting splashed or exposed to sand at the seashore.

Protection for water and dirt is accomplished by proper design of the laptop case. Guarding against damage from the shock of a fall begins with passive design elements that cushion the hard drive against damage.

More advanced safeguards include designs like IBM's Active Protection System for some of its ThinkPad laptops. Just as its name suggests, machines with IBM's technology include a motion sensor that continuously monitors the laptop's movement. Like the sensor in an automobile's airbag, it watches for sudden changes in motion that would include acceleration as a laptop tumbles off a desk or deceleration as it hits the floor. It reacts within 500 milliseconds (that's half a second to non-techies) to park the read/write heads of the drive in a place where they won't crash into the platters; then it stops the drive's spin.

Going Under the Covers of a Hard Drive

A modern hard drive, no matter how large or small, is basically a sealed box with a motor that spins one or more metal or synthetic platters (usually aluminum or a specialized ceramic) coated with an oxide that can record digital 0s or 1s. High-tech oxides can be made with compounds of iron, chromium, magnesium, or other substances. The platter is usually coated on both sides, meaning that each has two data surfaces. Also in the box is one or more read/write heads that move in toward the central spindle or retreat to the outer tracks as needed.

Most laptop hard drives spin their platters at 4,200 revolutions per minute, with some later models advancing to 5,400, 7,200, and 9,600 rpm — matching the speed of larger units designed for desktop computers.

The read/write heads in a hard drive are designed to fly on a cushion of air — much like the wing of an airplane — just above or just below the surface of the platter. I'm talking about a separation of just a few microns (a micron is a millionth of a meter, or about $\frac{1}{25,000}$ of an inch) from the platter.

Most hard drives place all of the heads on a single stalk that moves in and out. If a single platter is in the laptop drive, the stalk holds two heads — one for each data surface; if there are two platters, the stalk holds four heads, and so on. You can see within a modern hard drive, a sacrificial lamb from my workbench, in Figure 7-1.

Figure 7-1:
Inside a modern hard drive, its internal platters exposed.

So, when you put together the speed of the rotating disk and the closeness of the read/write heads, you can understand how the tiniest speck of dirt or sand could sit like a boulder on the surface of the platter. That is the reason hard drives are sealed units; they are assembled in high-tech clean rooms and protected by ultra-fine filters that allow them to breathe and get rid of heat but keep dirt away.

The laptop stores instructions and data in the form of 0s and 1s that are recorded on the surface of the platter as tiny magnetic points; to read back the information, the read/write heads look for changes in the polarity of the dots. The hard drive does not decode the meaning of the 0s or 1s; it is just a pick up, storage, and delivery mechanism to the computer's microprocessor.

The read/write heads are almost all variants of the same simple design first developed for use with magnetic audio tape: turns of tiny copper wire circle a *ferrite* (a form of iron oxide, once again) leaving a tiny gap on the side of the head that faces the platter. When electrical current is passed through the coil, it leaves a tiny magnetic marking on the data surface.

To read the information, the current is turned off, and the same gap senses the magnetic markings — actually the transition from one polarity to another — as it passes over the disk. The drive includes a tiny amplifier and a rectifier that converts the information into precise digital 0s or 1s.

How big is that hard drive in the window?

Designers of laptops and personal computers sometimes use the sort of fuzzy math that would make a politician proud. Some real numbers exist when it comes to capacity, but they are often hidden behind technological and marketing bafflegab.

Here's an example: Exactly how big is a 10GB hard drive?

- ✔ In precise technical terms, a gigabyte of information is equal to 2^{30} power, or 1,073,741,824 bytes.

- ✔ When the marketing department at a hard drive manufacturer (or a computer seller) describes the capacity of a drive, they often use a shorthand definition of gigabyte that means 1 billion bytes: 1,000,000,000. In that case, a marketer's 10GB hard drive is actually a 9.3132GB device, about 7 percent smaller.

- ✔ Back to technical specs: The hard drive has to devote some of its space to the index of files as well as electronic markings that denote the tracks, *sectors* (portion of a track), and *clusters* (groups of sectors). And if the hard drive is the *boot disk* for your system — the one that loads the operating system when the laptop is turned on — space also has to be left for that purpose. All told, the overhead required by the computer to manage the hard drive can range from 10–20 percent; pick the middle point and call it 15 percent. The supposed 10GB drive that is actually a 9.3132GB device may actually only have room for 7.9162GB of data.

✔ But wait: Remember that the disk controller doesn't fill up every possible cluster with data. The computer uses its own form of shorthand for efficiency in retrieving information; if the capacity of a cluster is 512 KB and a particular file is 514 KB in length, the controller is going to use two clusters, one of which will hold only a pair of lonely kilobytes of information.

✔ And then we have to deal with disk drive fragmentation. If you begin work on a chapter of a book, it may well start in one cluster and continue to the next; but when you come back to make edits, the file may be broken up into lots of little chunks scattered around the disk because that is where the available space exists. The result of fragmentation is first of all a slowing in the retrieval speed of data, and secondly an increase in wasted clusters. (Chapter 2 tells you how to defrag your computer.)

Just to add to the confusing math of hard drive capacity, consider the fact that many laptop manufacturers set up a hidden partition on the hard drive that comes with the system to hold compressed copies of much or all of the original operating system and utilities. They do this for your own protection — it's a convenient way to quickly restore your machine to its as-delivered configuration (although you will lose all data and any applications you have added on your own.) This hidden partition may eat up a few more gigabytes of space.

So, what's the bottom line? It's almost impossible to say with any precision. The first thing to do is to determine how the maker of your hard drive or computer defines capacity: Are they using the technical specs, where 1 gigabyte is equal to 1,073,741,824 bytes? Or are they using a marketer's 1 gigabyte of 1,000,000,000 bytes? And then reduce the number by 15 percent to subtract overhead. And then take out another 10–15 percent for various and sundry waste. In my personal shorthand, a 10GB drive is good for about 7GB of data, whether it is a designer gigabyte or a marketer's gigabyte. The brand-spanking-new "60GB" drive on a new laptop I purchased while working on this book actually netted a bit more than 53 real gigabytes of storage before I went to work on it to remove some of the supplied software and special offers that were of no use to me.

What's to retain here? More is better. If you have a choice between a 30GB and a 40GB hard drive in your new laptop and it makes economic sense to do so, go for the 40GB device — it'll give you, oh, 7GB more storage.

How fast is fast?

In most uses of a laptop the microprocessor, memory, and LCD screen cannot operate any faster than the flow of information they receive from the hard drive (or a CD or DVD drive). In a modern machine, in most situations it is a lot more likely that the microprocessor will sit around waiting for data than it is that the hard drive will pump information faster than the microprocessor can work on it.

A number of factors go into the calculation of speed:

- ✔ The revolutions per minute of the platters. The faster the platter spins, the quicker the read/write heads can move into position to a particular cluster and the faster the stream of data that comes off the disk. Designers talk about *latency* as a factor here, defining it as the average amount of time for the spinning drive to bring a particular cluster beneath or above the read/write head. Modern laptops generally use hard drives that spin at 4,200 rpm, although faster motors are beginning to be installed.

- ✔ The seek time for the read/write heads. This is the average amount of time required for the heads to move in or out to locate a track. Obviously, it is much quicker to move from track 49 to track 50 than it is to go all the way from 0 to 79. The hard drive mechanism can benefit from software utilities that attempt to reorganize data in a way that attempts to anticipate the system needs.

- ✔ The density of the data on the disk. The closer together the bits of information, the more data there is in a particular cluster and the faster the stream of data.

- ✔ The *data transfer speed* — the thickness and pumping power of the pipe between the disk and the processor. Although a number of data interfaces are in use on desktop machines (including ATA/IDE and a number of flavors of SCSI standards — more on these in the next section), nearly all laptops use a parallel ATA/IDE connection. In coming years, most hard drives are expected to migrate to the developing serial version of ATA (called *SATA*), which gives a slight speed boost while it reduces some of the complexity of the internal cabling.

When hard drives were first developed, each track had the same number of sectors, which was a simpler scheme but very wasteful because the outer tracks have much more space than the inner ones. Modern drives vary the number of sectors in each track, subdividing the outer circles into many more sectors than are found in the smaller inner ones. Therefore the stream of information from the outer tracks of a hard drive is much greater than from inside tracks: The outer edge is traveling much faster than the core and there is more information stored there.

Advanced hard drives also include *data buffers,* which are small blocks of RAM intended to help keep the transfer pipe filled at all times; they compensating for any differences in transfer rates amongst various devices.

Serial in the box

Serial ATA represents another step away from parallel wiring for high-speed communication. First I tell you why the techies are all excited, and then I tell you how it won't make much of a difference to you as a laptop user except that you'll have to make sure you know what you're buying when it comes time to upgrade a hard drive.

To this point in the history of the PC, nearly every hard drive has used parallel ATA as the transfer protocol for data. (A relatively small number of drives, mostly used in high-demand graphics or as servers, used high-speed SCSI serial interfaces.)

One significant disadvantage of parallel ATA was the fact that the motherboard and the drive had to be connected by a wide and unwieldy 40- or 80-wire cable and a 40-pin connector. Another problem was the requirement that 26 of the wires carry 5-volt signals.

Among the beauties of serial ATA is the fact this standard requires only four thin wires in a casing similar to a telephone cable. The first specification for SATA requires only four 500 millivolt (½ volt) signals; future versions are expected to allow use of signal voltages half again as strong at 250 millivolts or ¼ volt.

As a laptop user, you're not likely to be working under the covers of your machine moving cables and worrying about the proper flow of cooling — both problems that exist for designers and upgraders of desktop and tower PCs. But you will benefit when future motherboards use SATA because designs will become simpler, electrical demands a bit less, and throughput of data improved. The first drives and adapters offer only a tiny increase in true throughput — perhaps 1–5 percent — compared to parallel ATA, but future specifications are expected to double and triple throughput to 300 MBps and 600 MBps.

Serial ATA is a point-to-point interface with each device directly connected to the motherboard and able to use the entire bandwidth; *parallel ATA* typically uses a master and slave arrangement for pairs of devices, and in certain circumstances the two drives may have to share the same channel for loading or unloading data. And serial ATA is also capable of being set up to be *hot pluggable* (like USB and certain PC Card devices), allowing drives to be attached or removed from a laptop while it is running. The politically incorrect terms of *master* and *slave* refer to the fact that one device on the connector is considered to be the dominant piece of equipment, with the slave subservient to it or with a lower priority when it comes to demanding the attention of the microprocessor.

All that said, serial ATA drives have not yet arrived in consumer laptop designs. When they do, you'll have to take care to distinguish between plug-in hard drives (and CD and DVD devices) that expect a parallel connection and those that are looking for a serial attachment.

When Good Disks Go Bad

Steel yourself for some bad news: Your hard drive will die someday. I can't tell you when, where, or how. But I can promise that sooner or later the ravages of time, heat, physical shock, and the laws of physics will result in the drive grinding to a halt or otherwise failing.

Why am I so sure your hard drive will not live forever? Because they are mechanical devices. They have a motor that spins the platters, an actuator that moves the read/write heads in and out, and a set of electronics that has to exist within a sealed box. Add the fact that laptops move from place to place — sometimes with the hard drive spinning — and you've got a meltdown waiting for just the wrong time and place to happen.

Now, mind you, modern hard drives are amazingly robust. With any sort of luck your drive should last for many years, probably well beyond the obsolescence factor for your laptop. But you should always act as if the last time you shut down the machine is the last time you will be able to use it. Back up, back up, back up.

If you're lucky, you'll have some advance warning of an impending hard-drive death:

- ✔ An occasional hiccup where the drive won't come to life when you first apply power but comes back on a reboot.

- ✔ An intermittent warning from the operating system or the BIOS that it cannot communicate with the drive.

- ✔ A specific alarm from a disk-monitoring software utility.

- ✔ A steady (or irregular) increase in the number of bad blocks discovered by a system utility program.

Your response to any of these signals should be to double-check your emergency backup plans for your disk. Don't ever leave the only copy of an irreplaceable file on a hard drive, or anywhere else; always make sure you have backup copies on a CD, another hard drive, or other media.

In my system, I make copies of live projects on an external hard drive every other day — more often if I've done a lot of work or have any premonitions of disaster. And then, in a belt-and-suspenders preventive action, I also burn CDs with current projects at least once a week. Bottom line: The worst that can happen on my system is that I lose a day or two's worth of work. With CD-Rs costing somewhere between 10 cents and a quarter, they are the cheapest form of insurance you can get for your data.

I've already explained how data is stored in concentric circles, called tracks. Then there are the radiating spokes that extend from the center to the outside, creating pie-wedge sectors. Now get three dimensional. Every laptop hard drive has at least one two-sided platter, and some drives have more than one platter. A *cylinder* is the same track on all of the platters. (Think of a cookie cutter, separating the multiple platters into stacked rings.)

That's as far as I want to get on the technical side of the data structure in this book, because that's all the computer needs to know. The disk operating system that underlies Windows looks at data recorded across tracks, sectors, platters, and cylinders as a continuous stream of information as if it were recorded on a long piece of magnetic tape.

Getting with the Format

A hard drive has all of the parts when it comes out of the clean room at the factory, but its internal platter(s) are like a blank piece of paper. The computer has no way to know where to put information or how to retrieve it. It is a blank map.

The solution is to draw a set of circles, lines, and cylinders and create an index that shows what is where (along with other information, including when and how). The process is called *formatting* and includes three steps.

Low-level formatting

Low-level formatting is usually done at the factory. This involves addition of magnetic traffic signs that demark the tracks and divide each platter into sectors with codes noting the beginning and end of each. More sectors are at the longer, outer tracks and fewer at the shorter, inner ones.

Partitioning

Partitioning is a task done by your laptop maker or by you if you are replacing the original hard drive or adding a second new storage device. This process subdivides the wide-open space of the hard drive into useable areas recognizable by your operating system.

First of all, partitioning creates a *master boot record* (also called the *boot sector* or *MBR*) that contains the very basic index for the location of instructions and files that the computer needs to consult when it first comes to life; once the operating system is loaded it works together with the MBR to manage file

---

And brains to boot

Impress your friends: The term *boot* comes from the old phrase "lifting yourself up by your own bootstraps," which is, of course, a physical impossibility. Somehow the early computer designers figured out a way for a computer that when turned off is merely a collection of metal, silicon, and glass to figure out a way to bring itself to life by acting on the simple instructions in the boot sector.

---

storage and retrieval. For the record, the MBR is always located at cylinder 0, head 0, and sector 1.

Then the disk can be identified to the system as a single physical drive (usually called C, because the original PCs had an A and B floppy disk drive) or the disk can be divided into one physical and multiple logical drives. Some users prefer to subdivide a single large drive into several smaller logical drives; for example, using C for the operating system and applications, D for data, and E for graphics and music. The fact is that you can accomplish essentially the same thing through the use of folders and subfolders, and most modern applications assume that you will be organizing your system in that way.

The other reason to partition your hard drive into a physical and multiple logical drives is if you have an older machine whose BIOS or operating system is not equipped to deal with large drives. Along the course of history of the PC various roadblocks rose to partition size; any laptop younger than five years and running a modern operating system (Windows 98, ME, 2000, NT, and XP) will have no problem dealing with drives of 100GB and even larger.

Windows has a built-in partitioning utility, and hard drive manufacturers usually include an automatic partitioning program with their hardware. And if you want to try something a bit unusual, several specialized partitioning programs allow you to install multiple boot sectors — this could allow a sophisticated user to experiment with different operating systems. For example, you could choose to experiment with Microsoft's latest version of Windows in one partition while keeping your older version in another. Or you could try out Linux or another O/S in one boot sector and retain Windows in another.

One product that handles setup of nonstandard partitions is Norton Partition Magic, formerly marketed by PowerQuest Corporation.

High-level formatting

The third step is *high-level formatting,* which is the application of file structure and an indexing system to the hard drive. Think of this as a table of contents for your operating system, applications, and data.

The original organizational scheme for PCs used the *FAT* system, which was not a weight-loss program but rather an acronym for *File Attribute Table.* As systems became more sophisticated and capable of dealing with larger computer words and larger drives, Microsoft advanced through FAT12 (used on floppy disks), FAT16, and FAT32 versions. FAT16 can deal with partitions of just over 2 GB; FAT32 breaks through the barrier all the way through to 2 TB. (A terabyte is 2^{40}, or 1,024 gigabytes, or if you insist, 1,099,511,627,776 bytes. When you reach that point, you can bet that the marketing department will round up disk capacities to the next highest trillion bytes.)

The most current organizational scheme is *NTFS (New Technology File System),* which offers a number of efficiencies and essentially removes all limits on file size; files can be as large as the size of the entire drive or partition (As this book goes to press the current limit is 16 TB minus 1 KB, which is very, very, very large and bigger than any hard disk drive you're likely to see in a laptop for a long, long time.)

Nearly all current laptops use Windows 98 or a later version of that operating system in order to take advantage of features including USB (more on USB in Chapter 16). All can work with the old and relatively inefficient FAT system, but only Windows NT and Windows XP can work with NTFS. Here's a breakout of what works with which:

- ✔ FAT16 can be used on all versions of Windows including 95, 98, NT, 2000, and XP.

- ✔ FAT32 works with Windows 95 OSR2, 98, ME, 2000, and XP. Based on a 32-bit file allocation table, FAT32 made its way into a revised version of Windows 95 called 95B, or OEM Service Release 2. Subsequent releases of Windows also support it.

- ✔ NTFS disks are accessible to Windows XP and Windows 2000. Computers running Windows NT 4.0 with Service Pack 4 or later may be able to access some files, but this combination is not recommended.

What does this mean to you? If you buy a new laptop, it will probably come formatted as an NTFS disk, and that is just fine. The only reason to use FAT32 is if you are running an older machine or are mixing and matching older hardware and a current operating system, or the other way around.

If you upgrade your laptop from an earlier version of Windows to run Windows XP, you'll be given the opportunity to convert the disk from FAT32 to NTFS; the process does not delete data or applications on the disk. (Even so, I would recommend you make backups of irreplaceable data before making the update. Actually, you're already performing regular updates every few days anyway, right?)

It is somewhere between difficult and impossible to convert a later file system to an earlier one — for example to go from NTFS to FAT32, or from FAT16 to FAT — and no good reasons to do so except for an unusual incompatibility. You cannot directly convert to an earlier indexing system; the only way to do this is to copy all programs and data from the drive to another media — a properly formatted hard drive, a CD-R, a recordable DVD, or across a network to another machine — and then to reformat the drive under the FAT or FAT32 system. Reformatting will erase all data on the drive; if you manage to copy data to another media, you can later restore it to the re-indexed drive.

Driving Toward Installation

Any number of scenarios involve installing a hard drive. Follow the steps for those that pertain to your situation.

Putting a new hard drive in an old laptop

Putting a new hard drive in a modern laptop generally falls into one of three categories:

- **So darn easy** it should be required.
- **A small amount of hassle** but not so hard it's not worth doing.
- **Painful and worthy of question**, so maybe you should try a workaround.

I break each of these categories down, because I know you're really, really needing to know. That's probably the reason you've read this far into this chapter where you've just about learned everything you need to know to build your own hard drive from tin foil and paper clips.

The reason for the detail is to help you understand how a hard drive is built and organized. For one thing, you'll have a better understanding of error messages and utility programs. And then if necessary, you'll become a more educated consumer in buying a replacement or upgrade.

I talk first about the hardware side of a hard drive replacement, and explain installation of an operating system and transfer of data and applications later in this chapter.

So darn easy

Some of the most modern laptops place hard drives in bays where they can be removed and replaced as easily as a battery. All that is required is a match between the plastic frame and case for the drive and connector that delivers and picks up data and supplies power.

Turn off the laptop and remove the battery before taking the hard drive out of its bay.

Almost all such plug-and-run drives are sold directly by the laptop maker and some resellers. You cannot, though, buy a hard drive in a case designed for a Dell Inspiron 5160 and expect it to work in a Toshiba Satellite M35X, just to take two models at random. The hard drive and connector may be the same, but the plastic and metal frame and other attachment hardware are likely to be different. See Figure 7-2.

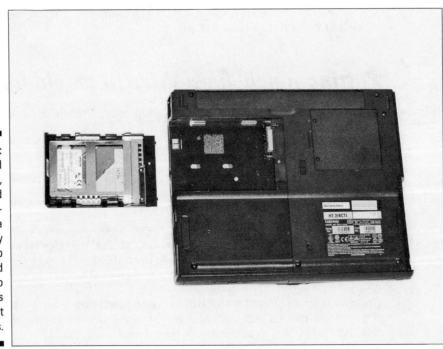

Figure 7-2:
A hard drive, removed from a plug-in bay on a Gateway Solo laptop and turned over to show its attachment points.

A small amount of hassle

It is usually possible to remove a hard drive installed in a bay and disassemble the plastic components and metal hardware to gain direct access to the tiny hard drive within.

1. **Prepare your work area.**

   Before you touch the hard drive you are removing or the new one you propose to install in its place, you want a clean, well-lit and stable surface. Ground yourself before touching either drive.

2. **Turn off the laptop, unplug the AC adapter, and remove the battery.**

3. **Take the hard drive out of its bay.**

4. **Keep track of every screw and piece you remove.**

   Have a pad of paper nearby and consider using a numbered, compartmentalized container for each part and make a corresponding entry in your notebook. One interesting solution is to use a clean egg carton with each of the cups numbered or lettered.

5. **Once you have taken out the old drive, put it aside and immediately install the new one in its place.**

6. **Install the plastic and metal pieces and plug the new assembly into your laptop.**

Painful and worthy of question

Older laptops were built with no concession to the user when it came to replacing the hard drive; the storage device was plugged in to an internal bay, buried beneath the top cover or hidden under the bottom plastic.

Before proceeding, it's worthwhile to distinguish between these two situations:

- ✔ Your existing hard drive is working properly, but you've run out of space.

- ✔ Your existing hard drive has stopped working, and you can no longer use it to boot the system.

It *is* possible to open up an older laptop and get at the hard drive, but the job may involve dozens of screws and the removal of all sorts of unrelated parts: the battery, the keyboard, the CD-ROM, and just about everything else. You should be able to read all of the gory details in the technical manual for your machine; if you don't have a copy, you may be able to find it on the web site of your machine's maker.

If all of this doesn't scare you off, be heartened by the fact that you will still probably be able to use an off-the-shelf laptop hard drive. It should match up with the connector inside the case and screw into place.

You have two alternatives here:

✔ Send the laptop to a professional repair facility and pay for its labor and expertise. This is a fairly expensive proposition, requiring about two hours of labor plus the retail cost of a new drive. See Chapter 4 for more about repair shops.

✔ Work around an inadequate hard drive by using an external storage device that connects. The external upgrade may be a bit more cumbersome than changing out an internal drive, but a lot less expensive and easier accomplished. Use the external drive for storage of data and new applications; keep the operating system on the original drive so the machine can be booted from that device.

If your internal drive has completely given up the ghost, you will have to either replace it or find some other way to boot the laptop.

If you're lucky, you may be able to burn, on a CD-R, a bootable version of the operating system and make a change to your BIOS setup so that the laptop looks for the boot information from the CD. It's a relatively obscure solution, but if it works for you let me be the first to congratulate you on saving a few hundred dollars.

Installing a hard drive into a holding case

You may be able to purchase the plastic holding case and other hardware for a hard drive from the maker or seller of your laptop. However, so many different models of laptops are on the market you'll unlikely find a one-size-fits-all drive holder at your local retail store or from any online site.

That's the bad news. The good news is that it is relatively easy to recycle the holder from the hard drive that was originally supplied with your laptop. The dance is the same, although the steps may vary from manufacturer to manufacturer and from model to model. (As a friend once described a change in government, "It's the same monkeys in different dresses.")

1. **Turn off the laptop, unplug the AC adapter, and remove the battery.**

   Do all three steps to assure that there is no power in the system that could generate a spark and damage components.

2. **Prepare your work area: You want a clean, well-lighted and stable surface.**

3. **Turn the laptop over so that its bottom is facing up.**

   You can protect the fragile LCD by cushioning your work surface with a mat or piece of soft packing material. You can use almost anything as long as it is not metallic or packing an electric charge.

4. **Ground yourself before touching the old drive and its enclosure and the new replacement drive.**

5. **Slide the hard drive out of its bay.**

   Depending on the laptop's design, you may have to remove one or more screws or release a catch, or both.

6. **Remove the small screws that attach the holder and drive case from the hard drive.**

   These are typically small Phillips-head screws.

7. **Set aside the screws in a safe place; make notes on any unusual steps you must conduct.**

8. **Carefully slide the hard drive away from the laptop.**

   Most sit in rails which extend all the way to edge of the case. Some laptops require you to release a catch before the drive will begin sliding. Others permit you to slide the drive an inch or so until it is released from the rail, and you'll have to lift it straight up to remove it.

9. **Unscrew several tiny screws that lock the little hard drive into the holding case.**

   Again, set aside the screws in a numbered container. You might want to make a rough drawing of the holder and the position of the screws.

10. **Lift or slide the old drive out of its holder and set it aside on a cushioned surface.**

   Handle old and new drives carefully, holding them only by their sides. Do not touch the exposed printed circuit board, and take care not to bend or dislodge the connector at the back. Do not press on the top or bottom of the drive, and make sure that you do not cover the drive's vent or "breather" hole with tape, a cable, or plastic parts.

11. **Insert the new drive into the holder and then reinstall all of the screws removed.**

12. **Install the new drive in the laptop.**

   Mate it to the rails you used to uninstall the old device. Press firmly but do not force the drive as you slide it the final one-third of an inch to bring the connector on the drive to its mate inside the drive.

13. **Reinstall any retaining screws you removed to release the hard drive.**

Jumping to conclusions

The specification for a standard ATA/IDE drive for a personal computer allows for one cable to serve one or two hard drives; one is usually designated as the "master" drive and the second as a "slave." In most setups, the drives are identified to the system by the placement of a jumper across a specific set of pins. A *jumper* is a small speck of plastic with a metal strip that connects the pins to which it is attached; it serves the same purpose as a switch. When it is in place between two pins, that particular circuit is completed; when it is absent, that circuit is open or disconnected.

Even though the hard drives produced for laptops are considerably smaller than those made for desktop machines, they follow the same technical and electrical specifications as their larger cousins. In theory, a 2.5-inch hard drive can be adapted to work in a desktop or tower PC and if it were attached to an IDE cable with two devices — two hard drives or a hard drive and CD or DVD drive, for example — one of the devices would have to be identified through the use of jumpers as the master and the other as the slave.

But let me get back to laptops, for that is the purpose of this book — it says so right there on the cover. Very few laptops have more than one internal hard drive, and the drive bays are directly connected to the motherboard's hard drive controller by a cable that makes no provision for a second device on the same link.

Helping you out a bit more, most hard drive manufacturers ship their equipment with a default setting as the master device. Check the instruction manuals that come with a new drive or consult the Web sites for advice about the need to make any changes in jumpers.

If your laptop does, in fact, allow for a second hard drive — some machines offer an extra bay that can be used for a hard drive, a floppy disk drive, a CD or DVD drive, or even be convertible to hold an auxiliary battery — consult the instruction manuals or call customer support to determine how that bay is electrically configured. It might require configuring the additional drive as a slave device (requiring you to set jumpers accordingly) or it may be connected to the motherboard by a separate IDE channel and devices installed in that bay may be considered master devices on a second channel. Once you find the answer, the only instance in which you are likely to have to make a change to jumper settings is if the device will be set up as a slave.

Like I said about that monkey in a change of dress, when it comes to setting jumpers, no two hard drives are going to be exactly the same. However, they are going to be very similar. In Figure 7-3 is a diagram of the back end of one typical hard drive.

As you can see, four pins at the right side (as you face the connector) are marked A, B, C, and D. The jumpers can only be installed horizontally or vertically, and not on a diagonal. This allows the following jumper connections: AB, AC, CD, and DB. (Some drive makers also allow for settings based on two jumpers, which makes for a fifth jumper condition: AC *plus* DB.)

Figure 7-3:
A typical back end of a standard hard drive, showing the location for jumpers and the polarity peg that assures proper positioning of the data cable.

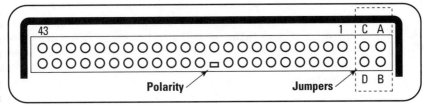

To have the drive operate as a master drive, no jumpers should be installed across any of the four pins. That's simple enough and that's the case on *most* new hard drives. To have the drive operate as a slave drive, a jumper has to be placed across CD.

To use a cable select scheme in which the design of the cable determines whether the drive is a master or slave, in this case you would jumper DB.

But *please* . . . don't assume that what I'm saying here is what you need to do with your particular monkey. Read the instruction manual and jumper accordingly.

I have seen some drives with three pairs of jumper pins, which allows for seven different jumper settings with one jumper in use and potentially a total of 17 different settings using three jumpers. But the fact is that modern drives are so sophisticated that just about the only hardware switch that needs to be set is the one that differentiates between master, slave, or cable select, and that only requires use of one jumper and four pins.

Configuring the BIOS and the drive

Today, most new drives come with a self-booting floppy diskette or CD that automates much of the configuration process for a new drive. The first step is make sure your system BIOS is set up to recognize the presence of a new hard drive. In the old days of computing, it was necessary to instruct the

BIOS about the type of drive, its size, and other specifications. Today, nearly all BIOS setups are capable of auto detecting IDE drives and determining their specifications. Chapter 6 has scads more on BIOS.

Read the instructions that come with the hard drive. If Autodetect is not available, go to the BIOS screen (reachable through a specific key combination during bootup — read the manual to find out which keys to use and when to press them) and identify the hard drive as a User Selected device. The manual for the drive will tell you the capacity (in GB), the number of sectors per track, the number of heads, and the number of cylinders in the drive. Some drives and BIOS systems will ask for even more details — it's all there in the instruction manual, but if you're lucky you won't need to go down this path and will instead be able to use Auto Detect.

Again, a modern drive should be able to automate the process or partitioning the drive and then formatting it. If not, you can follow the instructions given by Microsoft as part of Windows for the FDISK.EXE and FORMAT.EXE utilities. Or, you can purchase a third-party automated partitioning and formatting program.

Although most modern BIOS programs have solved the problem certain combinations of older machines and newer hard drives still are not fully compatible. You may have a 60GB hard drive (or so says the box it came in) but the laptop only reports 24GB of available storage. The hard drive itself may come with a utility that provides a means of breaking through the barrier of an older machine; an alternate solution may involve treating the one large physical drive as if it were two or more smaller logical drives. Consult your hard drive maker for advice if you run into this problem and there's not a solution provided on a CD in the box.

The Simplest Solution: External Add-ons

If your internal hard drive is too small or too slow, or (in some situations) if it has ground to a halt, the simplest solution may be to add a tiny, low-power external drive. External storage comes in four common types, all of them easy to add on; you have to judge the cost, weight, and power consumption advantages and disadvantages of each. Here are the four, in descending order of capacity.

USB external devices

The shelves of computer stores have begun to fill with fast, large, and inexpensive external hard drives that attach to a USB port for an instant expansion of storage. These drives can be huge, from today's new small end of 20–40GB to monsters of 200 or 300GB in capacity.

The only problem here is that most of the external devices are principally aimed at desktop computer users who don't much care about size, weight, and power consumption. If you buy an external USB drive of that sort, be aware that you will either have to provide electrical current from an AC adapter or add a fairly significant draw to your laptop's battery. An example of a full-sized Maxtor One-Touch external drive is shown in Figure 7-4.

As a laptop owner you should set your focus instead on devices specifically designed for battery-powered computers. These use low-power, lightweight drives that are often the same as those used as internal devices on laptops. As such they will work as an external USB drive without the need for an AC adapter, although one can be attached to the drive when you're working late in your hotel room.

If your laptop is capable of communication using the USB 2.0 standard (which I discuss in detail in Chapter 16), be sure to buy a drive that exchanges data at that speed. In most types of use, a USB drive is no slower than an internal device.

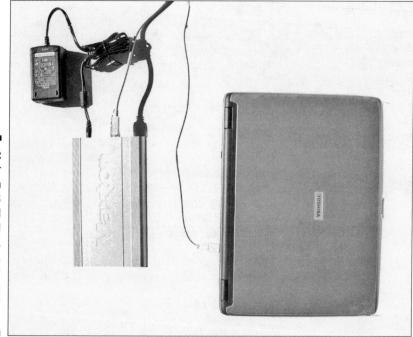

Figure 7-4:
A Maxtor One-Touch 40GB external USB hard drive, fast, capable, and requiring an AC adapter for power.

You can also build your own external USB drive, recycling a standard full-sized drive from a desktop computer. Inexpensive external cases hold the drive and small circuit board that converts the data interface from the direct IDE connection used within a computer to a USB circuit. Screw the old drive into the new holding case, attach a USB cable to the case and to the laptop, and (alas) attach an AC adapter to give it power. I show an example of a do-it-yourself external USB drive in Figure 7-5.

If your machine has an older USB 1.1 port, or completely lacks USB facilities, you can add the high-speed 2.0 connection by purchasing a PC Card with that facility. (There's an "if" waiting here, of course: If your machine is running a version of Windows earlier than 98SE — including Windows 98 and 95 — the operating system will have to be upgraded to permit use of the faster USB specification.)

Figure 7-5:
An external
USB drive
kit that
recycles a
desktop
hard drive
for use as
an attached
drive on a
laptop.

PC Card attached devices

A near-equivalent to a USB-attached hard drive is one that connects to the laptop through a PC Card interface. The advantage to these drives is that they are specifically designed for use with laptops (very few desktop PCs even have a PC Card slot) and they use the same tiny, low-powered hard drives employed for internal drives.

A class of do-it-yourself upgrades are meant to be used to hold the original hard drive of a laptop after it has been swapped out of its bay in an upgrade. One example, the EZ-Gig kit sold by Bix Computers at www.bixnet.com is shown in Figure 7-6. The kit includes a replacement hard drive, a small plastic case to hold the original drive, and a PC Card and cable. You can format the new drive and add an operating system and applications, or you can use the supplied Clone-EZ software to transfer the contents of the original drive to the new, larger drive before it is installed within the laptop.

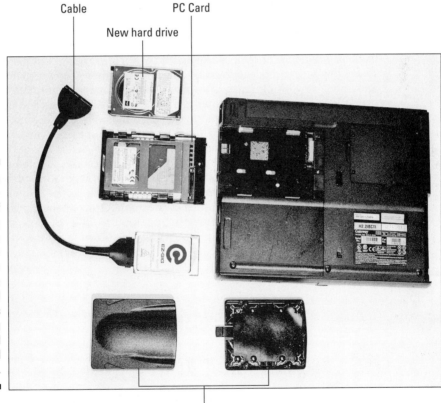

Figure 7-6: The components of an EZ-Gig kit, include a new laptop hard drive, a case for the original drive, plus connecting cable and PC Card interface.

PC Card drives

In 2005, Toshiba broke new ground with a tiny hard drive that slips into a PC Card slot and instantly delivers 5GB of storage without the need for cables, screwdrivers, or jumpers. The only downside to this device is that, because it is the first of its kind, it is more expensive and relatively small; both of those issues are sure to be solved in a short period of time. As this book goes to press, 5GB sold for about $150 in this format; expect to see larger capacities at lower prices soon.

Based on a 1.8-inch drive, Toshiba's device weighs only 55 grams (fewer than 2 ounces) and draws only 2 watts when working and half that amount when idle.

Flash memory keys

In 2005, you could purchase a key with 1GB of storage for just under $100. These low-power devices draw no power at all when they are in an idle state, and only a tiny bit of power is required to write or read information to or from them. Prices and capacities are already spiraling down and up in the right direction. The great advantage of flash memory keys is their tremendous portability; you can keep sensitive material on the key in your pocket or toss it into a safe. On the other hand, if you get too casual about the process, you could end up losing them easily. The other potential problem: A USB key sticks out an inch or two from the side of laptop, an invitation to disaster if they are bumped by other objects. (I'm not so much worried about the keys, which are pretty sturdy, but rather to the connectors on the laptop's motherboard or the possibility that the entire computer will fly on down to a hard surface.) An example of a flash memory key is shown in Figure 7-7.

Figure 7-7:
A flash memory key is an excellent way to securely transport information from place to place (as long as you don't lose the little fellow).

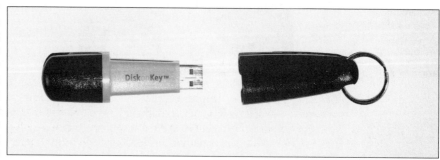

Chapter 8

Floppy Drives: Relics and Memories

A floppy drive used to matter. Really.

Today it seems impossibly slow, ridiculously small, and of little use in a time when we have networks, CD and DVD drives, flash memory keys, and wireless interconnects. And although the floppy drive is probably nearing the end of its usefulness on laptops and PCs, it still has a role for some users as a cheap and simple way to exchange information between one machine and another. Way back in ancient times we even had an affectionate name for its use: *sneakernet*. As in, pick up this disk and walk it across the room to that other machine and plug it in.

Its other use, also declining in importance, was as an emergency way to boot the operating system. Today most laptops have a CD or DVD that can hold the boot tracks and much, much more.

1.4 Million Bits of History

When the first personal computers came out, the first mass storage medium was the floppy disk drive. The original IBM PC, like the one that collects dust in the back of one of my storage closets, shipped with one 3-inch tall, 5.25-inch wide, single-sided disk drive that could hold all of 160 KB of data. And it truly was a floppy disk — a fragile circle of magnetized iron oxide on a plastic carrier within a bendable envelope.

But back at the dawn of PC time, about 1980, the cost of a hard drive was prohibitive — several thousand dollars for a few megabytes of storage. And so the first versions of *DOS* (the *disk operating system* that preceded and still in some ways underlies Microsoft Windows) were made to fit on a single floppy disk to boot the system and also hold a scaled-down word processor. And then you might store whatever files you had created on a second floppy.

Within a few years, led by Apple Computers, the bendable 5.25-inch floppy disk went away, replaced by a more durable 3.5-inch disk within a hard plastic case — stilled called *floppies* though they are not nearly so; the capacity of the smaller disk increased by leaps and bounds. Nearly all modern computers standardized on a 1.44MB capacity, roughly 10 times as capacious as the original device. (A number of attempts were made at adding 2.88MB floppies, and a few supersized designs went even higher. Iomega's Zip Drive and a few other competitors managed to squeeze 100MB to 250MB or more on special disks and drives that followed the same 3.5-inch form factor.)

With the arrival of small hard drives for storage and CD drives or Internet downloads to install new software, floppy drives became less important and eventually became vestigial parts of the PC and laptop — sort of an electronic appendix. Today there is little need for a sneakernet when homes and offices are interconnected by wireless hotspots or Ethernet cables. The emergency boot function has been replaced by bootable CD drives. And anyway, it was always a concern to knowledgeable users that a floppy disk was a great carrier for a computer virus; if an infected disk was left in the drive and if the machine was set up to check the floppy before it tried to load from the hard drive, a virus could sneak into the system *before* an antivirus program on the hard drive could detect and block it.

And almost every home and office with more than one machine has been updated to include some sort of network linking them — a wired Ethernet, a WiFi system, or a direct link between machines using a serial or USB cable. And there is also the advent of the *flash memory key,* a small chip of static RAM that plugs in to a USB port and can be walked between machines. (More on them in Chapter 7.)

The bottom line around here: On most of the machines in my office, the floppy disk drive has not been used in years. But until fairly recently, computer makers kept putting that vestigial drive into the desktops and laptops. Today, though, has begun to see the end of the line. Many modern laptop makers have decided to dispense with the floppy disk drive as a standard feature. In doing so, they:

✔ Save a few ounces of weight.

✔ Save a few dollars of cost.

✔ Open up 10 or 12 cubic inches of space that can be used for other purposes, including auxiliary batteries or second hard drives.

If you absolutely insist on having a floppy disk drive, you can buy one that attaches to the all-purpose USB port.

Getting In the Arena: Floppy Disk Mathematics

Floppy disks, like hard disks (but unlike CDs and DVDs) have a magnetic personality. They store information in the form of small notes put in place by an electromagnet. Inside the outer protective case is a circle of plastic (usually a tough and durable form called Mylar) that is coated with a compound of ferric oxide, which is a scientific version of powdered rust.

Okay, let me get my metaphors revved up and running. Think of a floppy disk as a circular arena, with a hole in the middle where your basic Jennifer-Christina-Madonna-Alicia is ready to pop up and perform on stage. Actually, that hole has a square opening and an additional rectangular locating slot that match corresponding pegs on a motor that sits inside the floppy disk drive. The pegs and the holes mate when the disk is inserted, allowing the system to automatically orient itself to a starting point.

Now, the arena surrounds the stage with concentric rows of seats. Each row is a complete circular — the end of one row does not connect into the row behind it. So, if you can envision this, you'll see that the rows that are closest to the center are much shorter (fewer seats) than the ones that are farthest away.

Dropping the metaphor for a moment: The rows of the arena are the *tracks* of a floppy disk. On what is now a standard 1.4MB floppy disk (called a *double density disk*), there are 80 tracks.

Back to symbology: The arena has 9, 12, or 18 aisles that radiate out from the center hole. The aisles split the rows into wedge-shaped sections which make it easier for buyers to find their seat; their ticket might tell them they are located in section 18, row 50, and seat 2. In computer terms, the radiating spokes split the disk into *sectors.* Again, visualize: The wedge-shaped sector may have just a handful of storage spaces (seats) at the very point of the wedge near the hole but have many more spaces at the outside of the circle. (There's also something called a *cluster,* which is a group of sectors linked together.) Okay, you're almost at the end of your excursion into metaphor, analogy, and simile. You've seen how the circular disk/arena can be subdivided into an indexed chart of memory locations/seats through the use of tracks/rows and sectors/sections.

But for the computer, it is very important that it have a quick, logical, and easily managed scheme to remember what information has been placed where, as well as to know what space is available for new recording. It does this by thinking in terms of those wedge-shaped sectors; when the computer wants to store a page of text, a snippet of sound, or a piece of an image, it finds an empty sector and starts recording from the beginning of that sector to the end. If the data fills up the entire sector, that's just peachy; however, if the sector has the capacity for 512 bytes but the information consists of just 64 bytes, three-quarters of the sector is going to be left empty and unused. That's just the way it is; the system trades wasted space for speed and simplicity.

Therein lies the answer to the burning question: How come I'm only able to fit (for example) 814K of data on a 1.4MB floppy disk? What you've got here is a bunch of short files that result in a lot of wasted space. Generally, sound and graphic files are large and result in relatively little squandering; text and data files are shorter and could be more wasteful. It also depends on whether the disk has been freshly formatted or whether there are bits and pieces of other files scattered around the disk; floppy disks (and hard drives) become increasingly fragmented over time, at least until they are cleaned up using a defragment utility — something I discuss in Chapter 2.

And remember the idea of clusters: A large cluster is more efficient for large files and extremely inefficient for smaller ones. Not that it really matters to users, but the computer numbers the tracks from the outside in. The outermost track is called 0, and the innermost 79. All of the tracks are squeezed into a band less than inch wide — 80 tracks at a density of 96 per inch.

Old-Style Physics in a Modern Machine

The analogies are now finished. Let me talk, briefly, about the mechanical side of the floppy disk drive. When you insert a floppy into a drive, a little catch slides back the cover that sits over the Mylar circle within. Once it is fully in place, the pair of pegs on the motor find their mating holes in the middle of the disk.

Within the drive, a pair of read/write heads move into position — one above and one below the disk. In a floppy disk drive, the heads actually touch the

My museum pieces

Yes, I am aware that there were some earlier and even more cumbersome arrangements for storage. The very first IBM PCs and machines from some other makers including Radio Shack, used audio cassette recorders to hold data. Another design, from Toshiba, used tiny micro-cassettes. Not only were they painfully slow, but they were not random access devices. If the file you wanted was stored at the end of the tape, you needed to fast forward all the way to that point to find it.

But we all sure thought those early machines were the bee's knees. I bought one of each new toy (the original IBM PC, which has the equivalent processing power of one of today's digital watches, listed for something like $5,000). It did, though, launch me on my writing career. I've produced more than 175 books since the birth of the PC, every one of them on a computer, and many of them were written in full or in part on a laptop perched on the seatback tray of an airliner, on my lap on a commuter train, on the table of the Nantucket ferry, and in hotel rooms.

Mylar disk; this is a very different design from that of a hard drive, where the heads float on a cushion of air a few microns above the surface of the disk. The motor spins the disk at a fairly lethargic 300 RPM (compared to 4,200 for a typical laptop hard drive and 5,400 or 7,200 in a desktop machine). The heads move in and out according to instructions from a controller on the motherboard; the controller consults an index (called the *FAT* or *File Attribute Table*) that exists on the floppy disk itself to find out what is located where.

The ferric oxide coating includes Teflon or other super-slippery compound to reduce friction, but the fact is that the contact of the read/write head with the disk itself will eventually grind away the oxide. Add to that the fact that a floppy disk drive is more or less open to the elements — the cover over the disk is not air tight, and the opening to the drive is a rather insignificant spring-loaded flap.

The bottom line: Floppy disks do not last forever and should not be used over and over again to make copies of essential data. And floppy disk drives are prone to mechanical failure because of the entry of dirt or because the internal read/write heads can become knocked out of alignment. (If a floppy drive's heads are misaligned, it may be possible to continue using the drive, but disks made using that particular device may not be readable on another machine with heads aligned properly, or misaligned in a different direction.)

Avoiding the Top Ten Stupid Floppy Disk Tricks

Floppy disks are far from indestructible; in fact, they are an invitation to disaster because they are removable and losable. Take great care not to expose them to danger, or misplace them; if I can restate that as a positive, in addition to taking care of them, keep multiple copies of any irreplaceable data.

That said, here are my top ten stupid floppy disk tricks, each of which is capable of ruining your day:

1. Storing them on the floor or other place where they collect dust that can clog the disk or gunk up the drive.

2. Keeping them on a radiator or in direct sunlight. Heat can warp the disk case and damage the media.

3. Placing a stack on top of a device that generates an electrical field, including speakers, some television or computer monitors, and motors (including pencil sharpeners).

4. Collecting disks near tools that have magnetic tips, including some screwdrivers and scissors.

5. Using a disk as a paperweight or a coaster for a cup of coffee.

6. Clipping a disk to a folder. Paper clips have sharp ends that could scratch and damage the disk, and some are magnetized.

7. Spilling a soda or a cup of coffee on a stack of disks. See also #5. Why do you have liquids anywhere near your computer in the first place?

8. Attaching them to a filing cabinet with a magnet.

9. Storing your only copy of a file on one floppy disk.

10. Losing your only copy of a file, stored on a floppy disk.

Chapter 9

Going Round and Around: CD and DVD Drives

*T*here is a horse-and-cart relationship between some of the more important components of laptop computers and more broadly based consumer
products such as televisions, home audio systems, and video and digital
cameras. Sometimes the horse comes first, and sometimes the cart.

When it comes to CDs and DVDs, although the technology is a natural fit for
computers, both actually arose from consumer applications. Compact discs
(they spell it with a *c* as a vestige of the European origins of the standard)
were developed as the digital replacement to stacks of wax: Those of us who
are old enough to call collections of music *albums* happily remember the
arrival of the CD. DVDs were first envisioned as a replacement for the analog
videocassette for VCRs.

The Music Came First

Both CDs and DVDs are considered *optical drives* since information is read in
the form of pulses of reflected light rather than as magnetic dots. CDs were
introduced to the market in 1982, just about a year after the first personal
computers began arriving in offices and homes. The storage device on the
original IBM PC was a cassette audio recorder and a clunky and slow 180K
floppy disk. Meanwhile, the first CD audio players worked with discs holding
as much as 600MB of data.

Overnight, the quality of music improved almost immeasurably, while the medium itself was nearly impervious to damage. Remember that old vinyl records were played by having a needle physically touching the tracks; over time the record would wear out, and a scratch could render the album useless. The CD, on the other hand, is read by a laser beam that never physically touches the disc. And so, properly stored, a CD has a much longer life than vinyl. CDs were an immediate success among consumers, and soon factories were pressing millions of copies of the latest offerings from Abba, the Eagles, and Frank Sinatra. The more music that was sold in CD form, the lower the cost of production of players and media, and that success subsidized the transition to computer use.

The other part of the story is that the recording method for a CD is digital instead of analog — one of the first applications of that sort of technology to a consumer product. This allowed for CD players that could use all sorts of electronic magic to process and improve the sound before it was finally converted to an analog signal and played through a set of speakers or headphones.

It was the digital storage scheme, though, that made the CD immediately attractive to computer manufacturers. It was a perfect way to store huge amounts of data that are kept in digital form anyhow. Suddenly a 1.44MB high-density floppy disk seemed puny when compared to a 600MB or 700MB CD.

The first trick was to find a way to shrink the size, weight, and power consumption of a CD player from a 10-pound shoebox to a 6-ounce plastic tray that could be built in to a computer or laptop. Once again the consumer side of the market took the lead: Products like the Sony Walkman and competitors quickly shrank the CD to a portable form.

The first use of CDs in laptops, then, was as a means to load operating systems and software onto the hard disk (spelled with a *k*) drive. CDs arrived too late for the very first few generations of laptops, but CD players were common by the mid-1990s. In addition to software delivery, engineers also added audio cards to allow portable computers to become highly sophisticated and somewhat expensive music players. Along with the music came large computer games delivered on CDs.

Then the emphasis switched back to the computer side: Engineers worked on finding ways to allow users to burn their own CDs as a form of personal storage. The arrival of the CD-R (CD recorder) began, once again with larger units for desktop computers; they quickly shrank to fit in laptop machines. The same pattern occurred with DVDs, whose almost-forgotten meaning is *digital video disc;* more recently, the official translation of the acronym was changed to *digital versatile disc,* but almost no one calls it anything but a DVD. DVDs first arrived in homes as a medium to carry movies; they are similar in concept to CDs but have a much larger capacity — large enough to hold several hours of video and audio.

Today, DVDs are beginning to supplant CDs as a medium to deliver huge quantities of data or software. Engineers quickly shrunk DVD players to laptop size, and were almost as fast coming up with several versions of recordable DVD systems, called *DVD-Rs.* And most recently, laptops began arriving with drives that could read both CDs and DVDs, and record either CD-Rs or DVD-Rs or both.

Seeing CD Devices

So, what can you do with a CD or DVD that you can't do with a floppy disk drive?

- ✔ Install a huge operating system from one disc.
- ✔ Install an office suite (word processor, spreadsheet, e-mail manager, calendar, and other applications).
- ✔ Play incredibly advanced computer games and simulations that reside on a CD or DVD without eating up valuable space on the hard drive.
- ✔ Offer access to huge encyclopedias, dictionaries, maps, and other data that would not be cost effective to permanently store on a hard drive.
- ✔ Record downloaded and copied (legally, of course) music to a CD that can be played on a computer or on a Walkman or other portable music player.
- ✔ Create a backup copy of essential data as an archive.
- ✔ Produce movies and digital photo slideshows and complex PowerPoint presentations to take on the road for clients and meetings.

How a CD works

CDs are manufactured in a factory by pressing a metal master into a soft plastic disk to imprint a pattern of pits and *lands,* or flat areas. The difference between the two can be interpreted as 0s and 1s of digital data. Today's CDs can hold as much as 800MB of data, although some drives are happier with slightly less ambitious recording schemes that store 600–700MB.

To read the disk, the CD player shines a focused laser beam of light onto a small section of the spinning disk; light reflects back from the flat surfaces but is absorbed or deflected by the pits. A photo detector reads the on and off light flashes to a signal that is converted to 0s and 1s.

In addition to the technical elegance of a CD, the concept is extremely attractive to marketers because the discs are so very inexpensive to manufacture. The first copy — the *master* — is the biggest expense but once the production line is up and running, each disc costs only a few pennies to make.

The first CD players for personal computers cost several hundred dollars and required complex *SCSI (small computer system interface)* or specialized interfaces; I have a closet full of the early machines. But because of the success of the technology on the consumer side, the price of the machines tumbled rapidly. Today the retail price of an external CD player is not much more than the cost of a pair of audio CDs; the cost to a laptop manufacturer for an internal CD player is even less. An example of a modern internal CD-R/DVD is shown in Figure 9-1.

How a CD-R works

I've already discussed how a CD manufacturer makes CDs by pressing them from a mold — very similar to the way in which old vinyl records were pressed. It is a very efficient way to make mass quantities. Obviously, though, that sort of system would not work for a home or office CD recorder where the user is making the discs one at a time. So the engineers got to work and came up with an alternate way to create discs with pits and lands. Recordable CDs have the same shape and a similar appearance to a prerecorded CD but they are built differently, with a special changeable layer between the top surface and the base.

Figure 9-1:
A combination CD-R and DVD player packed into a thin laptop case.

A CD-R works by generating a high-powered laser beam that physically melts a pit, or darkens the reflective properties of special CD blanks. A *CD-R*, by definition, makes a permanent record; once a pit is burned or darkened, it cannot be undone. Once recorded, it cannot be changed.

CD-Rs use a higher-powered focused laser beam that goes through the top layer to reach a temperature-sensitive recording layer. When writing information to the disc, the CD-R beam creates a pinpoint of heat of about 200° Celsius (about 400° Fahrenheit), which melts a tiny hole in the recording layer. An organic dye on the disc melts into the hole to create a reflective spot. When the CD-R is reading back the information on the disc, it uses the same laser beam, at a much lower intensity, to scan the disc. The pits or holes reflect light back to a sensor at different brightnesses, and these pulses are converted to 0s and 1s of data.

Over the years, engineers have come up with a number of dyes and other compounds for use with CD-Rs; the goal has been to improve the capacity, life, and speed of the discs (and to reduce prices). The most common early organic dyes included compounds of green cyanine, gold phthalocyanine, and silver-blue azo.

The difference between the various formulas may or may not make a difference on your CD-R. I have found that the discs from some manufacturers work better in one computer than another, and it has not always been a matter of price: Sometimes the less-expensive, non-name brand CD-Rs work best because they are not expected to push the boundaries of speed or capacity nor do they tout themselves as "Ultra Quality" or "Music Quality" or "Our Discs Are Better Than Anyone Else's."

A somewhat common problem is that a disc recorded on your laptop may work perfectly well when played back on that same machine but will not be readable in a desktop machine, or the other way around. Or you may find that a music CD you create on your laptop may not play on the CD in your car. My recommendation: If you experience any problems making or playing CD-Rs, buy a few samples of CD-Rs from various manufacturers and of differing colors and rated speeds and capacities and test them out to find the best match for your setup.

How a CD-RW works

A later technology is the *CD-RW*, which is capable of reading, writing, and rewriting CDs. They can record files to a disc, erase them, and rerecord them much like a hard drive can be used over and over again.

Price and prejudice

CD-Rs are very inexpensive; as this book goes to press you can buy a spindle of 100 discs for the equivalent of about 25 to 40 cents apiece; if you must have a separate *jewel box* for each disc, the price increases to about 60 to 75 cents each. At one time CD-RWs cost as much as $5 apiece, but the price differential has greatly improved in recent years; today you can buy a spindle of 100 CD-RW discs for the equivalent of about 60 to 75 cents each, or about $1.00 in a jewel case. Many compatibility issues have been solved, but you cannot be 100 percent sure that a CD-RW made on your laptop is going to work in a CD-R on your desk or a CD player in your car. Run some tests to find out for yourself. In my office, I've decided that the less expensive and more broadly compatible CD-R is the way to go; I buy them in 100- or 250-disc spindles and give no thought to making backup copies whenever and wherever.

That's the good news, and for some users this is the perfect technology — a huge, fast equivalent to the original floppy disk. The bad news, though, is that CD-RWs are more expensive than CD-Rs and are sometimes more persnickety about moving from one machine to another.

The trick behind CD-RW is the use of some more expensive inorganic or metallic compounds — often an alloy of silver with exotic elements like indium, antimony, and tellurium. And then there is a hyper-powered tiny laser, capable of heating pinpoints to 500–700° Celsius, about 900–1,300° Fahrenheit.

The high heat actually melts the crystals, changing them to a noncrystalline structure; when the laser reads back the information, these areas reflect back less light than the surrounding crystal. To erase a CD-RW, the laser shifts to a midway power of about 200° Celsius, enough to change the alloy back to a reflective crystal form.

A CD-RW should be capable of being recorded to, erased, and rerecorded dozens or even hundreds of times. However, just as with a floppy disk, don't plan on using a CD-RW over and over again as the only repository of irreplaceable data. You would be better off using a CD-R just once and placing that archive in a safe or other protected place.

How Fast Is Fast and How Big Is Big?

Although CDs, CD-Rs, and CD-RWs are very similar in design, especially when it comes to reading data recorded on them, they can and do vary in their specifications. All CDs store information in grooves that are 1.6 micron wide. A *micron* is ¹⁄₁,₀₀₀ of a millimeter; 1 inch is a bit more than 25,000 micros in width. If you've got a hair on your head to spare, pluck it out and take its measure: It's about 50 microns wide, or equivalent to about 30 grooves on a CD.

One major difference between a CD and a hard drive or a floppy disk is that there is only one long, spiral track. It's called a *serpentine track,* coiled in a continuous groove that runs from the innermost section of the disc to the outermost. (The outermost edge of a CD is the hardest area to manufacture accurately and the most easily damaged.)

The CD drive has to deal with the varying data densities of the inside (a small amount of data wound tight) and the outside (a great deal of data spread wide). The solution is *constant linear velocity (CLV),* which is a fancy way of saying that (in the first design) the motor was made to spin more slowly as the read/write head gets closer to the outer edge of the disc. More modern designs may run the motor at a single speed, or vary it only slightly; instead they may include a large memory buffer and sophisticated electronics that allow the computer to even out the data flow. Either way, the goal is to maintain the flow of data at a nearly constant speed anywhere on the disc.

Ratings for CDs include the following.

Capacity

CDs can hold between 600–800MB of data. As with a hard disk drive, some of that space is taken for *overhead* — creation of an index of files on the disc. Not all CD devices are capable of squeezing 800MB of data on a disc. Or they may be able to record that much information and replay the data on the same recorder, but the extra-large disc may not function properly on a computer's CD player or CD recorder in another machine or in an audio CD player.

The disc capacity is also affected by the nature of the data. If the disc is used to record audio or video, the information is written in a continuous stream — in the same order in which it will be played back. Thus, audio and video take up a bit less space on disc than word processing or spreadsheet files, which may be scattered around the track in smaller chunks.

The groove width is defined precisely, but disc manufacturers have a bit of leeway in deciding how tightly spaced the groove is scribed. A 650MB CD has about 333,000 sectors and can play about 74 minutes of audio; a supposed 700MB CD boosts the sector count to about 360,000 and 80 minutes.

And just for the record, if you will pardon the outdated pun, an audio disc can hold a bit more data because audio sectors have a capacity of 2,352 bytes, while data sectors can hold only 2,048 bytes (with the remainder held aside for error detection and correction). Therefore, a CD officially rated 650MB is actually equivalent to 747MB when holding music or speech.

Speed

CDs are marketed as being capable of a particular speed of use. But which use are they talking about?

- ✔ **For a CD player,** the speed rating of the device itself refers to how fast it can pick up and pass through the information it *reads* from the disc. And because more information is stored in the disc's larger outer tracks, modern CD players are capable of varying their speed of rotation, running much faster when the laser is reading from the outer tracks and slowing down when it is accessing the inner tracks.

- ✔ **For a CD-R device,** you see two speed ratings: one for the *read* function and a second for the *writing* function. Most CD-Rs are much faster at reading than writing.

- ✔ **For CD-RW machines,** you see three speed ratings: a *read* speed, a *writing* speed, and a *rewrite* or *erase* speed.

I have been speaking here about the machines; the CDs used for CD-Rs and CD-RWs state their speed limits, which may be greater or lesser than the potential speeds of the machines they are used on. Your best bet is to try to match the ratings between disc and machine as closely as possible; a disc rated at 52X for reading is not going to perform at that speed in a drive that promises only 40X playback. The most modern of CD-R and CD-RW drives are capable of reading identification codes on blank discs and set their recording speed accordingly.

The most important measure of speed for a CD-ROM drive is its *data transfer rate,* also referred to as *throughput* or its *read* speed. This tells you how fast the CD-ROM is able to transfer data to the computer's data bus. This is especially important when it comes to playing music from a CD or using a computer game that pumps a great deal of graphics to the screen; if the throughput is slow or uneven, playback will be unacceptably poky or choppy.

Here's where I come to the definition of X. The first CD players had a standard data transfer rate of 153.6K per second (usually referred to in technogeek shorthand as *150 kilobytes per second*), which is pretty slow by modern measures. But there was a reason: That was the speed used for playback by CD audio devices, and here is an obvious example of consumer products driving the computer market.

In any case, computer engineers quickly doubled that speed, and the next round of devices were called *double-speed,* or *2X devices.* As you can see, X has become a relative number. A 40X device is supposed to be capable of delivering information at forty times the speed of that original 150 kilobytes per second drive. As the drive speed increased, so too did the access speed of the read/write heads. That happens because the faster rotational speed brings a particular section of the track beneath the heads that much faster.

The typical access speed of a 1X drive was about 400 ms with a throughput of 150 kilobytes per second; a modern 52X drive may be able to get into position to access data in an average of about 85 ms and pump data to the computer at as much as 8MB per second.

Now when it comes to recording a disc, the write speed can have a major effect on the time required to burn a disc. An original 1X CD required about 74 minutes to record 650MB of data; a CD-R capable of a 48X recording speed could fill that disc in about 90 seconds.

Doing DVDs and DVD-Rs

The story of the DVD closely parallels that of the CD. It was first envisioned as a digital improvement on the analog videocassette as a medium to distribute movies and other video. But once it was adopted by the general public as a fabulous way to watch the latest thriller or comedy in high-, stop-action quality, the economy of scale brought the price of production down to the point where DVD players could be installed in laptop computers.

Not long after DVDs became nearly ubiquitous in home entertainment systems, engineers developed ways to allow users to record their own discs. Recordable DVDs have arrived in versions that can be used on computers, and also as a replacement for VCRs to make copies of television broadcasts.

The consumer side of the equation was responsible for the first specification for DVDS that received widespread use: a single-sided single layer with a capacity of 4.7GB. It just so happens that that size can accommodate a two-hour motion picture, complete with stereo audio and special video features. Engineers have designed compression schemes for audio and video that permit stereo surround sound, subtitles, and widescreen or letterbox versions of films.

And most recently, designers have figured out ways to produce multiformat devices for computers and laptops:

- CD and DVD combination players
- CD-R and DVD players
- CD-R and DVD-R devices

DVDs and CDs have more in common than they have differences; DVDs are, though, considerably larger in their capacity and their potential for advanced applications. While a CD maxes out at about 800MB in capacity, DVDs can presently hold about 4.7 or 9.4GB, and designs call for a doubling and tripling of that already stupendous size.

The disks are nearly identical in physical dimensions, so I concentrate on the functional differences:

- ✔ CDs record on one side of the disc, on a single layer of information, while DVDs can have a pair of layers of information on each side of the disc.

- ✔ CDs have a read/write head on one side of the disc, while DVD devices come at the disc from both sides.

- ✔ The serpentine, or spiral, layout of the single track on CDs and DVDs are similar, although DVD tracks are less than half the already miniscule width of a CD track, .74 micron instead of 1.6 microns.

- ✔ Just as with CDs, any prerecorded DVD should play without problem on a DVD player in a computer or in a home entertainment system. However, a DVD created in a DVD recorder may not play in another computer with a DVD player of a different manufacturer.

How a DVD drive works

DVDs use the same principle as CDs to read data; a laser shines on a layer of information recorded in the form of tiny reflective or nonreflective locations. If you've got a DVD *player,* it can only read DVDs and not record them; you may, though have a combination CD-RW and DVD player that allows you to record and erase a CD and play a DVD.

Recordable DVDs use a high-powered laser to heat a spot to change it from reflective crystal form to a nonreflective compound. To erase or rewrite a block of data, a lower-powered laser reheats spots on the disc to change them back to reflective crystals. Both CDs and DVDs are 1.2mm thick, but a DVD's laser can focus on one or another of two 0.6-mm deep substrates. DVD drives use a shorter wavelength of light to help them focus on smaller and thinner locations. A DVD's *pits* and *lands* (holes and flat surfaces) can be as small as 0.4 micrometers, less than half that of a CD-ROM, which makes holes as deep as 0.83 micrometers — I'm talking about tiny dimensions either way, but you get the idea: DVDs work in even tinier increments than CDs.

DVD speed ratings follow a similar theory of relativity to that of CD drives. The first DVD players were capable of reading data at about 1.3MB per second; subsequent drives could download at double and quadruple that speed and are called *2X* or *4X* drives. Since DVD drives can also read CD discs, you also see a CD rating, typically in the 32X or 40X range. And then you'll also find writing and rewriting speeds for CD and DVD discs.

DVDs and world affairs

In their great wisdom, manufacturers of prerecorded DVDs decided to attempt to cut down, if not prevent, piracy of copyrighted video and other material by assigning geographic "regions" that limit unofficial traffic from place to place. The first time you try to play a regionalized DVD on your computer, you will likely be asked to set your DVD to play discs from your region; you can choose a geographic area from a list presented as part of the properties of the drive. North America is Region 1, while Asia and Europe are in different regions.

You can change the region a limited number of times, usually no more than five. After the remaining number of available changes reaches zero, you cannot change the region even if you reinstall Windows or move your DVD player to a different computer. That is the official word. Unofficially, you may be able to find software that unlocks a DVD from a region other than your own. And you may be able to find utilities that will reset the region chosen for your computer as necessary. Spend a little time searching on the Internet for either fix.

All data stored on a DVD is encoded in digital 0s and 1s, and a signal intended for display on a computer will work anywhere the device is used. However, if the signal is to be output to a television set, it is encoded for one or the other of the two incompatible major television systems in use around the world. *NTSC* is the 525-line standard used in the United States, Canada, Japan, Mexico, Taiwan, and a few other countries. *PAL* is the 625-line standard common in most of Europe and Africa, Australia, China, and elsewhere. Very few DVD players intended for use in NTSC countries will play a PAL-encoded disc. On the other hand, most DVD players sold for PAL countries are multi-standard and work with televisions of either design.

Pick a standard, almost any standard

When it comes to buying and using media for a DVD recorder, you've got to be compatible. That's because manufacturers have not. (Been compatible, that is.) Over the years several competing specifications existed for recordable DVDs. Not all types work with each other. Here is a tour of the various standards.

DVD-R

The original specification for DVD-Recordable, developed by the DVD Forum with the first machine offered to the industry in 1997 at a bargain basement price of about $17,000. The original capacity was 3.5GB or 3.95GB, which was later expanded to 4.7GB. The discs, which now cost as little as 60–75 cents apiece, use an organic dye for one-time recording.

DVD-RW

The DVD-Rewriteable followed the same 4.7GB specification as the DVD-R when it was released in 1999. Early versions of DVD-RW record only on discs identified as meeting the DVD-R or DVD-RW standard and are best suited for video and audio; data error detection and correction facilities are limited. Discs use a chemical that changes their phase from reflective to nonreflective when touched by heat. These discs sold for about $2.00 each in 2005.

DVD+RW

This competing rewriteable standard was supported by a consortium of man-ufacturers in competition with the DVD Forum and introduced in 2001; today discs sell for about $1.75–2.00. It has the same 4.7GB capacity and has some advantages, including higher speed recording and improved facilities to handle video, audio, and data. Discs use a chemical that changes phase from reflective to nonreflective when struck by the laser beam's heat. The original DVD+RW drives can read prerecorded DVDs and CDs, and usually can also read DVD-Rs and DVD-RWs, but can only record on DVD+R or DVD+RW discs. If that sentence doesn't make sense, go back and pay attention to the differ-ence between the dash and the plus in the names. DVD-R is not the same as DVD+R. Don't blame me, I'm just the messenger.

DVD+R

This write-only version of a 4.7GB DVD was created and supported by the same group of manufacturers responsible for DVD+RW. In 2005, these discs sold for about 60–75 cents apiece.

DVD-RAM

This 4.7GB specification seems destined to fall by the technological wayside. It requires use of a cartridge to hold the disc; Type 1 is a sealed container, while Type 2 permits the disc to be swapped. Inconvenient, and a bit more expensive, it also is not particularly well suited to laptop use.

DVD+R DL and DVD+RW DL

These Dual (or Double) Layer discs allow a laser to change its focus between one or the other layer with a capacity of about 86GB. In 2005, dual-layer DVD+R sold for about $5 apiece.

What does this mean to you as a user? Get the right one for your player. If you have a brand-new laptop, it may well have a DVD+RW or DVD+R device that can also use DVD-RW or DVD-R discs. Sorry, but I can't see your machine from here: Check the documentation that came with your machine or call customer support for advice.

When a Good CD or DVD Goes Bad

CD and DVD drives, of whatever specification or manufacturer, are targets of opportunity for unfortunate accidents — especially when in versions installed in laptop computers. Here's why they are susceptible.

Arrested development

They have moving parts, including a motor that spins the disc and a stepper motor to move the read/write heads across the radius of the platter. The tiny motors have become extremely reliable and will probably live a long and full life, but any moving part may one day stop its motion.

Suggested treatment: Keep all ventilation holes clear, and make sure that your laptop fan is operating properly; heat is the enemy of many parts of a laptop, including drive motors. Take care to mount discs carefully and do not force the drive to work with a misaligned or damaged disc.

Twisted logic

On a laptop, the entire mechanism slides out of the body of the machine on a lightweight set of rails. Discs have to be mounted carefully to avoid twisting the mechanism out of alignment. And you really, really, really do not want to drop your computer with the drive drawer open.

Suggested treatment: Use a light hand when you mount a disc; examine the mechanism to see if you should support the tray with one hand while you install the disc with the other. Do the same when you remove a disc. Always make sure that the drive drawer is closed when not in use. And don't drop your laptop.

Cloudy views

The lens that focuses the beam of the tiny laser is exposed to the elements each time the drawer is opened. Dirt or dust that settles on the lens can cause it to lose its eye for data. It is also possible for the CD or DVD itself to be dirty or coated with an oil or other substance that makes it impossible for the LCD to focus on the data layer. If necessary, gently wipe the disc with a clean cloth dipped in water or a very weak water-alcohol mix; wipe in a circle, following the tracks around the disc instead of scrubbing across them from the outside in or the inside out. After cleaning, if you can read the material from a disc, copy it to your hard drive, throw away the CD or DVD, and rerecord it to a fresh, clean disc.

Itchy & scratchy discs

Try not to scratch your CD or DVD collection. That said, a small surface scratch may not mean the end of the world or the end of your data. Let me do some rough pluses and minuses: A DVD's data density is two to four times as much as that of a CD, and therefore a DVD scratch is likely to damage more data. However, DVDs set aside about 10 times as much space for error detection and correction, and so the problem may be fixed automatically. If the DVD is being used to hold a movie or audio, a serious scratch may result in a momentary loss of signal or a frozen frame, but the show will go on.

I am not recommending that you treat your CDs or DVDs with disrespect. Try to store them in their jewel cases or in lined envelopes. Keep them out of the direct sun and off of radiators and other sources of heat. But you can also be assured that these modern discs are much more resistant to damage and protective of content than were old vinyl records.

Suggested treatment: Keep your workspace clean and avoid working in excessively dusty or dirty places. If dust does enter the drive, use a can of compressed air to blow dirt off the lens — aim the spray away from the interior of the laptop and be sure to keep the can upright and at least six inches away from the lens to avoid contaminating the lens and motor with any of the propellant used in the air sprayer. Check with the manufacturer of your laptop for any special advice for cleaning the lens of the laser beam.

A bad marriage

Not all CDs and DVDs use the same design for their lasers and optics, and not all recordable and rewriteable CDs and DVDs use the same chemical compounds for their recordable layer. Although the most current drives are much more flexible in their demands than earlier ones, you may run into situations where a drive refuses to write to a particular design or brand, or is unable to read data recorded by a different drive.

Suggested treatment: Most manufacturers make recommendations of compatible brands or types of blank discs for recording. But you shouldn't feel that you must use only Sony brand discs with a Sony drive, just to use one example. Run tests to find which brands and colors of discs work best in your laptop as well as in any desktop machine you may want to play recorded CDs or DVDs.

When a disc gets stuck on you

If a disc is not properly installed on the spindle in an optical drive, it can jam the drawer when it closes or prevent the motor from rotating the disc; in the worst case, the mechanism can be damaged.

Take special care in placing a disc on the spindle, pressing it gently until it clicks into place. The disc must be lying flat and unwarped, with its printed label side facing upward. Support the drawer from underneath to keep it from warping as you apply pressure from the top to seat the disc into the circular spindle. Make sure the drive tray closes properly; never force it shut.

If the drive does not come to life, press the disc eject button on the drive and hope that it pops out to give you access to the disc. Some systems also have an eject button that is part of the CD or DVD playing or recording software. Additionally, there may be a special-purpose eject key on the keyboard that works in conjunction with the Fn, or Function, key shift.

By the way, each of these steps requires that your laptop be connected to a power source. If none of these steps frees your disc, try the following:

Shut down the laptop through Windows and then restart the machine. Once Windows restarts, try ejecting the disc through use of one of the previously described buttons. If you still cannot eject the disc, shut down the computer and turn off all power. Locate the manual eject button on the disk drive, a small hole nearby the power eject. Use a straightened paper clip or a tiny screwdriver to press the button until the drawer is released; carefully pull the tray open and remove the disc. (Never use a pencil to press the manual eject; the soft lead may break off and fall inside the computer, which could cause internal damage.)

Check the documentation that comes with your laptop or the maker of the optical drive. (You can find the name of the manufacturer of the drive and its model number by checking the properties of the CD or DVD drive from the Control Panel.) If you can identify a maker and model number, check the web site for that manufacturer and see if it has any specific recommendations. As an example, Toshiba states the following in its manual for a current laptop: It recommends silver-colored CD-Rs, followed by gold, with green-colored discs the least reliable.

If you are having a problem loading a program from a commercially created CD-ROM, consult the software's documentation and check that the hardware configuration meets the program's needs. Some installation programs will fail but not inform the user why they have stopped.

Computer dementia

CD and DVD drives make great demands on the system and, depending on the type of information stored on the disc, to the sound card and graphics adapter. Any corruption, accidental deletions of drivers or applications, and even inappropriate settings or file associations can cause a drive to suddenly become missing in action.

Suggested treatment: If your CD or DVD stops playing or recording, the first thing to do is to go to the Control Panel and check the device properties. Make use of the Update Driver option to look for a new driver or make sure that the one in place is the correct one. You can also use the Roll Back Driver option to go back in time to the previous driver.

If your machine is running Windows XP, you can also use System Restore to return your system to previous settings. System Restore goes back somewhere between a few days and a few weeks, depending on how many changes you have made to your system recently. You can access System Restore by clicking Accessories➪System Tools➪System Restore.

Keeping the Drive Alive

Most problems with CDs and DVDs can be solved by careful cleaning of the drive lens or by resetting or updating the drivers and applications that control them. But if the failure is an electrical or electronic one, or if the drive has been physically damaged in a fall (please don't drop your laptop), you have two-and-a-half choices.

Get thee to a repair shop

There is no cost-effective way to repair an optical drive. Parts and labor to fix a broken unit will easily exceed the cost of a new replacement unit. If your laptop is still under warranty, rush it to a service depot and have the computer manufacturer or retailer replace the unit. That's the easy solution.

Here's where the half-a-choice comes in: If the machine is out of warranty, you can purchase a compatible unit, or an upgraded optical device that combines CD, CD-R, CD-RW, DVD, or DVD recordable functions, and install it yourself (or have a technician do it for you).

The replacement unit itself should cost between $50–$100 and will probably be an improved, more advanced version of your original optical drive. That's the good news. An example of a tiny replacement CD-R/DVD drive ready for installation is shown in Figure 9-2.

The bad news is that installing a replacement CD or DVD drive is a very labor-intensive process on most laptops. Some machines make it very easy by installing the optical drive in an easily swappable bay, similar to the ones used for hard disk drives or batteries; most makers, though, tightly integrate the CD or DVD into the case directly.

Figure 9-2:
A replacement CD-R/DVD drive ready to replace an existing internal optical drive. Connectors from one device to another are the same; device driver software identifies the hardware to the operating system.

If you don't have a drive in a bay, the installation process for a CD or DVD will entail major disassembly of the laptop. You'll likely have to remove the bottom cover and perhaps the top cover and keyboard to gain access to the mounting screws for the drive and the connecting power and data cables. If you're brave enough to do the job yourself, figure on a slow and careful disassembly, reassembly, installation of new drivers, and testing that will require at least an hour and probably more.

If you're going to hire a professional to do the work for you, you'll have to pay for that time plus the cost of the drive and any shipping costs. I'd estimate a bill in the range of $200–$300.

Can it

For most users, a much better solution is to declare the broken drive — as the British say — redundant. By that I mean, fire the bloke.

Leave the CD or DVD drive in place and instead purchase an external optical drive that attaches to a high-speed USB 2.0 or FireWire IEEE 1394 port. Expect to pay between $75–$150 for a fully capable external drive. Chapter 16 tells you more about USB and FireWire.

The unfortunate news is that you will have one more piece of equipment to lug around (plus, in some designs, an AC adapter). But you only need to bring out the optical device when you need to use it. You may not be able to use the external drive on an airplane or in other situations where the laptop itself is running on battery power.

On the plus side, the external drive may have some added features including the ability to output directly to a television set without the need for the computer. And the external drive may not draw down the laptop's battery.

Mixing and matching dos and don'ts

Can you play an audio CD on a DVD player? Probably. Nearly all DVD players are capable of reading and playing audio CDs and accessing information on a data CD. However, standard CD players cannot read anything from a DVD — the tracks are too close together and the data is stored at a different depth. However, modern laptops are now offered with combo drives that include a CD-R or CD-RW and a DVD player or a DVD recorder.

Can you use a CD-R with a DVD? It depends. Some of the organic dyes used to record data on a CD-R cannot be seen by the laser in a DVD. You may have to experiment with different colors and brands of CD-Rs to find compatibility. Some modern combo CD/DVD devices employ multiple lasers of different wavelengths so that they can work with just about any kind of disc you challenge them with. You may see features called *dual laser* or *dual optics* or a MultiRead logo on a DVD; these devices promise a higher degree of compatibility, but you'll still need to conduct your own tests.

Can you use a CD-RW with a DVD? Probably. The metallic recording substrate used in CD-RWs are easier for a DVD to read. Once again, though, experiment to be assured of compatibility.

Can you record a CD-R or CD-RW from a DVD recorder? If the recordable DVD is of recent manufacture, the answer is probably. They can either adjust their laser beam or have multiple lasers of differing wavelengths for this purpose. Older DVD recorders may be unable to downshift to work with CD-RWs and are even less likely to be compatible with CD-Rs.

Chapter 10

Tripping the Keyboard Fantastic

Despite all of the fantastic advances in technology that have occurred since the day a human first scribbled a pictogram on the wall of a cave, for most of us the primary interface between our minds and our computers is somewhere between two and ten fingers. We issue instructions with graceful swoops (or fitful hunt-and-pecks) across the face of a keyboard, and the glides and clicks of a mouse, trackball, stick, or other pointing device.

On nearly all desktop computers, the keyboard and pointing device are independent elements and can be replaced or upgraded by unplugging and substituting a new device. On a laptop computer, the keyboard and pointing device are integrated into the box, which complicates matters.

There's one other difference: On a laptop, the keyboard is usually slightly smaller than the main section of a desktop's input device, and the action of the keys — the distance they travel in a downward direction — may be less. Most laptop keyboards do not include the numeric keyboard and redundant pointing keys of a full-sized board, although designers have become very creative at adding multiple functions through the use of additional levels of shift; you commonly find a Fn or Function shift that converts a laptop's key to a special purpose, which is printed on its face in a different color than the standard assignment.

This chapter explores a few possibilities for repair and replacement of a laptop's keyboard and mouse and then looks at ways to work around limitations — and failures — with external devices.

Spongeworthy

The earliest designs for keyboards used individual switches beneath each key. More modern (less expensive and generally more reliable) designs use a two-layer, flexible, printed circuit held apart by rubber domes, spongy foam, or tiny springs.

Working the Board

A keyboard experiences two possible types of failure: mechanical and electronic. Let me begin with the mechanical side. A keyboard is a box of switches; when you press or release a key you are making or breaking contact with a tiny grid of wires beneath. The contact or release is recognized by a specialized processor that determines the switch location and converts the signal into a standard scan code for the key. That code is passed along to the computer's CPU.

On the mechanical side, one of the most common sources of a problem involves dirt or other foreign substances interfering with the key's action. It is also possible that a spring, dome, or foam piece can become damaged. The other common cause of mechanical failure is unintentional administration of aqueous, caffeinated, or phosphoric substances. In other words: spilling water, coffee, or soda on the keyboard.

Keyboard Maintenance Department

Look at some basic rules for proper keyboard hygiene:

 ✔ **Keep your laptop away from food and drink.** This is especially important — and difficult — when you are using the machine on the seatback table of an airliner.

  Think about your work habits: Do you sit at the keyboard like Homer Simpson, with a sugar donut in one hand and a brew in the other? Cookies, chips, and sandwiches produce crumbs that can fall into the crevices around keys.

  Be especially alert when a flight attendant reaches over to hand a drink to someone sitting beside you. (This is one reason you might want to request a window seat if you are planning to use a laptop on a flight.) And watch out for the spray of sticky soda when a can is opened near you.

✔ **Keep your hands clean.** Keep a package of wipes in your computer bag to remove food residue, oils, and dirt.

✔ **Pay attention to the environment in which you are working.** Is it excessively dirty? Is machinery in the area putting sawdust or, even worse, metal filings in the air?

If you absolutely must use a laptop in that sort of an environment, you have a few options:

- Purchase and use a keyboard *skin* that lays over the top of the keys to protect it. The skin will slow down your typing and otherwise make it difficult to use the laptop, but it keeps junk from getting below the keys.

- Buy a *mil-spec* or *ruggedized* laptop, which is specifically designed for use in dirty, wet, corrosive, and other exciting places to work. You'll pay a thousand dollars or more above the price of a standard laptop for the privilege.

✔ **Keep a lid on it.** When your laptop is not in use, keep the cover closed and store it in a clean and stable location.

Cleaning Up Your Act

If you use your laptop regularly, clean it every few weeks or so; if the portable is only powered up for an occasional trip, perform your electronic ablutions each time you prepare to pack your bag.

Running interference

Practice some preventive maintenance. Make sure the computer is turned off and disconnected from power sources; for the highest degree of safety, remove the battery pack as well.

✔ **Flip it.** Carefully turn the laptop upside down, holding it above a trash can or — if you have some prurient interest in what you'll find or are looking for a lost contact lens — over a clean white sheet of paper or cardboard.

✔ **Fan it.** Use a soft-bristle brush to gently floss between the keys. For a deeper, more satisfying cleaning, use a can of compressed, filtered air to blow away dirt and other evidence of your existence. (If you do this over a clean surface, you will be amazed at what tumbles out: crumbs, eyelashes, flecks of skin or nails, and the occasional non-computer bug.)

You can purchase cans of compressed air at computer, photo, video, and artist supply stores. Be sure to follow instructions for use; don't shake the can or turn it over — always hold it upright — to avoid spraying out any of the propellant in liquid form. The spray from canned air can be very cold as it converts from liquid to gaseous state. Take care not to spray the LCD screen, which could cause it to temporarily freeze and possibly crack.

You can also use a vacuum cleaner, but be careful not to use a super-powered system that might suck up a key or cause damage to the LCD screen. Keep the vacuum's nozzle or brush an inch or so away from the keyboard. You can also purchase a small handheld vacuum specifically intended for cleaning a computer, although you might be able to find better uses for your money.

✔ **Scrub.** Clean the keys with a damp (not soaking wet) lint-free cloth or swab. You can use water or a specialized keyboard cleaning solution. You can also mix your own solution with water mixed with 50 percent or less of isopropyl alcohol. Follow up by gently drying the keys with a damp cloth.

Don't use an industrial-strength solution, an ammonia-based cleaner like Windex, or any other off-the-shelf preparation (other than a keyboard cleaner). These solutions could discolor or degrade the plastic and possibly leave behind an electrically conductive residue.

Getting tipsy

If, despite my entreaties and those of everyone you know and love, you manage to tip a glass of sticky cola or a cuppa java on your keyboard, don't panic . . . but act quickly. If the machine is turned on, shut it off immediately; in the case of a major spill don't even bother with an orderly shutdown of Windows — just shut off the power. Unplug the power cord and remove the battery to eliminate all sources of electricity.

Start by wiping down the keyboard with a damp lint-free cloth. Use just enough water to get at the mess and make repeated passes. You can use a small, clean watercolor brush — dipped in water — to get at the small spaces between the keys.

If you're lucky, you'll be able to get at all of the Diet Dr. Pepper or mochachino grande by careful cleaning from the top of the board. Allow the keyboard to completely dry before you reapply power. (You can blow *cool* air — at its lowest speed setting — from a hair dryer to quicken the process.)

If you're talking about spill of Exxon Valdez proportions, it may be wise to remove the keys from the board and clean beneath them.

Shampoo and a wash? I'll pass.

You'll see in some computer books and magazine articles breathless accounts about how some user has rescued a keyboard by putting it through the rinse cycle in a dishwasher or hosing it down with a garden house. Not here, though.

First of all, these guys are talking about detachable, replaceable keyboards for desktops and not one that is integrated into a laptop computer. You absolutely do not want to wet down all of the other components attached to a keyboard that is part of a laptop. Secondly, I'm not convinced that a full soak won't kill a keyboard or make it unreliable. And a replacement keyboard for a desktop computer can be purchased for as little as $10.

Going deep

Deep cleaning a keyboard requires removal of the keys, which is a job that ranges in difficulty from extremely easy to nearly impossible. Begin by consulting your laptop's instruction manual or calling customer support; you don't want to break the plastic by incorrect technique.

In most designs, you can lift up individual keys by using a hooked tweezer or a chip-lifting tool. Position the tool squarely above the key and hook its arms beneath the cap; lift straight up.

But wait! Before you do that, do the following:

1. **Make sure you place the laptop on a sturdy, well-lit surface.**

2. **Have at hand several small light-colored boxes to hold parts as they are removed.**

3. **Make sure you know the keyboard layout.**

   Your instruction manual may include a drawing of the design. Or you can make a drawing or use a digital camera or video camera to take a close-up picture to consult. (Make sure you have another computer or a television screen you can use to view its image.)

4. **Remove just one or two key caps at a time and keep track of all parts.**

   There may be a small rubber dome or spring beneath the cap. Be aware that some keys and domes or springs may have different shapes in various areas of the keyboard.

5. **Use a dampened brush or small piece of cloth to clean beneath the key.**

6. **Carefully dry off the area before replacing the cap.**

7. **Examine the key carefully before reinstalling to avoid forcing it into the wrong place.**

In extreme situations, you may want to lubricate the keys or the underlying switches. This solution is for a problem I hope you don't face: seriously stuck or seized switches. Before you lubricate, follow the preceding instructions to remove and clean the keys. Purchase a dry film lubricant from an electronics supply shop, and use a fine watercolor brush to apply a tiny bit of the solution on a corner of an obscure key, like the PrtSc or Pause/Break cap to make sure that the lubricant does not damage the plastic. Allow the solution to fully dry before deciding whether to proceed. If the lubricant seems to be appropriate for your system, *very lightly* apply a tiny amount of the lubricant into all of the guide notches of each key. Then apply the lubricant to the moving parts of the switches. Allow all pieces to completely dry before reassembling the keyboard.

When the Keys Don't Stroke

Every once in a while a computer user ends up with a dead keyboard. (As the guys from *Monty Python* would say, "Dead. Demised. A stiff. Bereft of life. Kicked the bucket. An *ex-keyboard.*")

Here the cause is usually electrical or electronic. An electrical breakdown could be a frayed or broken connecting cable; an electronic problem could be caused by failure of the keyboard's processor, which translates key strokes into scan codes that the CPUS recognizes and acts upon.

If your laptop's keyboard is demised, you have three choices.

Poking your head in

Open the laptop, removing whatever pieces stand in the way of getting at the connections to the internal keyboard. (These may include plastic casings, the hard drive, the battery, and sometimes much more.) Check the ribbon cable and power connector that go between the keyboard and the motherboard. Sometimes the problem is caused by nothing more than a loose cable. Remove and reattach the cable, reinstall the parts you removed, and try the system.

For this, and all other work that takes you inside the covers of your laptop, be sure to consult the repair manual for your machine. You may have received a copy of the manual at the time of purchase, or you may find the manual on the Internet, available as a PDF or HTML (Web page). Place the computer on a sturdy, well-lighted surface and provide yourself with numbered or lettered containers for parts. Keep a notepad and pen nearby to keep track of all of the steps you have taken. One excellent ad hoc container for parts is an empty egg container; mark each of the dozen holes and track which is which in your notes. Be sure to ground yourself before touching any internal part of the machine.

Going shopping

If adjusting the cables does not fix the problem, you can choose to replace the laptop's keyboard with a new unit. Depending on the make and model, and whether you buy from the original manufacturer or from a parts dealer, a replacement keyboard will likely cost between $30–$100 for a do-it-yourself job that will take about an hour of time and moderate to advanced mechanical skills.

When shopping for a replacement keyboard you may find three types of offerings:

✔ An *original equipment manufacturer (OEM)* replacement, a new unit exactly as used by the laptop manufacturer. Note that very few laptop marketers — including Dell, IBM, Compaq, HP, and Gateway — actually make their own models.

✔ A compatible replacement, a new unit that is promised to work in your laptop although not specifically designed for that purpose. Be very careful to ensure that the seller guarantees the replacement will fit in your machine and work properly. Be very specific about the model number and the serial number, and be sure you agree with the seller's return policy in case it turns out to be not quite so compatible as promised.

✔ A refurbished replacement, which can be either a new unit removed from a laptop where other components have failed or a used unit that has been repaired by a competent technician. Be sure you understand any warranty offered by the seller.

Working around

The third option to deal with a failed keyboard is to find a way to work around the built-in unit. Unless the motherboard fails — which is a much more serious issue than a mere keyboard — you should be able to attach an external keyboard to a laptop. This is generally an acceptable workaround if the laptop is going to be used on a desk, but probably not a great solution for the seatback tray of an airliner.

You can use any desktop replacement keyboard with a laptop; the only issue is to match its connector to an available port. Some laptops offer a PS/2 keyboard or mouse connector; another option is to purchase a keyboard that uses a USB port for attachment.

A USB keyboard can be attached while the laptop is running. To add a keyboard that uses a PS/2 port (an option available only on older models), the safest method is to turn off the laptop and install the plug for the new board before reapplying power; this prevents accidental shorts or static jolts to the system.

Tapping In to Keyboard Replacement

No two brands and makes of laptops are exactly alike, and the complexity involved in replacing a keyboard varies greatly. If you're very, very lucky, the keyboard can be replaced after the removal of just a few screws from the top or bottom and a careful unplugging of the data and power cables. More likely, though, the job will require some pretty amazing feats of micromanaging tiny screws, teensy washers and spacers, and fragile plastic case parts, as well as temporary removal of all sorts of electronic components that stand in the way of access to the keyboard.

Ask yourself a few questions before attempting to do this on your own:

- ✔ Do I feel comfortable opening up a desktop computer to install memory in an internal slot? (Consider that a level-3 task on a scale of 1 through 10.)
- ✔ Am I dexterous enough to replace a clasp on a fine gold charm bracelet, keeping track of all of the parts and reassembling it so that it looks good as new? (About an 8 on a scale of 10.)
- ✔ Would I rather pay a technician to do the work for me, receiving a warranty (usually 30–90 days) for the job and the replacement keyboard? (Expect to pay about $100–$150 for labor, plus the cost of shipping the unit to and from the service center.)
- ✔ Is the laptop worth an investment of between $30–$250 for a replacement keyboard? (The low price is do-it-yourself and the high price is a worst-case price for a professional job.)

Place the computer on a sturdy, well-lighted work surface with sufficient elbow room for you, and space to hold tools and parts at arm's reach. Make sure the computer is disconnected from an AC source and remove the battery. Remove any attached cables or peripherals.

And then you want to have the following things:

- The repair or maintenance manual from manufacturer or downloaded from the Internet support page of maker
- One or more small flat-blade screwdrivers
- One or more small Phillips-blade screwdrivers
- One or more nonconductive plastic picks to lift parts
- An antistatic strip or grounding plate
- A set of labeled storage containers for parts
- A notebook and pencil to note your progress

Table 10-1 shows the dos and don'ts for removing and replacing a keyboard.

Table 10-1	Replacing a Keyboard — Dos and Don'ts
Do	*Don't*
Do be cautious when removing a cable. Pull on its connector, not on the cable itself. Putting strain on the cable could pull wires out of their attachment points.	Don't touch the connectors or pins on any cable; the natural oils on your fingers can interfere with electrical conductance.
Do note the orientation of any cable as you remove it from its connection point; there should be matching arrows or triangles. If none are obvious, make a small arrow mark on the connector and its matching attachment point to help with reinstallation.	Don't crimp or twist any ribbon cables, which can result in a short.
Do hold any component by its plastic or nonconductive edges. Touching metal parts, including connectors, could send a static charge into the electronics or add oil from your fingers that adds resistance to the electrical connection.	Don't bend pins or twist cables out of their holders; look for release catches on the sides of connectors.

Here's a sample of the process for the removal and replacement of a keyboard on just one machine, a Dell Inspiron laptop. You can get a sense of the work involved in Figure 10-1.

1. **Remove the AC adapter and battery.**

2. **Remove all attached cables.**

3. **Lift the notched right edge of the hinge cover and pry loose the cover from the hinges and bottom case.**

   Use a nonconductive, non-scratching plastic scribe or (carefully) use a small flat-blade screwdriver.

4. **Turn over the laptop and remove the four keyboard screws — three labeled with a K in a circle, and one labeled with a K/M in a circle.**

   Take care not to strip their home in the case.

5. **Lift up the hinge cover to expose the keyboard screws.**

6. **Partially lift the keyboard out of the bottom case, resting it on the display hinges so that the keyboard connector is exposed.**

7. **Pull up on the keyboard connector to disconnect it from the interface on the motherboard.**

8. **Remove the keyboard from the bottom case.**

9. **Place the new keyboard on the display hinges. Carefully press the keyboard connector cable into the interface on the motherboard.**

   Press down evenly to avoid bending pins or damaging the motherboard.

10. **Insert the four plastic securing tabs on the keyboard into the matching slots in the palm rest at the front of the laptop. Lower the keyboard into the bottom case.**

11. **Check to see that the keyboard is properly seated in the case, and then replace the four keyboard screws.**

12. **Replace the hinge cover.**

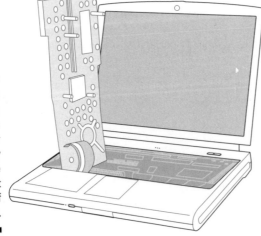

Figure 10-1:
Replacing a keyboard is major surgery within the tight confines of a laptop.

Chapter 11

Putting Your Finger on Pointing Devices

A mouse — or a trackball, pointing stick, or touchpad — gives you a way to reach into your computer's display to issue a command, move a graphic or block of text, or scroll a screen up and down, left and right. It is an all but essential part of operating systems based on a graphical user interface; the most common *GUI* (techies actually call this a *gooey*) is Microsoft Windows in its various incarnations. Other GUIs include Apple's various operating systems, as well as Linux.

Whatever the controlling device is called, the end result is the ability to move a pointer on the screen with great precision and execute various high-tech activities including point-and-click, grab and hold, highlighting, painting, sampling, and more.

Keeping the Ball Rolling

Pointing devices translate the movement of your hand or finger (or some specialized tools for people with special needs) based on either *mechanical* or *optical* sensors. Let me differentiate among the most common types of pointing devices.

Rounding the mouse

A *mouse* is a rounded block of plastic with a sensor on the bottom that translates movement across a mouse pad or a desktop into movement on the screen. For Windows-based systems, the mouse has at least two buttons; the left button is generally used to select an item or execute a command, while the right button brings up context-sensitive menus. You also see mice that add a central scroll wheel that can be used by itself or in conjunction with the left or right button to move the screen or menus up and down. Mice can be of either mechanical or optical design. A mechanical mouse's insides are described in the preceding section.

A *mechanical mouse* has a small rubber or plastic ball on its bottom or top. As a mouse moves across a surface (or as your fingers move a trackball's ball), the ball turns small rollers or shafts, which cause metallic contacts or brushes to sweep across a segmented conductor. As the brushes make and break electrical contact, a microprocessor counts the number of contacts and the time interval between them to determine the direction and speed of movement. In most designs, there are two rollers or shafts, mounted at a 90-degree angle; if both rollers are moving, the mouse is smart enough to figure out that it is being moved on an angle. The end result is a signal sent to the computer's CPU for action.

An *optical mouse* has no moving parts. Instead they employ an electronic sensor that uses a special mouse pad with a highly reflective surface and finely etched lines to determine movement and create signals. An alternate design uses a high-intensity *light-emitting diode (LED)* that illuminates the lines on a pad. In theory, an optical mouse is capable of discerning extremely fine movement — as fine a resolution as $\frac{1}{2000}$ of an inch, which is 2 to 10 times as delicate as a mechanical device — and many of the latest designs no longer require the use of a special optical pad.

Perched in between are *optomechanical mice,* in which a moving ball turns rollers with slots or perforations; an internal LED shines through the openings and an optical sensor detects the pulses and converts them into a signal. The advantage of optomechanical devices is high precision without the need for a specialized mouse pad.

Keeping your eye on the trackball

Think of a *trackball* as a mouse turned upside down. You use your fingers to rotate an oversized ball that uses sensors that translate that movement into signals to the computer. Trackballs can use mechanical or optical sensors. A *mechanical trackball* rolls against a set of rotary switches that sense up, down, or side-to-side movement. An *optical trackball* moves in front of a photoelectric or photoreflective sensor that reads the movement of a pattern on the ball. The optical trackball may be slightly more sensitive than a mechanical equivalent.

The advantage of a trackball is that the device itself does not move around on the desktop. It can be stationed in one place alongside the keyboard or — as is sometimes the design for laptops — integrated into the keyboard or clipped onto its side.

Another advantage for some users is an ergonomic one. Using a trackball requires little or no movement of the wrist or shoulder, reducing for some the incidence of repetitive stress injuries or other problems caused by lifting the hands from the keyboard to move a mouse.

I'll go on the record here: I *love* trackballs, and have changed over my desktop machine to exclusively work with one. I also have a small clip-on trackball for my laptop that I sometimes take with me on extended trips. I find the use of a trackball much less demanding than the constant reach for a separate mouse. That said, many other users find trackballs too sensitive and difficult to use. The only solution here: Try one and see if you like it.

Pointing the stick

Some laptop designers offer keyboards with a tiny *pointing stick* — often topped with a nub like the eraser on a pencil — usually placed somewhere near the middle of the keyboard, often above the B key; the pointing stick functions like a miniature and highly sensitive joystick. Its central location may appeal to lefties, as it does not discriminate against those with a sinister hand.

The stick senses finger pressure as it is pushed in one direction or the other. It is able to move quicker in response to more insistent signals and slower to more subtle nudges. Most systems add a left and right button at the bottom of the keyboard.

Pointing sticks are also an example of a technology that not every user finds immediately easy to use; many users become quite adept at moving around on the screen with the little stick, while others find themselves hopelessly fumble-fingered. I suggest you spend some time at the computer store, or borrow a friend's machine, to make certain you are comfortable with this design.

Pointing sticks rarely require any special maintenance other than ordinary cleaning of the keyboard (which I describe in Chapter 10). If the eraser-like nub wears out or falls off, you should be able to purchase replacement pointers from the original equipment manufacturer or from a computer parts supplier.

Getting in touch (pad)

Another way to control the cursor movement is to use a *touchpad,* which can be integrated into the keyboard or placed alongside. The pad senses the movement of your finger in any direction and converts that into a signal to the system.

A left and right button is usually alongside the pad, although some designs also permit you to tap the pad to send an equivalent signal; for example, Gateway's Enhanced EX Pad design interprets a one-finger tap as a left button click, a two-finger tap as a middle button click, and a three-button tap as a right-click. It takes a bit of practice to become fully proficient.

A centrally mounted touchpad is another device that is friendly to lefties. An example of a modern touchpad is shown in Figure 11-1.

Breaking in to tablets

Tablets are close to a direct translation of writing on a paper-like surface to the screen, and for that reason are particularly attractive to artists and graphic technicians. They are essentially large touchpads, although some designs an electronic *radio frequency (RF)* or infrared field to detect the motion of a special stylus.

Figure 11-1: A touchpad on a modern laptop can be adjusted for more sensitivity, and special tap codes can select icons or other onscreen elements.

The Zen and Art of Mouse Maintenance

The good news about pointing devices is that 1) they don't fail very often, 2) replacing them is relatively inexpensive, and 3) you can easily work around a failed or inadequate device by attaching an external unit.

Keep your keyboard clean and occasionally spray it with a can of compressed air to clear away any dirt or donut crumbs that might interfere with the use of a built-in pointing stick. Carefully clean finger oils and dirt from any touchpad with a damp cloth; you can also add a small amount — less than 50 percent of the solution — of isopropyl alcohol. Chapter 10 details the steps if you want a deeper clean.

If a built-in pointer or touchpad fails, they can be replaced as part of a new keyboard. Or, you can easily attach an external pointing device to work around the problem or upgrade your system.

Mouse skitters

If your mouse or other pointing device stops working or begins to react unpredictably, you should determine whether the problem is a mechanical one — a broken part, a crimped or disconnected cable, or poor personal mousekeeping, including dirt, oil, or sticky stuff on the moving parts.

The easiest way to test an external mouse or other pointing device is to temporarily replace it with a known-good equivalent. If you find that the USB mouse from your desktop works perfectly well when it replaces the external mouse, you have established two important details: first, that the USB port on your laptop is working properly, and second, that the problem is with the original mouse.

You can also try plugging in a new pointing device to the same port. Because I earn my living in front of a computer, I always keep in my closet at least one spare trackball (my preferred pointing device) as well as an extra keyboard. They are intended for use with my desktop machine, but can easily substitute for a laptop device for testing or workaround purposes.

For an external device, check the cable at both ends for crimps, damage, or loose connectors. This sort of injury should be obvious to the eye. Unless you're working with an expensive special-purpose pointer, it probably does not make sense to attempt to repair a broken cable; it is inexpensive and much easier to replace the entire unit.

Go to Start➪Control Panel➪Mouse icon and visit the specialized controller; the screen will differ slightly based on your laptop manufacturer and the pointing device. In Figure 11-2 you can see basic and advanced settings for the built-in touchpad of a current Toshiba laptop.

Figure 11-2:
The Mouse
Properties
report
allows
adjustment
of the button
configura-
tion, double-
click speed,
and other
basic and
advanced
user
settings.
Sometimes
a seeming
problem is a
mismatch
between the
way you use
the pointer
and the way
it is set up to
respond.

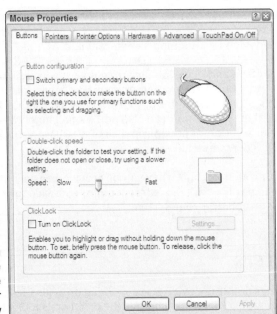

Cleaning a mouse or trackball

Checking on the cleanliness of a mouse or trackball is easy. Remember that over the course of its life, a mouse may travel miles and miles on a desktop, picking up all manner of dirt, oils, and other contaminants. The upside-down trackball is susceptible to the oils and other substances on your fingers, as well as anything else that settles on it from the air.

As preventive medicine, make the effort to clean your desk and any surface you will be working on. (Stop and look at the airline seatback tray table before you put your laptop there; is it sticky and dirty?) If you've just put on suntan lotion, makeup, or other oils, wash your hands before touching the pointing device or the keyboard.

To cure a messy external mouse or trackball, do the following:

 1. **Unplug the mouse or trackball from the laptop and move it to a clean, well-lighted work surface.**

USB devices can be removed from a laptop that is running. Devices connected to other ports should only be removed when the laptop is turned off.

2. **Release the ball.**

   • To release the ball on a mouse, look for a rotating ring that surrounds the ball. Most devices include an arrow to indicate the direction the ring should be turned to be removed.

   • On a trackball, the ball is usually held in place by a clip or spring and can be lifted directly out of its socket.

3. **Use a can of compressed air to clean out any dirt or dust sitting in the well of the mouse or trackball.**

   You can also use a clean, soft-bristled brush.

4. **Lightly moisten a lint-free cloth with a weak solution of water and isopropyl alcohol; clean the interior of the well.**

   Take care not to displace the ordinary position of the rollers or contact switches within.

5. **Clean the ball with water or a water and alcohol solution.**

   Check the instruction manual or manufacturer web site for any other tips on cleaning.

6. **Once you are certain all of the parts are completely dry, carefully reassemble the pointing device and reattach it to your laptop.**

   USB devices can be *hot swapped,* meaning they can be plugged in or removed while the machine is running; devices that plug in to a PS/2 connector or a serial port should be installed with the machine turned off.

Cleaning an optical mouse or tablet is simpler because they use no moving parts.

1. **Disconnect the device from the laptop.**

   Devices that use the USB port can be removed while the machine is running; otherwise, turn off the laptop before disconnecting any external peripherals.

2. **Place the optical mouse or tablet on a well-lighted, sturdy work surface.**

3. **Use water or a weak solution of water and isopropyl alcohol to clean the sensor window on the mouse or the surface of the tablet.**

4. **Allow all surfaces to completely dry before reattaching the device to your laptop.**

   Once again, the laptop should be turned off except for devices that connect to the USB port.

Cleaning a touchpad

Touchpads are sealed and not likely to be the source of problem because of dirt or dust, although they can become slippery or sticky from the transfer of oils or other substances from the fingers of those troublesome humans who use them.

1. **Tilt the keyboard up and to the side and spray compressed air to dislodge dirt or crumbs.**

   You tilt the keyboard so the can of air can be held upright while spraying. If the can is held at too sharp of an angle, there is the possibility that some of the liquid propellant will mix with the air and make the situation worse.

2. **Clean the surface with a mild cleaning solution such as a weak form of window cleaner.**

   If you are uncertain about whether a solution is appropriate, test a tiny dab of the liquid on the bottom of the case to see if it dulls the surface or leaves a residue.

3. **Remove the tiny pointer and soak it in cleaning solution.**

4. **Wash off the cleaner and allow the pointer to completely dry before you return it to its place.**

Most laptop manufacturers sell replacement caps, and you may be able to find generic caps at some computer supply stores.

Fixing the settings

If you suspect that the problem is related to computer settings, stop and think: What has changed since the last time the pointing device worked properly? Have you installed any new hardware or software? Has your system's antivirus utility set off any alarms about attempted invasions that may have garbled settings or drivers?

1. **Under Windows, go to Start➪Control Panel➪Mouse Properties➪Hardware tab.**

2. **Check the Device Status.**

   What you're hoping to find is a report that says, "This device is working properly."

3. **If that's not what you find, click the Troubleshoot button and follow the steps outlined there.**

   You can also reach the same place in a slightly different manner. Go to Start➪Control Panel➪System icon➪Device Manager.

You see a listing of the various pieces of hardware in your system, like the one shown in Figure 11-3. Depending on the version of Windows you are running, you may see an icon for Mouse or the politically computer-correct icon of human interface devices (HIDs).

4. **Click the + (or double-click the icon) to expand the category and show all installed devices under that icon.**

On this Toshiba model the built-in touchpad is from a component manu-facturer called Alps. The absence of an exclamation point or X mark tells you that the system has recognized the existence of the device and its drivers and that things appear to be working properly.

Figure 11-3: The Device Manager reports on hardware within a modern laptop.

5. **Scan all the items for any red Xs or a yellow exclamation point.**

An X indicates that a device has been automatically or manually dis-abled and is unavailable. A yellow exclamation point tells you the system perceives a potential conflict of resources.

Depending on the type of problem, the built-in intelligence of the device, and its ability to communicate with the system and the operating system, you may see either a mere notification of a problem or conflict, or you may see a specific problem code or text notification and a suggested solu-tion. Consult the instruction manual for the device or go online to the manufacturer's web site to seek more information.

6. **Open the mouse or human interface device category and examine the properties.**

Do so even if you don't see any warning signs.

7. **Choose the Driver tab of the device property for your mouse or HID.**

You have these options:

• Check the date and version number for the device.

- Search for an updated driver from a local disk or over the Internet.

- Roll back the driver currently in use to the previously installed driver (under Windows XP).

If you are still stymied, visit the web site established by the device manufacturer and visit the support or knowledge base section in search of suggestions.

If the mouse or other pointing device is working only intermittently, there may be a problem with software settings. Or the settings may have been garbled by an improper shutdown, a power surge, or other momentary problem with your laptop.

Go to the mouse control panel and start by resetting everything to the manufacturer's suggested settings. (These may be called the *default.*) Check through the choices for speed, acceleration, sounds, colors, and other options to see if any are assigned to unexpected or unwanted choices. The gateway to the device driver and additional pointing device settings is through Device Manager or by double-clicking the mouse icon within Control Panel. Figure 11-4 shows an example of the Properties page, with additional tabs, for an Alps Pointing Device. Note that you can launch a troubleshooting wizard from this tab as well.

Figure 11-4:
The General tab for the pointing device reports that it appears to be working properly. Although this is an internally connected touchpad, the system considers it a piece of hardware that is plugged in to a PS/2 mouse port.

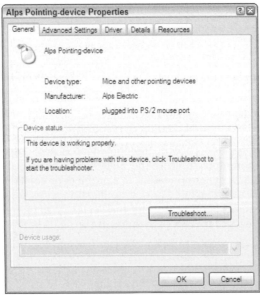

Attaching an External Unit

Mice and other external pointing devices are easily attached to any of four available ports on your laptop:

- **PS/2 port.** This port is specifically intended for use with keyboards or mice. This small round connector was first used on a series of IBM desktops; it is still used to connect some mice and keyboard devices.

- **USB port.** This works with any USB device. You can also obtain a small adapter that permits a pointing device with a PS/2 connector to plug in to a USB port.

- **Serial port.** Using a serial port may require configuring the device to work with available memory and system resources.

- **Wireless or infrared port.** Many types of pointing device are available in cordless versions that communicate with a laptop using WiFi or Bluetooth RF communication or infrared. (Infrared devices were introduced with much fanfare in the late 1990s but have been largely supplanted by RF technology. More on this, if you're interested, in Chapter 14.)

For any device other than a standard mouse, you are likely to be asked to install a small piece of software called a *device driver* on your system; even with a simple mouse, there may be extended facilities available in a driver supplied by the manufacturer. In many instances, the most important part of a pointing device is the software: The best allow you to customize the assignments for buttons and wheels, choose an online cursor design, and adjust the sensitivity (how rapidly it moves across the screen). Most software also permits an adjustment of the acceleration of the mouse; you might want it to begin moving slowly and pick up speed only after you make large strokes across the screen.

Any time you install a new pointing device, and once or twice a year thereafter, make a visit to the device manufacturer's web site to look for an updated or improved version of the driver. Make sure that any download matches the operating system in use on your machine.

Chapter 12

Seeing the Light: LCDs and Video

· ·

In This Chapter

▶ Learning to love and protect an LCD

▶ Delving into the technology of a computer display

▶ Dealing with video display misbehavior

· ·

*T*he first transportable computers were nothing more than desktop computers squeezed as tightly as possible into a plastic or metal suitcase with a small 5- or 7-inch cathode ray tube (CRT) monitor. Oh yes, there was a power cord, too. Today laptops are smaller than a pizza box and feature a larger, sharper, and dramatically more colorful LCD screen. And with a battery instead of a power cord? Oh the places they can go.

Listing an LCD's Wonders (and One Downside)

An LCD has lots to offer:

✔ They use much less power than a standard computer monitor.

✔ They produce little or no heat.

✔ They don't flicker or strobe, and individual pixels can be sharper than a monitor.

✔ They require a much narrower frame around their edges, meaning that a 15-inch LCD delivers about the same viewable surface as a 17-inch CRT monitor.

✔ They don't weigh 75 pounds and take up 2 square feet of desk space.

The one thing that isn't so great:

> ✔ They can crack, crumple, scratch, freeze, or break off. They're relatively fragile to begin with, and are part of a portable computer. That means they move from desktop to traveling bag to overhead compartments and under-seat storage, motel desks, and other temporary homes. Be careful out there: LCD screens are the most vulnerable part of your laptop.

Evolving from CRT to LCD

If you're old enough to have seen some of the first computers — house-sized boxes filled with vacuum tubes, relays, and click-clacking memory made up of tiny rings and magnets — or if you are a fan of old science fiction movies, you'll remember that the next result of all the beeping, whirring, and groaning of this mostly mechanical beast was a panel of flashing lights. These first computers were used mostly as elephantine calculating machines for things like toting up the U.S. Census or determining the aiming angle for an artillery piece.

The next step in the computer evolution was the connection of a primitive *teletype,* an electric typewriter that clanked out a report, at first in numbers, and eventually in some form of English-like words. It wasn't until the mid-1960s that government, universities, and big businesses began using television-like monitors to display numbers and words. By the time of the arrival of the first Apple II in 1976 and the IBM PC in 1981, monitors were able to display primitive graphics.

What do I mean by primitive graphics? The first monitors were character based — essentially a video representation of a typewriter. The computer would send a message to place the letter *e* in the 16th column of the 7th row and a video controller would send instructions to illuminate the predefined outline of that letter. The first games and images were created using alphabetic characters, artfully arranged. Figure 12-1 shows a version of a stick figure that everyone thought was so cool when the computer would set it to marching across the screen.

Figure 12-1:
This primitive graphic used to thrill computer users.

Look familiar? They should be if you use a cell phone or an instant messenger to exchange little tidbits of useless information. Modern users make little smiley faces from characters, like this: :-) or ;-).

From there the race was on to develop ways to draw more complex forms and eventually to address the entire screen just like a television set. Today a computer monitor offers a sharper, more stable, and generally superior image than the family TV.

By the late 1980s designers began to move away from AC-powered CRTs in portable computers and started using small, thin, and low-power *liquid crystal display (LCD)* screens that a battery could power. The first laptops used small monochrome screens. The next step was a full-sized monochrome (dark gray characters on a light green screen was state of the art), and eventually they reached the spectacular full-color widescreen LCDs in use today.

Sizing Up the Screen

A laptop LCD has two essential dimensions: its diagonal size, which is a measure of its physical size, and its resolution, which tells you how many individual dots the system is able to display on the screen. In general, bigger is better. . .up to a point.

The physical size of laptop LCDs has progressed from 9 or 10 inches (measured from an upper corner to a lower corner) to widescreens as big as 17 inches. The ultrawide screens are stunning to view and very useful on your desktop, but you may find them to be hard to fit on an airline's seatback tray.

High resolution is a good thing to have at any size, but the larger the physical screen size, the more important it is that the LCD be able to work with many more dots.

Resolution is measured in *pixels,* which is a concatenation of picture elements; you can call them dots. A mid-range model like Toshiba's Satellite offers a 15.4-inch screen with 1,280×800 resolution. Apple's impressive 17-inch PowerBook G4 and Toshiba's Qosmio G15 each support a resolution 1,440×900 pixels: about 1.3 million individual dots.

Unlike a computer monitor and its associated *video display adapter* (electronic circuitry that converts 0s and 1s into information the monitor uses to create an image), most LCDs can only work at one preset resolution as determined by the actual number of pixels built in to the display. If it is important to work at a nonstandard resolution, some displays work with specialized software that can emulate other settings.

Taking a Brief Aside into Technology

Quickly, let me explore just enough about video display technology so that you shop wisely or make sound troubleshooting decisions.

In its most simplified descriptions, a video monitor works like this:

1. The computer produces a stream of data (made up of 0s and 1s) that describes the image to be displayed onscreen.

2. The information creates the equivalent of a page of information within a block of memory within the computer or on a video adapter.

3. A page of information is sent from the computer's video port to the monitor.

4. The monitor decodes the data stream to identify a particular position on the screen as well as its color and brightness.

5. Electronics on the monitor use a magnetic field to move a stream of electrons across, down, and then back up again across the inside face of glass tube that is coated with special phosphors (which momentarily glow when hit by the stream).

In its most simplified descriptions, an LCD is very similar, only different:

✔ The laptop produces a page in much the same way as a desktop computer and sends the signal within its closed case to a specialized piece of electronics, which reverses the intensities and colors.

✔ Protected behind a clear plastic front panel and a solid back panel is a sheet filled with an unusual substance called *liquid crystal,* which exists somewhere between a liquid and solid state. These crystals are *thermotropic,* meaning they change their state based on temperature. In most designs, the crystals allow light to pass through them in their natural state and block the light (appearing dark) when touched by electricity.

✔ At the base of the panel is a small fluorescent lamp that serves as a backlight. The screen appears completely white if all of the LCD's pixels are in their off, or clear, orientation.

Many older laptops do not have a backlight and are instead *reflective,* meaning that they rely on light bouncing off the back of the screen. In the best conditions (a well-lit office) reflective screen is good, but when lights are low (think of that airplane seatback tray) the image can be difficult to see. A few modern machines allow the user to turn the backlight on or off to save battery power; most current machines have software settings that give full brightness when the laptop is plugged in to an AC outlet and turn down the lamp when the battery is running the show.

✔ The LCD's controller for a modern active-matrix LCD addresses a specific row and then a specific column; the pixel at the point where a positive charge and a ground meet receives power and goes dark. *Active-matrix designs* include tiny transistors at each meeting point of a column and row, yielding a sharper and faster-to-refresh image.

Everything else is a matter of little details. The amount of voltage can be adjusted to make the dot fully dark or just barely darkened; a typical LCD has the equivalent of a 256-level grayscale. The other part of the equation involves color, which is created through the use of three subpixels with red, green, or blue filters.

Doing the math

Each of the LCD points on a typical laptop's screen can be set at an intensity from 0 to 255, which is the same as saying there are 256 possible settings. With three pixels at each location for a color monitor, that means an LCD's palette is made up of about 16.8 million colors (256 red × 256 green × 256 blue = 16,777,216).

For the record, that range of colors is much wider than most humans can discern. However, each color is a specific *digital* value; a standard television set uses a continuous and essentially infinite range of *analog* colors and brightness levels to display our daily drivel and some extraordinarily gifted (or extremely picky) viewers claim to prefer an analog image to a digital one.

Dead pixels

A modern laptop with a screen resolution of 1,280×800 has 1,024,000 addressable points and three times that when you consider subpixels with colored filters. That's a lot of little points of darkness, and the reality is that some pixels may be dead on arrival while others may fade away with time. If you use a white background on your LCD, a dead pixel may appear black or gray; if you use a black background, a dead pixel may only be noticeable if it lights up white or colored.

And so it is not unusual to have a few dead spots, or even more than a few. In fact, many laptop makers will not make substitutions for an LCD under warranty until the percentage of bad pixels is more than a few percent, which is quite a few.

Dead pixels, alas, are not repairable. The only option is to install a new screen at a cost of several hundred dollars . . . and even then you have no guarantee that there won't be a few gaps here and there. The good news: The human eye and brain have an incredible ability to fill in the gaps.

Holding a Bad Video Display Card

Depending on the design of your laptop, the video display circuitry may be built right into the motherboard, or it may exist as a tiny daughterboard that attaches to a connector on the motherboard. If a video adapter on the motherboard fails, you'll almost certainly have to decide whether it makes economic sense to replace the entire motherboard. If a video adapter on a daughterboard fails, replacement materials cost less, but you still face the cost of labor to make the swap.

The most difficult thing about diagnosing a possible problem with a display card is that you generally won't be able to see any error messages on the LCD. The first step is to determine if the problem is indeed caused by the video card or instead is a problem with the LCD settings or the display itself.

If your laptop is equipped with a diagnostic utility, use its facilities to test the video card, video memory, and the LCD itself. Figure 12-2 is an example of a test using the CheckIt Diagnostic. The following sections offer troubleshooting steps for a suspect display.

Figure 12-2: Part of the test of a laptop's video card, a component of CheckIt Diagnostics. In this section the utility is testing an AVI video file.

Plugging it in

Make sure that your laptop is plugged in to an AC source or has a fully charged battery available. Turn on the machine and watch the LEDs and any other indicators; check the instruction manual for any special details about your particular model that might give you a clue about the nature of the problem.

Turning it up

Make sure that the LCD brightness setting is high. Some laptops have a setting that turns off the LCD and diverts the image to either a standard graphics port for use with a computer monitor or to a video output for use with a television set. On most machines, the setting is *transitory* — it resets to a default LCD setting when the power is turned off. On a handful of machines, though, a slide switch or other physical control that diverts the signal away from the LCD.

Bringing on the BIOS

Do you see any information on the screen during the bootup? If you see any details from the BIOS Setup, press the key that displays the setup screen; consult the instruction manual to find the key required for your laptop. Some of common keys includes Esc, F1, F2, or F10.

Read the BIOS screen and look for a setting that identifies the primary display type. I have seen some of these possible settings over the years on various machines:

✔ LCD (default)

✔ Computer monitor or CRT

✔ Video or television

✔ Auto select (If any external display is connected at power-on, the display adapter will use that device; otherwise the LCD is used.)

✔ Simultaneous (Both the LCD and CRT screen modes are enabled at startup.)

Have you made any recent changes to the BIOS setup that might have accidentally resulted in a switch to CRT or video output instead of LCD? The setup can also end up being inadvertently changed by electrostatic shock or by a virus. (You are running a capable, fully updated antivirus program, right?)

Letting your little light shine

Let the machine fully boot. If you ordinarily have to enter a password to load Windows, wait until the drive stops spinning — you should be at the point where the password is expected — and type it in and press Enter; if you don't have to type in a password but have to press Enter to continue, do so.

I'm assuming you do not see the friendly Windows home screen. But: Did you see any semblance of a picture, as an image that appeared and then faded away? That is often indication of a problem with the LCD or its associated circuitry and not the display adapter.

Try shining a strong light on the screen. Can you make out your Windows desktop or an application? This is another indication that the problem may be with the LCD circuitry or with the fluorescent backlight that illuminates the screen.

Watching the boob tube

If you still do not have an idea of the cause of the problem, attach a television set or a computer monitor to your laptop. Consult the instruction manual for your computer to determine any key combinations or special settings you must use to divert the signal.

Various laptops have differing commands. On a current Toshiba machine, for example, the key combination is Fn/F5 to toggle external video on or off; on an older Gateway machine the command is Fn/F3. Other machines will automatically recognize the presence of certain types of external displays.

If you can see an image on an external monitor, this is an indication that your video display adapter is probably functioning properly. Bear in mind that a display on a television set is going to be at a lower resolution and likely present a faded or limited color set.

Working from the keyboard of your laptop and using the external display, check to see if any settings have been made to disable the laptop and see if the driver is functioning properly. Here are the steps under Windows XP. The process is similar under other recent versions of Windows including 98, 98SE, and ME.

1. **Click Start⇨Control Panel⇨System icon⇨Hardware tab⇨ Device Manager.**

2. **Expand the + mark to the left of Display Adapters and read the report under Device Status.**

   If the report reads "The device is working properly," the circuitry is responding to queries from Windows, and the operating system has found a working device driver. You can click the Driver tab to get more details about the software associated with the video adapter.

   If the report tells you there is a problem with the adapter or the driver, follow the troubleshooting steps displayed on the General tab. You may be asked to reinstall a driver from the laptop manufacturer's recovery disc or by downloading it from the Internet.

3. **Go back to the Control Panel and double-click the Display icon.**

4. **Choose the Settings tab and check the settings.**

   Here is where you can choose the screen resolution and color quality. If the proper driver is being used, you should not be able to select a screen resolution or a color quality that is beyond the capabilities of the laptop's display adapter or the circuitry on its motherboard. However, you can experiment with a lower screen resolution and a lower color quality to see if this repairs your problem.

5. **Click the Advanced button.**

   This button allows monitor adjustments (in this case your internal LCD).

6. **Select Hide Modes That This Monitor Cannot Display if that is not already checked.**

7. **Choose the Troubleshoot tab, which is customized to your system.**

   Try various settings to see if you can fix the problem.

If none of these adjustments bring your LCD back to life, it would appear that the problem is with the LCD. In Chapter 3 I discuss options for repair or replacement of an LCD screen. It comes down to a financial and not a technical decision.

Part IV
Failing to Communicate

The 5th Wave   By Rich Tennant

"In preparation for takeoff, we ask that you turn off all electronic devices, laptop computers and mainframes..."

In this part . . .

In the early days of computing people thought it
was magical when they could connect two machines
(at a pace that seems quite comfortable to a snail) using
a telephone modem. The first PC modems could send
or receive (one direction at a time only, please) at about
150 bits per second. Today's standard dial-up modems
are about 370 times faster. And a broadband cable or
DSL modem is up there in "Hoowhee!" land, as much as
25,000 faster than where the PC first started talking to bul-
letin boards, nearby machines, and the World Wide Web.

In this part you get wired and unwired. I discuss the fastest
growing form of communication for laptops: wireless interconnection. You also explore modems, serial ports, parallel
ports (if your machine has held onto this disappearing act),
and current speed champions for communication by wire:
USB and FireWire ports.

Chapter 13

Networks, Gateways, and Routers

. . . .

. . . .

*T*here was a time when computers were islands. You would bring your work to the machine (in a stack of punch cards, a roll of paper tape, or a reel of magnetic tape) and feed in the data and instructions. After a few seconds, a few minutes, or even a few hours of chugging and clanking and clicking, the computer would spit out the answer: 12 or OK or a new roll of paper or tape with the information sorted in a new order.

The idea of one machine "talking" to another was about as remote as the concept of a human having back-and-forth real-time interaction with a computer.

How Many Computers Do We Really Need?

Way back in the ancient history of computers there was a fairly widespread belief that the world only needed a handful of huge computers to control things like the electrical power grid, the U.S. Census, and certain celebrities' egos. In 1977 Ken Olsen, founder and CEO of Digital Equipment Corporation (DEC), told an industry gathering that he saw "no reason for any individual to have a computer in his home."

I covered Olsen in the 1980s, and I sorta kinda know what he meant. At the time Olsen made his pronouncement, DEC was the number-two computer maker in the world, just behind IBM. DEC was renowned for making refrigerator-sized components that could be linked together into tractor-trailer-sized multiprocessors; these were the *smaller* versions — called *minicomputers* —

of IBM's house-sized monsters. Olsen's belief was that all processing could be centralized, and those relatively few people who needed access to the processor and its data could do so through desktop *dumb terminals,* which were essentially a keyboard and a monitor with a long cable that connected to a computer.

Ironically, both IBM and Digital have both seen their fortunes change dramatically since then. IBM made a dramatic move in 1981 when it introduced the first personal computer; for a while that machine became the tail that wagged the company's dog, but eventually Big Blue got out of the manufacturing side of the desktop business, and then the laptop business, to concentrate on its core business of business services, electronic storage systems, and still-huge mainframe computers.

DEC watched its core business of mid-sized computers be eaten alive by armies of PCs that ended up on every desk in an office from secretary to chairman of the board. The company was eventually taken over by Compaq Computer, which was born as a PC competitor to IBM; Compaq later was gobbled up by Hewlett-Packard, which was a more nimble version of DEC.

Anyhow, to come to a point here (You were wondering?), the irony is that in some ways Olsen was correct. Nearly three out of four homes in the United States have PCs, and more than half of these users have more than one machine with a network connection between them; at the same time nearly every computer on the planet is in some way linked to the World Wide Web. The Internet is essentially one gigantic computer, with users able to use the resources of others. Somewhere out there are millions of books, hundreds of thousands of pieces of music and video, global e-mail and instant messaging, and even shared processing.

Working the Net

And so, the personal computer — and your wired or wireless laptop — have become not-at-all-dumb terminals in a global network. You don't need to have a disk with a copy of the Seattle phone book in your computer; it's out there on the Web. You don't need to balance your checkbook with pen and paper; instead you can reach into your bank's mainframe and look at all the transactions recorded there. And the idea of carrying around a thick book full of airline schedules — as business travelers we used to do that not that long ago — sounds ludicrous today. Why do that when you can log on to the Internet from your wireless laptop and check times, gates, and prices?

The first step: making your computer network-capable. For that you need one, two, or all three of the following pieces of hardware:

✔ A *network interface card (NIC),* which connects your laptop to a wired Ethernet network. Nearly all current laptop models come with this facility built in to the motherboard; look for a slightly oversized version of a telephone plug on the side or back of the machine.

If your laptop does not have a NIC, you can easily add one with an adapter that plugs in to the USB port. An older solution used an adapter that attaches to the computer through the PC Card slot. (PC Card slots are credit card-sized devices whose first uses were to add NICs, modems, and flash memory cards. That sort of connection is likely to be slower than its more modern USB equivalent (which can connect to almost any external device) and also results in a somewhat fragile connector extending out the side of your laptop, an accident waiting to happen. Chapter 16 details USB and PC Cards.

Add-on NICs are relatively inexpensive, selling for as little as $20–$50, and easily installed; USB adapters require the least involvement by the user, especially if you are running a current version of Windows. You may have to load a software device driver from a CD or from the Internet; follow the instructions provided by the manufacturer.

✔ A *wireless adapter* that allows your laptop to exchange information with a home or office network equipped with a wireless base station, or to sign on to the Internet through a wireless *hotspot* (public-access networks) in airports, hotels, and coffee shops. (A *base station* is a receiver/transmitter attached to a desktop machine; for laptops a mini version of the same device can be included on the motherboard itself or as a small plug-in device for USB or PC Card slots.) Again, many laptops now come equipped with wireless facilities; those that don't can be upgraded through the use of a USB or PC Card adapter. Two other possibilities not in widespread use among laptops are infrared and Bluetooth (a specialized variation of wireless). For more details, see Chapter 14.

✔ A *modem* that allows connection to the Internet or to a dial-up office intranet. This used to be the only way for laptop owners to communicate out of the box, and many laptops still come with a telephone modem. In current use, though, users are much more likely to connect via wired Ethernet NIC to a broadband (high-speed, high-capacity) cable or DSL connection to the Internet or to a wireless adapter that ties into a shared broadband connection. Read more about modems in Chapter 15.

Anytime you disconnect a network (Ethernet) cable, remove it first from the computer and then from the wall jack or router. To install the cable, begin at the jack or router and then plug it in to the computer. Why? To avoid the remote possibility of an electrical surge.

The Basics of an Ethernet

I can get deep into the technical details of the Ethernet here or I can acknowledge that current versions of Windows and hardware are quite good at handling all the hard work of configuration and setup. So let me not get too deep into the details; I've included a little sidebar for those who really want to know a bit about how a network works.

Ethernet for those who have to know

The best way to think of Ethernet, or at least the best one that I can wrap my arms around is this: Think of a high-speed single-lane highway that runs in a circle. Vehicles can get on or off the road many places, but if they stay on the highway, they'll eventually come back to where they began and then start another circuit.

Now think of what you would have to do if you were a driver trying to get onto the road; you can't just zoom onto the road without finding a gap in the traffic large enough for your vehicle. And then once you're on the road you've got to maintain speed while looking for the correct exit, but you can only get off the road if there is room on the off-ramp; if another vehicle is in your way, you'll have to go all the way around the circle and try again. That's an Ethernet, in a very simplified description. Technically, a NIC using that protocol employs Carrier Sense Multiple Access With Collision Detection, a fancy description for a scheme that monitors the stream of traffic and looks for an opening.

Information or instructions are broken up into small pieces, called *packets;* the data is enclosed within some extra coding that identifies the sender and specifies the intended recipient. When a NIC finds an opening in the traffic, it sends out a packet; if two devices on the network send a packet at the same moment, there will be a *collision.* After a randomly assigned wait, each computer is instructed to resend the packet.

I've described the Ethernet as a circle, a design called a *ring.* In fact, the most common design for an Ethernet is called a *hub-and-spoke,* with a central hub or switch and each of the attached computers located at the end of a spoke that travels to and from its NIC. Another design is called a *bus,* and it sets up with all of the computers branching off a single main line.

The same concept is applied for wireless networks, which are set up very much like wired systems — without the wires. A central wireless hub receives all of the incoming information and instructions from wireless computers and retransmits packets to appropriate addresses. Because the wireless design works almost the same way as a wired Ethernet, an office or home can create a network that intermixes devices with and without wires.

Today's most common wired Ethernet systems in homes and offices are based on cables and hardware called *10Base-T* and capable of moving data at as much as 10 megabits per second of data, or 100Base-T which ups the speed to 100mbps. State-of-the-art is *Gigabit Ethernet,* which can zoom along at as much as 1,000 Mbps.

Just like a single-lane highway, nothing can travel on an Ethernet faster than the slowest component on a particular link. If you have a 100Base-T hub and 10Base-T NICs, communication takes place at 10 Mbps.

If you are merely adding a new or upgraded laptop to an existing wired network, all you need on the hardware side is the NIC and an Ethernet cable.

On the other hand, if you are creating a network from scratch, here are the hardware components:

✔ *NICs* for all computers. If not already installed on your laptop, they can be added to a PC Card slot or (preferably) to a USB port. Some devices can also be added to a network and used as a device by any attached computer; as an example, some printers can be *network attached* with a specialized NIC and circuitry.

✔ A *hub* to serve as the central connection point for cables from computers and other devices. The hub can also be connected to a router and broadband modem (more about these in a moment). The hub (some techies call it a *concentrator*) can also be used to connect two networks or to connect to a wireless transmitter to extend into a *WiFi* (wireless fidelity) system; in that use it is considered a *router.* If you add in a hardware *firewall* as one layer of protection against Internet pirates and ne'er-do-wells, what you've got is a *gateway,* a combination of switch, router, and firewall.

An intelligent version of a hub is called a *switch,* and it speeds up the process by connecting directly from the sending device to the receiving device without sending the packet all the way around the ring or down the full length of the bus. In the process it cuts down on time-consuming collisions (data packets bumping into each other). You can read about these concepts in further depth in the accompanying "Ethernet for those who have to know" sidebar.

Building a Firewall

If I were in charge, the Internet would be fantastically fast, infinitely vast, virtually without cost . . . and most importantly, completely free of cyberjerks. I'll leave it to you to come up with an answer as to why some people dedicate whole chunks of their otherwise empty lives to spoiling a good thing for others. End of sermon, except to say that any user of the Internet — and especially those who maintain an always-on, high-speed broadband connection — need to erect hardware and software barriers against thieves and vandals.

A *hardware firewall* works by plugging the entryways into the network and into attached computers except for those specifically granted permission to come in. Firewalls are not perfect — a truly dedicated hacker may be able to get through — nor do they fully protect against the contents of e-mails and downloads that you permit to get through. (You have to be on guard against those by yourself, and use a capable antivirus software program to sweep your mail and downloads and block suspicious activities.)

Although the market offers some very capable *software firewalls,* I am not a fan of the concept. They work in much the same way as a hardware firewall, examining every incoming packet to see if it was really intended for your machine or just randomly jiggling the handles looking for an unlocked door. But the difference is that the software firewall is already *inside* your computer, running under your operating system. That's too close for comfort for me; I like the idea that a hardware firewall sits outside the computer with an electronic shotgun.

Chapter 14

Feeling Up in the Air

A wireless network is just like a wired one, except for the lack of wires. It's that missing physical link that makes wireless computing so very attractive, because it allows you to move a laptop from room to room in your home or office and stay connected. And perhaps best of all, it permits traveling laptop users to link up to the Internet, an e-mail server, and even to a private office network while on the road — in airport lounges, in hotels, and at designated public-access wireless Internet *hotspots* in coffee shops, business centers, and other places.

It's in the air: Millions of users, with laptop owners at the forefront, are cutting the wires that bind them to the Internet, to devices like printers, and to networks that connect one machine to another. Wireless systems follow the same basic principles as a wired network: Each device has its own ID, and packets of information are addressed to assure that only the intended recipient receive the data; unfortunately, although designers of wireless systems have gotten very good at protecting data, the mere fact that the information is floating in the ether invites snoops to attempt to intercept communication. Be careful out there!

Look Ma, No Wires

Like almost everything else in personal computing, the tools and process of going wireless have become cheaper and easier over time. If your laptop does not already come equipped with a wireless (*WiFi*, short for *wireless fidelity*, a geeky pun on the almost-forgotten HiFi, high fidelity audio systems of the 1960s) card or have one built in to the motherboard or case, you can add one for $50–$100. That capability permits you to communicate with existing wireless networks in homes and offices, as well as in public places like libraries, schools, Internet cafes, and airports.

If you need to set up your own wireless network, you need to add a WiFi *router,* a transmitter/receiver that plugs in to a standard computer or into the router of an existing wired network. Cost: $75–$150 for the state of the art. (Chapter 13 offers more router information.)

The only other possible expense is for a software *firewall* (a program that is intended to block unauthorized intrusion to your machine) and antivirus protection — but that is something you should already have in place for all of your machines. Most current Windows operating systems come prepared to work a wireless network or can be adapted to do so with software device drivers provided by hardware makers. I recommend, though, that you consider Windows 98SE the entry-level version for wireless computing and Windows XP (kept current with at least Service Pack 2) as the optimal operating system.

Minding your wireless Ps and Qs

By industry convention, the most common wireless technology is based on the 802.11 standard, which dates back to the late 1990s in its original form. As of this writing there have been three significant versions of the 802.11 standard, each better than the one before. You've got your original *a* version, followed in rapid succession by *b* and *g.*

There were, of course, proposals for c, d, e, and f, but for various reasons they were deemed not ready for prime time or not technically or economically feasible. As we go to press, 802.11g is the latest and greatest, but wireless propeller heads are hard at work and itching to let loose any or all of these: 802.11e, 803.11h, 802.11i, and 802.11n. And just for a change of pace, a whole new group of new schemes falls under the 802.15, 802.16, and 802.20 standards. What? Did you think they had already reached the limit of laptop capability?

The good news, though, is that the big bubble of machines released to work with the 802.11g specification almost certainly means that when even better WiFi hardware and software are available, they will have to be *backward compatible* with previous equipment. That means that if (or more likely when) speeds, reliability, and range improve, at the very worst your current machine will operate just as it does now; in the best case, manufacturers will offer inexpensive plug-in adapters (USB, PC Card, or dedicated slot; more on these in Chapter 16) that upgrade a machine to the new standard.

Certification and compatibility

Any manufacturer can produce a device that works within the unlicensed frequencies used by the various WiFi standards. However, to carry the official Wi-Fi Certified logo, a manufacturer has to be a member of an industry association set up to grant that seal of approval.

While unofficial devices may work quite well, only a product with the certification logo is guaranteed to meet interoperability tests with other standards and other manufacturers. WiFi equipment works anywhere there is compatible equipment, but a handful of countries have

either banned it or have not yet permitted its use. Some European countries limit the number of channels that can be used by a transceiver, while some nations (including Italy) officially require a license for use of the airwaves. A handful of totalitarian regimes are very nervous about all sorts of high-technology and may start muttering something about CIA if they determine you are carrying a radio transmitter. When in doubt, check with your country's embassy or local authorities.

Here's a guide to the standards in use now:

- ✔ **802.11a** was first out of the gate, at least on paper, and offered a great deal of potential. It was fast, supported a bandwidth of as much as 54 mbps, and its radio frequency was far enough away from garage door openers and other appliances to avoid interference. On the downside, though, its *transmission range* — the distance its signal can carry — was relatively short, about 60 feet or so. It works well within a room or house, but not much farther. The standard works in the 5-GHz frequency range, between 5.725–5.850 GHz, which is also used by some wireless phones.

    The higher a signal's frequency and the more data it carries, the shorter its effective range.

- ✔ **802.11b** quickly supplanted -a for many users because of a tradeoff of greater range over speed and lower cost. This standard sends signals in the frequency range of 2.4–2.4835 GHz. This standard has a bandwidth of about 11mbps but a signal range of about 300 feet, although in certain settings the signal can be affected or stopped by household or business appliances. Got a 2.4 GHz wireless phone in your house or office? Same radio frequency. The same goes for microwave ovens, Bluetooth communication devices, and certain medical and scientific tools.

    And so early WiFi users had to choose between range and speed. Just to make the decision more difficult, 802.11a and 802.11b use different frequencies and technologies, meaning that it is difficult or impossible to mix and match systems that use solely one or the other.

✔ **802.11g** takes the best of a and b. It supports a bandwidth of as much as 54mbps and the broader range of about 300 feet. Because it uses the same 2.4-GHz radio frequency as 802.11b, it is compatible with hardware designed for that earlier standard. And engineers have made great improvements in dealing with interference. Finally, the g version is somewhat less susceptible to hacking by snoops and thieves than earlier standards.

Determining whether wireless is worthwhile

Many years ago I worked as executive editor and editor-in-chief for a major New York publisher, a company that had a near-lock on magazines about PCs. In fact, those two initials were used in the title of their flagship publication and several others.

Our division was growing at an extraordinary rate, adding cubicles and moving desks into hallways and storage rooms. The old Manhattan building we occupied had plaster walls and ceilings and very limited extra space for more phone lines or (for what were then) thick and heavy Ethernet cables for networking big and clunky PCs. And a visit from a fire warden gave official notice that we'd have to deal with a licensed electrician and use metal conduit if we proposed to stick new wires in the walls.

Hot spots in the big city

How can you find a hotspot for wireless computing? If you subscribe to a cell phone service or a cable television/cable Internet company that offers hotspots, you can check out its web site and search by city or ZIP code. You can also search through the web sites of national chains that are installing hotspots at many of their locations: these include FedEx Kinko's, Starbucks, Borders Books, Panera Bread, and several hotel chains.

You can also visit national web sites that allow you to search by airport or ZIP code; most of these give you the locations for paid commercial access. One such web site is www.jiwire.com.

Finally, you can try one of the national providers of hotspots:

✔ www.tmobile.com (Operated by T-Mobile cellular)

✔ www.myconnect.com (Operated by Toshiba Computers)

✔ www.boingo.com (A third party that sells access under its own name as well as rebranded services for small and large ISPs)

One of the magazines I supervised was installed in one of those former windowless closets. And so I took my expense account to the nearest Radio Shack and bought up half a dozen sets of cordless phones and every possible connector and adapter in the store. We attached to a wired phone outlet in another office and extended antennae into the hall. Though the communication was sometimes sketchy, we were able to make phone calls and hook up our slow dial-up modems to the makeshift wireless system. The range of these phones was no more than about 50 feet, and the modems operated somewhere between 300–1,200 bps — about 2 percent of the speed of an 802.11g WiFi network. But our makeshift network worked, in a sort of a limited way for an off-night.

I use this bit of ancient PC history just as an example of wireless communication serving as a way to get around architectural barriers. That is one of two very good reasons to use WiFi today.

Good reason number one: Easy installation

Assume you live in a house or apartment and want to share information between two or more computers, or share a single incoming broadband connection throughout the house. You can connect machines in two ways: one is to run wires along the floor, across the ceiling, through the walls, down to the basement, and up to the crawlspace. Obviously, this can be done but it can be difficult, messy work, and may not be possible to do so in rented space. And if you hire an electrician or a computer technician to do the work, it can be a very expensive project. The same problems apply in office settings. It can be expensive and difficult to retrofit old offices to new communication technologies, and you may run into additional wrinkles, such as building and fire codes, that make the job practically impossible to accomplish.

But if you think of WiFi communication instead of cables and wires, many problems are quickly solved. Modern wireless systems transmit across a room and through most walls. If you need to go more than 300 feet, or if the walls or ceilings are extremely dense or contain steel beams, metal studs, or other signal-blocking materials, you can purchase *repeaters* and *signal boosters*. Place them in such a way to bend signals around otherwise impenetrable corners or find places in the walls or ceilings where communication links can be made.

The cost of WiFi equipment is a bit more than that of cabling (depending on the distance to be spanned) although like everything else in computing, the price spiral is in a downward direction. But the payback comes in avoidance of electrician or technician hourly rates. And a wireless system is not a permanent thing; it can be picked up and moved to a new location quite easily. It is also, as the techies like to say, easily *scalable*. You can add more machines and *access points* (hotspots) with ease without the need to string more wire.

Good reason number two: Hotspots and public access

One of the reasons we are gathered together between the covers of this book is that we have a need for a laptop computer. We enjoy the benefits of moving from place to place with our business or our personal information with us at all times.

For laptop users, WiFi is a way to quickly connect to the Internet or to a private intranet or *local area network (LAN)* while traveling. On the Internet side, there are already thousands of places where you can turn on your laptop and gain access to the World Wide Web with a few clicks. Some of these places are hotspots that are part of a commercial subscription service; for example the T-Mobile cellular phone company offers access points at many Border's Books, FedEx Kinko's, and Starbucks around the United States and elsewhere. For a monthly or daily fee you can stroll into one of these locations and check your mail, do some research, or use the coffee shop as a temporary office.

In many other public places, like airports and business centers, you can turn on your WiFi-equipped laptop and sign up for a few hours or days' worth of service. On the high seas, a growing number of cruise lines offer wireless Internet to paying passengers, allowing relatively low-cost communication from some very remote locations. Several major airlines have introduced wireless Internet access aboard its international flights (for a fee, but nevertheless pretty cool).

You'll also find a growing number of free Internet connections in restaurants, hotels, and libraries. These WiFi locations are set up to accept any visitor. Many hotels that cater to businesspeople offer wireless services to their guests. And many travelers are able to link up to their corporate network anywhere in their home office or at branch locations by walking in with their WiFi-equipped laptop.

Knowing the Dos, Don'ts, and Won'ts

Pay attention to those little letters after the numbers in the wireless standards. If you're setting up a new system, going with the most current is generally best — 802.11g or later. Shoppers who look only at the price may end up buying old technology that may be limited in its capabilities and unable to interoperate with other wireless components. In the worst case it may be unable to properly communicate with wired networks in offices.

If you're lucky, when you plug in your components and follow the manufacturer instructions and the built-in Windows configuration process, your wireless network will be up and running immediately. (Windows 98SE, 2000, ME, and XP walk you through the process with increasingly simpler instructions.)

The flippin' switch

I was frustrated at the inability of my brand-new laptop to communicate using its built-in 802.11g WiFi card. Windows reported to me that it recognized and was ready to work with the hardware; T-Mobile confirmed to me that the hotspot was live and operational, and that my account was active. The instruction manual for the laptop made brief mention of the need to "turn on" the WiFi card, but I assumed that meant I needed to activate the wireless facilities through Windows, and this I had done.

And so I made a phone call to technical support for the laptop, made by a reputable company whose name begins with *Toshi* and ends with *ba.* I reached a technician after a 20-minute wait on hold during which I was regularly thanked for my patience. (Why do companies thank you for something you have not yet offered?) We solved the problem in about 10 seconds: This model laptop (and as it turns out, quite a few others from the same company and others) has a tiny slide switch on the side that turns on or off the wireless card. Turning it off saves battery power and avoids interference with other systems, which is good. Failing to mention its existence in the instruction manual, not so good.

Sometimes, though, the wireless network does not work properly when first started or even more vexingly, may work intermittently. Try these troubleshooting steps to prepare a WiFi system:

Getting on the bus

Access points or WiFi cards need to be connected to the bus or ports of any laptop, desktop, or device that expects to communicate over the wireless system. (The *bus* is the data superhighway that connects to and from the microprocessor.) Preconfigured wireless-capable laptops are, by definition, ready to go with internal connections. If using a WiFi card, it needs to be properly attached to either a USB port or plugged squarely into the pins of the PC Card socket. (Chapter 16 talks more about PC Cards and USB.)

Powering up

Make sure all components are properly powered. Access points need a source of electrical power. That sometimes means an AC wall source; if attached to a laptop from the battery, that means through the USB port or through a special port for a wireless card.

If you attach a WiFi card to the PC Card socket of your laptop or to a special-purpose compartment in the case, you have no choice about the power source or the power drain on your ability to use other external devices — except by turning off the switch for the WiFi transceiver or physically removing it from its PC Card socket. (Be sure to use the Windows facilities to "stop" a device attached to the PC Card port before removing it from a machine that is up and running. Windows displays a utility to permit safe removal of a USB or PC Card in the notification area, usually located at the lower-right corner of the screen. Click the utility to open it and then choose the device you want to stop.)

If you are using an external WiFi transceiver that is attached to a USB port, you may improve its, the laptop's, or another device's performance by using a *powered* USB hub, which plugs in to an electrical outlet to assure sufficient voltage for all attached devices. Of course, if you're going to plug a powered USB port into a wall socket, you might as well do the same for the laptop itself. This sort of solution works well while moving from office to office; it is less worthy if your machine is meant to be used entirely on battery power.

Fighting frequency

Be aware of possible sources of *radio frequency (RF)* interference or objects that shield radio signal transmission:

- Wireless telephones, especially those that use the 2.4 GHz frequency
- Certain household appliances, including microwave ovens, television sets, baby monitors, and even improperly shielded PCs
- Radio frequency remote controls for garage doors and other electrical equipment (Note that most modern remotes for televisions, VCRs, and many other high-tech devices use pulses of infrared light; infrared controls may occasionally interfere with each other but don't effect RF devices.)
- Another office's or neighbor's WiFi system
- A high-powered transmitter, especially the sort used by radio or television stations or by police or military authorities

Signal blockage comes in many forms, too:

- Large metal objects like filing cabinets or refrigerators
- Metal netting in plaster walls
- Decorative metal ceilings
- Certain types of wall coverings or flooring that has metal or other dense substances

None of this should be any surprise to you if you use a cell phone. You know that even within a single room there may be spots where the signal is strong or weak, or places where the connection is completely gone. And you know that a strong signal may suddenly fade away, perhaps because some other source of interference has entered the arena.

Keeping Your PIN to Yourself

Finally, it is worth noting that using a wireless network is a little bit like shouting out your bank account number across a packed baseball stadium and also somewhat like leaving the door to your home or office unlocked.

What do I mean by that? Well, first of all, you are disclosing some valuable private information in a public place. An eavesdropper — ranging from the electronic equivalent of a peeping Tom to a professional thief who is looking to steal your savings — can park outside your home or office or sit across the coffee shop or airport lounge and attempt to tap in to the flow of data coming to or from your machine over the Internet.

Don't think, though, that this is all that easily done. The eavesdropper has to pick your particular stream of information out of the thicket of 0s and 1s bouncing around the room, has to determine what they mean and to which accounts they apply, and has to grab the beginning, middle, and end of the data from the chopped-up packets of information that move from place to place. That's why I liken it to yelling your information across Fenway Park; someone else may or may not hear you, may not understand everything you say, and may not grasp the significance of what they hear even if they get it all.

My second analogy, that of leaving your house or office unlocked, may be more troubling. Even though in the real world leaving an unlocked door is not a problem for most of us — simply not all that many thieves walk around jiggling doorknobs — when it comes to computers, alas, technology has automated the jiggling.

A dedicated computer hacker or professional thief can use electronic tools that quickly probe hundreds and thousands of ports on a computer that is connected to a network (wired or wireless) in search of one that is unlocked. If he can find one open to outsiders and that leads to personal data stored on the computer's hard drive, he can attempt to steal from your bank accounts or steal your identity for other purposes. If he is merely malicious, he could plant a virus on your system.

So who you gonna call when it comes to security? The answer for laptop users is the same as for desktop computer owners: Every machine should have at least one level of electronic firewall as well as a capable, continually updated antivirus program.

A *firewall* is a piece of hardware or a software program that sits — in reality or in logic form — between your machine and the outside world. In a wired environment, the firewall may exist in the router that connects a single machine to others or the entire network to an incoming broadband Internet service. As a piece of software, a firewall is constantly on the lookout for any activity not specifically authorized by the user or that is suspicious, like an inward reach for data not initiated by your actions.

An *antivirus* is a second line of defense. A good program performs a number of actions, including scanning all incoming (and outgoing) e-mail for malicious code as well as keeping an eye on the microprocessor for unusual functions. Those functions range from requests to alter the hard drive's boot tracks to unsolicited probes of the drive's contents. (Chapter 7 details hard drives.)

This is another reason to update your machine to use the latest WiFi standard; at the time of publication that is 802.11g. This standard, though not perfect, includes improved security elements called *WiFi Protected Access (WPA)*. This replaces the earlier (a and b) scheme called *Wired Equivalent Privacy (WEP)*, which was not all that private.

Keep your operating system up to date. Microsoft and Apple are constantly adding patches, fixes, and new features. If you're using Windows XP, it definitely makes sense to upgrade to Windows XP Service Pack 2 to take advantage of new and improved facilities.

And then keep an eye on the developing later standards. The coming 802.11i version is supposed to include a new security method called *Temporal Key Integrity Protocol*, which will build an even higher and tougher wall between your machine and hackers.

To this I add one more suggestion: Always conduct your business as if you assume that someone is out there trying to steal your secrets. If you are in a strange location, like a coffee shop or hotel, try to avoid doing your banking or managing your portfolio. If you absolutely must do so, regularly change your password for these accounts and keep a close eye on balances and transactions for any activity you did not authorize. Your e-mail account is probably of little interest to a hacker, but nevertheless you should regularly change the password.

And finally, while you are working, keep an eye on your screen and its indicator lights; also keep an ear tuned to the sounds of your hard drive. If you see or hear something unusual when you are going wireless — something that is different from what you see or hear when your machine is attached to an Ethernet cable — sign off the WiFi connection *and* shut off or remove the WiFi adapter.

Staying beneath the radar

Right out of the box, most WiFi systems are configured to be open to any machine that speaks the same language, which could include your next-door neighbors and some guy in a car down the road. It takes a few extra steps to make it difficult — but not impossible — for someone else to sneak into your wireless cloud.

The basic way to lock up a home network is to instruct the router to block any computers not on a list you provide; this is called *MAC (media access control) filtering*. This is based on the unique identification number stored on network adapter cards; the ID is randomly generated, and it is highly unlikely to find identical sets. Following the instructions provided by your router maker, enter the MAC address for each device in your wireless network into the memory of the router, and it will block foreign access.

You can look up the MAC address of a computer running Windows XP with these steps:

1. Go to Start⇨Run.

2. Type **CMD** and click OK to go to the operating system that percolates beneath Windows.

3. When you see the command prompt, type **IPCONFIG/ALL** and press the Enter key.

You'll find all sorts of information about your network adapter, but the one you are looking for is called Physical Address. Herein is the MAC address, which will look something like this: 00-88-AD-78-35-97.

If you have both an Ethernet adapter and a wireless card in your machine, you'll find a listing for both the wired adapter and wireless card; the one you want is for the WiFi adapter and is listed as the Ethernet adapter Wireless Network Connection. As I indicated, MAC filtering is not perfect; a moderately talented sneak can often find a way to fool the router. Be sure to keep your firewall and antivirus hardware and software current.

Facilitating WiFi in a Laptop

Almost every new laptop now includes a wireless transceiver built in to the motherboard or attached to it through a special port in the case. However, if your laptop does not include wireless facilities or if its standard is outdated, you can easily upgrade and update.

Sans current facilities

The following options are for adding wireless to a laptop that does not have any existing facilities.

Holding the card

Check the instruction manual or consult the manufacturer's telephone support service or web site to see if the laptop has a built-in compartment for holding a small wireless card. The good news is that this is a neat solution to upgrading your computer. The bad news comes in two parts: First, the wireless card is almost certainly a *proprietary* part, meaning that you must purchase the manufacturer's card at whatever price it sets. The second part of the bad news is that some manufacturers do not encourage end users to install cards in this special slot. This hesitance may come from concern that an improperly installed or poorly shielded card can cause interference with other devices that use radio frequencies.

On the transceiving end

You could purchase a PC Card wireless transceiver. These devices, available from a number of competing manufacturers (which means that prices should be reasonable) are plug-and-play upgrades to a laptop.

The disadvantages of using a PC Card for wireless include the fact that your laptop may have only one or two such slots available; to counter this, some manufacturers have combined a wireless transceiver with a *network interface card (NIC)* adapter, which allows the single card to permit your computer to connect to either a wireless network or a wired Ethernet. Another possible disadvantage to using a PC Card for wireless is that these devices usually include a small antenna that projects from the side of the laptop; the nub of an antenna is an unattractive nuisance, easy to break off, destroying the card or even the PC Card slot itself.

My advice if you plan to use a PC Card wireless adapter is to get into the habit of removing the card every time you turn off the machine, before you put the laptop away in its case. You should also find a small carrying case for the adapter — a box about the size of a deck of playing cards should fit the bill.

Buddying up to USB

The third option to expand a laptop for wireless is to add a device that connects to the USB port. Most of the latest technology is moving in this direction, and like PC Card devices, this is a plug-and-play solution. Most USB wireless adapters are about two inches long, about two-thirds the size of a tube of lip balm.

Like PC Cards, USB wireless adapters are available from a number of manufacturers, which helps keep prices down and features improving over time. And although USB devices do project from the side of the laptop (actually sticking out a bit more than do PC Cards), they are less likely to damage the computer if they are dislodged; the USB port is close to the edge of the case. I still recommend removing and storing the little wireless devices when the laptop is put away in a case.

And USB devices can be installed directly in the port on the laptop or attached to a hub that connects by wire to the computer; adding a hub allows use of multiple USB devices.

Already got the goods

Upgrading to a better wireless transceiver or working around a broken WiFi adapter is easily done.

Upgrading or replacing wireless facilities

Although it is possible to physically remove a wireless adapter that is installed within a laptop case, I recommend against doing so. This is tight work with delicate connectors, and may void your warranty. And as I've already noted, you'll have to buy the laptop maker's own card, almost certainly a more expensive solution than using an external PC Card or USB device. The only reason to remove a built-in card is if it is somehow causing operational problems with your laptop or if you cannot switch it off with a hardware slide switch or software command.

To disable the drivers associated with built-in hardware, follow these steps:

1. **Remove or disable the existing wireless circuitry.**

   If the card is installed in an internal slot, you may be able to switch it off so the system does not seek to use it; you'll probably also have to remove or disable drivers for the cards that are installed within Windows.

2. **Choose Start⇨Control Panel⇨System to display the System Properties panel.**

3. **Choose the Hardware Device Manager.**

4. **Look for the + mark next to Network adapters; click that symbol to expand the list of hardware managed there.**

   Depending on the configuration of your machine, you may see several devices here including a NIC used for a wired connection to an Ethernet, a 1394 adapter (to support high-speed FireWire communication), a Bluetooth adapter (for that particular type of radio frequency communication), and a Wireless Network Connection. It is that last piece of hardware you need to disable.

5. **Double-click the wireless component to display its properties.**

   At the bottom of the properties page is a section called Device Usage.

6. **Click the Device Usage down arrow and select Do Not Use This Device (Disable).**

   This instructs Windows not to use the drivers associated with it.

Note that the instructions I have given in this section are from Windows XP; the language you see onscreen in earlier versions (dating back to Windows 98SE) may be slightly different, but the steps are the same. If you run into problems disabling the internal wireless facilities, consult the instruction manual for your laptop or call the support desk of the manufacturer for further assistance.

It's much easier, of course, if your previous wireless adapter had been a PC Card or USB device. Here all you need to do is remove the old and plug in the new. Follow the instructions that come with the new device to install any needed drivers or other software.

Setting up a wireless network at home

Adding a wireless network in your home or office is as easy as one-two-three . . . and four and five. Here's my list of steps:

1. **Select a compatible and capable set of wireless equipment for the base station and each of the devices attached to it.**

   - The *base station* is the receiver/transmitter attached to whichever computer you choose to be your network hub. If you plan to share an Internet connection over your private wireless network, the base station should be attached to the machine that is also connected to the modem.

   - The *wireless router* assignment is to convert signals coming from a wired network or from a broadband Internet connection into a form that can be broadcast.

   - The *wireless transceiver* (also called a *wireless network adapter*) is the broadcaster and receiver necessary at each device that seeks to communicate with the router. Your newer-vintage laptop may come equipped with a transceiver. Some new printers and other peripherals (extras) may have a built-in transceiver, too. You can easily add a USB or PC Card wireless transceiver to a laptop.

Keeping it in the family

Although any device that has an official Wi-Fi Certified label on it should be interoperable with any other such device, you will probably find it easier to create a network that uses hardware from the same vendor. For example, stay within the Linksys, D-Link, or Microsoft families rather than mixing and matching devices from these or other makers. But as I write these words, I'm glancing over at the table alongside my desk that holds my communications gear, and no two of the various pieces of equipment there is from the same maker. I see a Linksys cable/DSL hub and router, a Motorola cable modem, a D-Link telephone adapter, and a Belkin USB Ethernet wired adapter.

2. **Turn off the cable modem or DSL modem.**

   You're now connecting the wireless router. Carefully follow the instructions that come with the hardware; doing things out of order can result in improperly configured devices, and you will be unable to get to the Internet to seek assistance.

   If there is no on-off switch, disconnect the AC adapter that goes to the modem. Do *not* disconnect the modem from the incoming cable television/ Internet feed.

3. **Connect the wireless router to the modem.**

   In most setups, you'll be using an Ethernet cable. Now you're configuring the wireless router.

4. **Attach the network cable that is usually supplied with the wireless router to a computer and one of the open network ports on the router.**

   Use any port *except* those labeled as Internet, WAN, or WLAN.

5. **Open Internet Explorer or another compatible browser and go to the particular address specified by the router maker.**

   This is very similar to going to a particular web site on the Internet; note that the address does not include the www prefix, because you are not going onto the World Wide Web. Table 14-1 lists the default addresses, usernames, and passwords for four of the largest makers or distributors of router hardware.

Table 14-1	Default Addresses, Usernames, and Passwords for Routers		
Manufacturer	*Address*	*Username*	*Password*
3Com	http://192.168.1.1	admin	admin
D-Link	http://192.168.0.1	admin	*(blank)*
Linksys	http://192.168.1.1	admin	admin
Microsoft Broadband	http://192.168.2.1	admin	admin

Once you reach the internal setup screen of the router you are asked to make some important decisions. Most users can use the default settings — in fact, unless you have reason to make changes, don't alter the defaults.

6. **Make these three settings:**

   • **Wireless Network Name.** In technobabble, this is also referred to as an *SSID.* (Just for the record, an SSID is a Service Set Identifier.) Whatever name you give your network is converted into a 32-character code that is part of the header for every packet sent over your wireless network between a mobile device and the router.

Try to pick a network name that is a bit unusual and certainly not one that is embarrassing; I can sit right here at the desk in my office and read the name of the wireless network in use at my neighbor's house about 150 feet away.

- **Encryption.** You have the option to select **Wireless Encryption (WEP), Wi-Fi Protected Access (WPA),** or no encryption. You're generally best off choosing WPA, if available, or WEP as a second-best choice. If you're connecting at a public hotspot, the operator may insist that these encryption schemes be turned off and the company's own system used.

  You may also be asked to type in a passphrase that the router will use to generate *encryption keys* (a form of code) that protect the security of your data. You don't need to remember your passphrase — it is there to see anytime you go to the router's configuration screen. You should, though, make the passphrase complex enough that a hacker is not likely to guess what it is. Don't use your name or your birthday or your favorite sports team. Instead, use a nonsensical combination of a word and numbers, something like 5217Dummies7021Rule.

- **Administrative Password.** Here's where you've got to choose a complex password that you memorize or somehow track. You need this password to make future changes to the router's settings. Once again, I suggest a combination of numbers and an unusual word or phrase.

7. **Once you've made your settings, follow the manufacturer's instructions to save them.**

8. **Reconnect the computer to the router and turn on the PC's power.**

   Current versions of Windows should automatically detect the presence of a new wireless adapter; you may have to install a driver from a CD. The computer should communicate with the router and any other PC on the wireless network (and on a wired network if it is attached to the router as well).

9. **Make sure that all of the computers are properly protected behind firewalls and antivirus software.**

Setting up a wireless network

A basic home or small office wireless network is based around an *access point* — a transmitter/receiver that can communicate with laptops, desktops, and

A scheme for passwords

Unless you have a photographic memory, you may have to find some way to write down your passwords. That's only natural, but don't make it easy for someone to steal them. Don't write them down and tape them to the side of your computer monitor. Don't keep them in your wallet. And don't use passwords that are so very obvious as your date of birth or your wife's maiden name; trust me, hackers are smart enough to try those first.

Here are a few tips to safer computing:

✔ Establish a base of four or five unusual words that are easy for you to remember but hard for an outsider to guess. Let's say, just as a random example, that you're a serious baseball fan — serious enough to remember the starting lineup for the Los Angeles Dodgers on September 9, 1965 — the day Sandy Koufax pitched a perfect game, besting Chicago Cubs pitcher Bob Hendley who gave up only one hit and one run. Your secret set of words might include Koufax, Torborg, Parker, and Lefebvre — the pitcher, catcher, first baseman, and second baseman. Baseball scorekeepers assign those particular four positions as 1, 2, 3, and 4.

So if you choose *9koufaxlefebvre65 as* a password, you could write in your notepad that the password for your bank account is ##14##. You will remember that ## refers to 19 and the second ## is 65 because that is your base. And you'll know to substitute baseball position 1 and 4 as the meat of the password. And you can reverse spelling, choosing a password like *19grobrot65rekrap* and noting it in your pad as ##%2##%3. Use the % sign — or anything else that works for your — to signify that a word's spelling is reversed.

✔ Use a password-protection program such as Norton Password Manager. Under that program you create one very complex password and enter it each time you turn on your machine or reboot it, and then let the software automatically fill in passwords for most web sites you visit.

✔ In any case, change your passwords at least every six months — and immediately if you suspect that someone has gained access to any of your accounts without your permission.

other devices equipped with wireless transceivers. Figure 14-1 shows four pieces of equipment: the access point, a *hub* that interconnects various wired devices in your system, a router that examines incoming data from one network and correctly reroutes it to another network, and a broadband Internet connection — usually a cable or DSL modem.

You can also purchase a combined hub and router, or an all-in-one unit that has a hub, router, and access point. One version of a magic black box also brings together the cable or DSL modem.

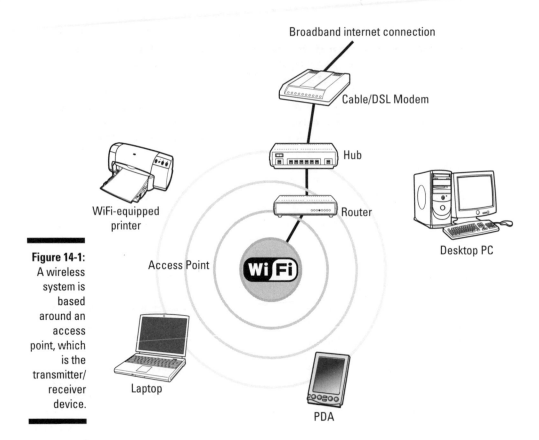

Broadband internet connection

Cable/DSL Modem

Hub

WiFi-equipped printer

Router

Desktop PC

Figure 14-1:
A wireless system is based around an access point, which is the transmitter/ receiver device.

Access Point

WiFi

Laptop

PDA

Networking Other Ways

I've exhaustively explored wireless communications. (I know I'm tired of the subject, and I suspect by now so are you.) And I've touched on traditional wired Ethernet networks, which connect laptops and desktops to each other through a central hub. Just for the record, you have a few other means of interconnection of machines.

The original quick-and-easy means to transfer files from one machine to another earned the nickname of *sneakernet*. This high-tech process involved copying files to a floppy disk on one machine and then carrying the disk to where the files could be uploaded and used. Sneakernets have evolved a bit: You can burn a CD-R on one machine and bring about 600MB of data, photos, or music to another machine in that way. You can also use a tiny flash disk, which is a form of non-volatile RAM; various makers now package as much as several gigabytes of memory in another one of those USB lip balm-like packages. These sticks of memory can be formatted as if they were hard drives and carried from one machine to another. (Chapter 9 talks about these things at length.)

A second method of transfer involved special cables that interconnect ports on two machines. Early PCs used a *null modem* cable that allowed swapping files between serial ports; a more current method uses a cable between USB ports.

Less common solutions — and those being rapidly supplanted by quick and inexpensive wireless networks — include use of a home or office's electrical power lines or telephone cables. Both of these wired systems are relatively slow, subject to interference, and may not work at all if your electrical wiring or telephone system is not continuous from point to point; data may be lost if there are electrical subpanels or telephone splitters or amplifiers.

And in any case, for the purposes of this book I am looking for ways to easily move your laptop and its data and applications from place to place. The best solutions here are wireless communication or wired Ethernet.

Harald Bluetooth is in the room

There's one more wireless technology that holds a lot of promise for certain types of devices, although it has not yet grabbed hold of much of the laptop market: It's called Bluetooth.

Bluetooth is a standard that allows for very quick and easy interconnection between all sorts of equipment on an ad hoc basis. For example, you could walk into a room with a Bluetooth-enabled cell phone or *personal digital accessory* (*PDA,* like a Palm Pilot) and immediately be able to exchange data with any like-minded device. Bluetooth can also be used to allow for cordless mice, connections to printers and other equipment, and even wireless LANs.

Bluetooth operates at a frequency of 2.45 GHz, which is right in the middle of the WiFi 802.11b and 802.11g range. It does, though, include some sophisticated facilities to avoid interference from other devices.

TECHNICAL STUFF

Not down in the mouth

Why Bluetooth? I guess I can't go any further in this section without explaining how a modern communications standard ended up with such a colorful and odd name. The answer lies in the fact that one center of high technology — specifically the cell phone industry — is in Scandinavia with companies including Nokia (which sounds Japanese but is actually Finnish) and Ericsson (which is a Swedish company which also has a 50-50 joint venture with the Japanese firm Sony).

One of the heroes of Scandinavia was this guy Harald Bluetooth, who was king of Denmark in the 10th century; during his reign he united Denmark and part of Norway. As a uniter, not a divider, his name was deemed appropriate for a communications standard.

A strong point of Bluetooth is that the hardware does all of the work. Once any two devices find each other, they negotiate between them for all of the technical details of the conversation: things like exchanging electronic addresses, selecting the best protocol for data, and setting in motion a timing sequence for frequency hopping (which I explain in a moment).

The conversation between devices determines if one or the other device needs something from the other, or if one unit needs to control the other. Once they've established an electronic handshake, they establish a personal-area network, also called a *piconet*.

One way in which Bluetooth devices avoid interference is by working at a very low power level. The standard calls for transmitting at 1 milliwatt, which is one-thousandth of a watt; by comparison, a typical cell phone uses one to three watts (one thousand to three-thousandths as much power) to communicate with the nearest tower.

Of course, using lower power limits their range; in a typical home or office a Bluetooth unit works no more than about 32 feet, although some manufacturers claim a range of about 50 percent more. That works fine across a room, and the signal will penetrate most walls, but it's still a limited area.

A key element of the technology behind Bluetooth is *spread-spectrum frequency hopping.* It's pretty much all in the name: The devices in a piconet continually change the exact frequency, using any one of 79 tiny slices of the radio pie and hopping randomly to another 1,600 times per second. What this does is make it extremely unlikely that there will be any sustained period of interference between Bluetooth devices. Even if by chance two units end up on the same frequency for the moment, they bounce to a different randomly selected one almost immediately. Bluetooth includes the ability to reject (or ask for a resend) any time there is corruption in a tiny packet of data it receives.

Adding Bluetooth to your laptop

Bluetooth technology is already being used in some cell phones, PDAs, cordless computer accessories (including mice, headsets, and keyboards), and home appliances (including stereo systems and universal remote controls that can send signals through walls and floors).

You'll be hard-pressed to find any standard laptops that come equipped with Bluetooth technology, but it is very easy to add: Purchase a USB Bluetooth adapter and plug it in to your laptop. You may have to add a driver (supplied on CD with the adapter or downloaded over the Internet). Software supplied with the adapters adds a Bluetooth icon to the system tray that opens to a connection wizard for modems and a synchronization page to facilitate communication between a pair of Bluetooth devices.

Interested in infrared

For a brief moment in the evolution of the personal computer and the laptop, there was the era of the *infrared (IR)* device. Everyone has been using this technology for years. In fact, it is at the heart of one of the most important essentials of modern life: the television remote control.

It appeared that infrared would be a natural medium for use in connecting laptops and computers to printers and other devices, and to each other. You may well find that a laptop or printer one or two generations old may have infrared circuitry and a small red-filtered window for use in communication. But IR had one big disadvantage: Devices had to be able to "see" each other across the room. The signals might be able to bounce around a desk or off the ceiling, but not through a door or wall. It was for that reason that IR was quickly bypassed by WiFi, which can travel greater distances and penetrate most walls.

Infrared communication for computers is an adaptation of the IEEE 802.11 standard, permitting interchange of information at about 1.6Mbps — if nothing is in the way and the communication angle is no more than about 15 degrees off center. IR is radiation of a frequency lower than visible light (below red light) but higher than microwaves. The low end of the visible spectrum starts with radiation that has a wavelength over about 700 nanometers. (A nanometer is one-billionth of a meter.) Microwaves top out with a wavelength of 1mm and range down to about 30cm. IR communications devices range in wavelength from .85–.90 micrometer. (A micrometer is one-millionth of a meter.)

An *infrared port* is a specialized version of a standard serial port. Windows 98 and later include built-in support for IR ports, often using an industry standard name of *IrDA;* if you're still holding on to an old system running Windows 95, that operating system can be updated to support IR if you can find the code on the Microsoft web page or elsewhere on the Internet. Current versions of Windows include an Infrared Wizard that configures the IR serial port and troubleshoots communication between devices.

As I've said, IR has become a vestigial part on modern laptops and peripherals with the exception of a handful of cordless mice and keyboards. If you have the capability and it works for you, that's fine; if you're buying a new system, there is little reason not to use WiFi instead.

If an existing IR connection suddenly stops working, check the Device Manager to see if it reports a conflict or a hardware failure. Consider reinstalling the device driver if it's outdated or corrupted. If you are convinced your IR circuitry has somehow failed, or if you need to add IR connectivity to a laptop to communicate with another device, the simplest and least expensive solution is to purchase a USB device that adds an IR channel; such hardware is available for as little as $20.

Chapter 15

Modems: The Essential Translators

*M*odems are the entry ramp to the information superhighway. They are — trust me on this — relatively simple devices that are absolutely essential when it comes to translating between the digital 0s and 1s that exist within a laptop and the analog electrical pulses that travel over telephone wires, cable television coaxials, and fiber optics, and through the air in wireless radio or infrared communication.

Okay, let me break this down: I have previously examined the digital nature of the computer, where everything is stored, transported, and manipulated in the form of binary math. Numbers are created out of 0s and 1s and are used to represent letters, characters, the elements of a graphical image, and the representation for music and other audio.

A computer's special-purpose circuits are perfectly capable of moving huge blocks of data over relatively short distances using 8-, 16-, and even 32-wire-wide parallel paths. But when the computer needs to send and receive data over a greater distance, the pathways are not conducive to parallel transmissions and not set up to transmit discrete digital 0s and 1s.

It All Started with Mr. Bell

Why, you might ask, don't computers merely send 0s and 1s in digital form across the phone lines in the same way a PC does when it sends information to a printer? The answer goes back to the original purpose of the telephone system: to send a version of the human voice from one place to another.

When Scotch-born Bostonian Alexander Graham Bell patented his telephone in 1876 — beating by just a few hours a similar claim by Chicago inventor Elisha Gray, which is why we old fogies grew up complaining about Ma Bell instead of Ma Gray — he created a system that was based on analog signaling.

Think of an *analog* signal as an *analogy* rather than a discrete code. The pitch and volume of the human voice were represented by the peaks and valleys and frequency of an electrical wave. That system works very well from point to point — if you can string a continuous pair of wires from one house or office to another a reasonable distance away. But because of electrical resistance in the wires, once the signal travels more than a few hundred feet it needs to be boosted back to original levels by an amplifier. And then there is the issue of being able to connect any one telephone to another on an *ad hoc* basis: That requires switching of the signal from one circuit to another.

Bell's design was intended to be analog all the way, including amplifiers and switches. It is for that reason that telephone services generally cannot carry pure digital 0s and 1s any distance. (You might be able to send signals within a home or office, but once you hit a switch or a non-digital amplifier, you've got a problem.)

So, a standard telephone modem converts the digital bits to an analog warble. When a modem first connects, you can usually hear the two devices whistling at each other to agree on a speed and communication method; if you were to lift a telephone handset on the circuit you would hear the audible conversation of computers. When a computer communicates over a telephone, the 0s and 1s are modulated into a high or low warble of tones. At the receiving end, the warble is demodulated and the highs converted to a 1 and the lows to a 0. Therein comes the name of the device: *Modem* comes as a *concatenation* (combining) of the phrase *modulator-demodulator*.

AM/FM

If the computer were instead using radio waves for communication, it could employ a number of encoding schemes with the most common being *AM* (amplitude modulation) or *FM* (frequency modulation). You'll recognize those terms from conventional radio stations.

An AM signal conveys information by the volume or intensity of its signal. If a computer sends data by amplitude modulation, the radio wave is made up of peaks and valleys; think of a high spike as a 1 and low spike as a 0 and you can understand the basics. FM signals convey information by sending out a wave with uniform peaks and valleys but varying time intervals between them, sort of a Morse code of dashes and dots (or in computer terms, 1s and 0s). The same sort of method is used when data is sent by infrared or by pulses of light over a fiber optic cable.

Typing Your Modem

The original concept of a modem was a way for a digital computer to produce a communications signal that could be sent over the standard pair of copper wires that exist within the telephone cable that goes into most homes and offices. (Techies, as is their style and need, have even made up a name and acronym for this century-old technology: *POTS,* for *plain old telephone service.*)

In this section I talk about the three most common direct-connection modems:

 ✔ Dial-up telephone modems

 ✔ Cable modems

 ✔ DSL telephone modems

Cable and DSL modems, because they are capable of much greater capacities, are considered *broadband technologies.*

Chapter 14 talks about two other gateways to the Internet and to various devices in your home or office: WiFi and Bluetooth wireless communication. For many laptop users, dial-up telecommunication is becoming less and less attractive, replaced by WiFi communication that can connect to high-speed Internet at commercial hotspots, Internet cafes, hotels, and at the offices of clients. *Hotspots* are public-access points within range of a wireless transmitter/receiver for the use of visitors, subscribers, and workers.

Telephone modems

The first telephone modems for personal computers poked along at an anemic 110 bps; the first modem I worked with, in a wire service newsroom, was a box of wires and flashing lights that could move the news to a teletype machine at about 75 bps.

Over the first two decades of the PC and laptop, modems advanced fairly rapidly from 1,200 to 56,000 bps. Engineers have done an amazing job of squeezing every possible bit of performance from the old phone system, but today not much effort is being applied to new research here. It is at that 56K point that consumer modems reached the limits of POTS.

And even though your modem may claim the ability to communicate at 56,000 bps, the truth is that in many parts of the United States and elsewhere around the world, the POTS has not been upgraded for decades. I've worked in places where the realistic speed limit for communication over old copper

---

Web enabler

Adding in necessary bits to mark the beginning and end of 8-bit computer words plus an error checking bit, the net throughput of a 300 bps modem might be equivalent to about 27 bytes per second. If modems had not advanced beyond that point, the World Wide Web would never have been possible.

---

telephone wires is 33,600 bps. (Fast modems are designed to automatically *step down* to the transmit and receive at the fastest rate available across the entire connection from your home or office to the phone company's switching office, and then across the city or country or around the world to another local switching office, and from there on the *local loop* to the destination home or office.)

One large advantage of telephone modems is that they are *dial-up* devices. That means that you can call any other computer that has a modem, or make your choice among various connection points for *ISPs* (Internet service providers). That also makes them highly portable; a dial-up modem in your laptop can connect to any standard analog telephone line while you are on the road, and dial up to your home office or to a connection point for an ISP.

Consumer modems are *asynchronous* devices, meaning that the stream of data is not dependent on timing. Words of computer data are surrounded by additional start and stop bits that identify them. By contrast, specialized modems used in certain direct connections or over leased lines may be *synchronous,* meaning that data marches to the beat of a clock and therefore does not require some of the extra bits used in consumer models.

Be careful before you attach a standard dial-up modem to an office or hotel phone system. Within a modern structure, the phone system may be digital or use a nonstandard design up to the point where it connects to the POTS and the rest of the world. If you have any doubt about the design of a phone system, ask before you plug in. A mismatch could result in frying your modem and possibly causing damage to your laptop.

Cable modems

Today, for many users the best way to get past the limitations of a telephone modem is to instead use a cable modem. The beauty of this design lies in the fact that it does not in any way have to work around Bell's old copper wires.

Rather, cable modems are designed to work with the "fat" pipe that delivers dozens or hundreds of television signals into your home.

Another advantage: Just as you can instantly tune into the Left-Handed Model Dump Truck Shopping Network anytime you turn on your television set, the Internet on a cable modem is constantly available to your computer. There is no dialing up and no sign-on delays. Using the Internet doesn't interfere with your use of the same cable for television; the provider installs a properly designed splitter to send one feed to your laptop or desktop computer and the other to the television sets.

And yet another advantage: It is very easy to add a router or gateway between the cable modem and your computer; doing so permits you to attach several laptops or desktops to the same Internet connection. (Chapter 13 takes you through routers and gateways.) You can also add a WiFi router that spreads your incoming signal through your house, allowing you to bring your laptop from room to room. It also allows desktops in the house to share the same incoming feed. Although you will be dividing a single connection, the truth is that rarely will more than one of the machines be making a major demand on the pipe at the same time. Because the incoming signal is so fast, split-second differences in demand are inconsequential.

Even better, many cable television providers have upgraded their systems to use fiber optic cable that is faster, with even greater capacity, and more reliability than even the cable television coaxial. Typically, *fiber optic cable* is used for long distance runs from headquarters to a distribution box on the street near a group of homes or offices; from there the pulses of light that travel on the fiber optic cable are converted to an electrical signal that is carried on a *coaxial cable.* (This type of cable uses a copper core surrounded by an insulator and then a ground; if you've ever attached a TV to a cable television outlet, you've probably handled a *coax.*)

TIP

Get it right to begin with

If the quality of your cable television service is not very good before you add cable modem Internet, you're probably asking for a further degraded TV signal and a less-than-optimal Internet connection. Insist that your cable television connection be brought up to specifications; the company may have to add an amplifier at the street or in your home to improve a weak signal.

My office is attached to my home, which has (gulp) six and sometimes seven televisions. I also use the cable feed to provide incoming FM radio signals for my stereo system. And so when the installer came to wire my office for a cable modem, he determined that there were too many splits in the incoming cable to allow my computer to get full speed. And so I requested and received a separate cable — without any splitters — from the outside of the house directly into the office.

Amazingly, even with five traditional networks, six news channels, seven shopping stations, eight sports channels, and a couple dozen strange offerings that must be of interest to someone somewhere at sometime if not you, there is still space on a television cable for two channels of the Internet. (Why two? Most cable Internet offerings are unbalanced, meaning that the download stream of web pages, audio, video, and e-mail is under heavier demand than the upload stream of commands, e-mail, and whatever else you might send from your machine to the rest of the world. In an *unbalanced system*, more of the available bandwidth is made available to the incoming stream than the uploading stream.)

On the machine in my office, I typically receive a download speed of about 3mbps and an upload speed of about 236kbps. To put that in perspective, when I am receiving a web page or a video feed, it is coming in at about 60 times faster than a dial-up modem could deliver; when I am uploading, my data goes onto the Internet at speeds of four to six times faster than is possible using POTS.

Today, the download speed of a cable modem and a cable system varies from about 1.5–4 Mbps with expectations that some more advanced systems will reach 5 Mbps speeds in coming years.

A number of technical designs (called *protocols*) exist for cable modem, but nearly all current devices adhere to a standard called *DOCSIS (Data Over Cable Service Interface Specification)*. As a user, all that matters is that your modem meets the requirements of the cable company; once you're connected to the Internet, it does not matter what type of modem is used by any person or service you connect to. You may receive a free loan of a cable modem when you contract with a cable company for the service or you may be required to rent one from the company; it may be cheaper to buy your own cable modem, although the cable company may decline to offer support for something it did not provide.

And the next step in the evolution of the use of the fat television cable is to also bring in a telephone signal; among early major providers are Vonage and AT&T (a distant cousin of the original Ma Bell). The technology is called *VOIP,* for *Voice Over Internet Protocol.* You'll add a telephone adapter to the cable router. It will not be long before you can purchase a portable VOIP telephone adapter to allow direct connection of your laptop to a cable television Internet feed. (And just to make things a bit more complex, something called *digital telephone service* uses a portion of the cable television line to carry signals that, once they reach a switching office, are then routed over traditional telephone wires, satellite, or microwave connections.)

To this point, I've written of nothing but good news. Cable modem users have a few areas of possible concern:

✔ In general, I have found cable companies somewhat better at dealing with customer service than are phone companies, although Ma Bell's deregulated descendants and competitors have improved their attitude somewhat since comedian Lily Tomlin's character Ernestine used to snort, "We don't care. We don't have to. We're the Phone Company."

✔ If your cable system is prone to regular outages or if you have had other problems with the cable company, consider carefully whether you want to give over your Internet connection to them.

✔ The cable between your home or office and the central office of the cable company is shared by all users along the way; this is different from the way most POTS wires are set up. This may or may not be a problem — it depends on how many users are on your particular line and their usage habits. It also depends on whether your cable company has upgraded to more capacious fiber optics in your area. The only way to find out what kind of service you will receive is to try it out; if you find the useable speed too slow for your needs, ask the cable company for advice or consider alternate communications methods.

✔ The cable company should be able to deliver at least the minimum speed it advertises.

✔ Cable modems, because they are constantly connected to the Internet, are an attractive target for malicious hackers. Don't even think about using a cable modem without a *hardware firewall* (often built in to a router) or a *software firewall,* or both. A firewall is a system, either hardware or software, designed to prevent unauthorized access to your system from external sources. And make sure that you install and keep current a capable antivirus program.

DSL modems

I have previously described how POTS is limited to about 56,000 bps, or a bit less depending on the age or capabilities of the phone company's components between your home or office and its destinations. But an alternative, a system called *Digital Subscriber Line (DSL),* that is typically capable of speeds of downloads as fast as 1.5 mbps in residential settings; that is about six or seven times as fast as you'll receive with a dial-up modem but still only a fraction of the potential speed of a cable modem. Premium-service DSL offerings promise download speeds of as much as 5 mbps. (Your results may vary, faster or slower, depending on the quality of the wire in your area, the distance to the central office, and other factors.)

DSL takes advantage of the fact that POTS uses only a small slice of the available frequency range of copper wiring, sending analog voice signals in the range from 0–4 kHz; that narrow band works well over long distances. (The fact that POTS uses such a narrow band to carry voices is the reason phone conversations sound relatively thin or tinny compared to face-to-face or FM radio.) Standard dial-up modems modulate their signal into the same 4 kHz-wide band. The advanced engineering behind DSL sends its signals in a fatter (and higher) section of bandwidth on the copper wire, between 25 kHz and 1 MHz.

The advantages of DSL include the fact that the connection between the home/office and the phone company's switching center is not shared by other users; the speed you receive when your connection is installed should not go down and could possibly go up if the phone company improves its facilities. Another advantage is that users can continue to use their telephone line for standard telephone conversations, removing the need for a separate phone line for dial-up Internet service.

On the downside, though, DSL may not be available in areas where the POTS is very old. And the farther your home or office is from the phone company's central office, the higher the likelihood that DSL service may be slower or unreliable. (In most instances, you want to be no farther than one or two miles from the central office; that's probably not a problem in an urban setting, but out in the country the nearest phone company facility may be much more distant.)

And, just as I warned about cable modem providers, you need to make a judgment about the quality of customer service you expect from your phone company. If they don't deliver decent quality and reliable POTS, don't expect them to be able to make you happy with higher-tech DSL.

You may receive a free loan of a DSL modem when you contract with a phone company for the service or you may be required to rent one from the company; it may be cheaper to buy your own DSL modem, although the phone company may decline to offer support for something it did not provide.

Pitting Internal versus External Connections

Dial-up modems are often offered as internal devices on laptops, built directly into the motherboard as a *Winmodem* (a scheme that uses the CPU for some of the functions of the device, sometimes also called a *soft modem*) or installed in a mini-PCI slot in the case. Another option for internal installation is the use of a PC Card slot. The other option for dial-up modems is as an external device, attached to a serial port or a USB port. (More on USB in Chapter 16.)

Cable and DSL modems are almost always part of a desktop installation and therefore are external devices.

 Whatever the design for your modem, the use of a router generally permits sharing a connection amongst more than one laptop or computer. Sharing a dial-up modem is likely to be less satisfactory than using the greater speed and capacity of a broadband device such as a cable or DSL modem.

On a desktop machine, I usually recommend use of an external device for several reasons:

- ✔ They offer LEDs and other indicators that tell you the link status.
- ✔ They can be turned on or off independently of the computer itself.
- ✔ They can be easily replaced if they fail, a much simpler task than dealing with an internal part.

Laptop users *can* have it both ways, using a tiny internal modem plugged in to the PC Card slot, a mini-PCI slot, or a miniature device attached to the USB port. The least attractive option for laptop users is to work with a full-sized modem that requires a serial cable.

Troubleshooting an external dial-up telephone modem

An advantage of an external modem is the ability to isolate it from the computer itself for testing. To do so, start by checking the modem itself.

Is it plugged in to a power source and turned on?

The source of power may be an AC adapter or a USB port. When power is applied, do the modem LEDs or other indicators illuminate? Are any flashing or otherwise giving you a report on a built-in self-test for the device?

Is the cable from the modem to the laptop properly connected at both ends?

Older modems typically attach to the serial port on a laptop; newer models generally use the USB port or install in a PC Card slot. Check for crimps, cuts, or damage to pins. Make sure the cable is squarely attached so that all pins make contact.

Don't assume that a cable will last forever. They can die a thousand deaths: stretched to the point where wires break or pull out of their internal connectors; broken or thinned by repeated heating and cooling, or burned through by a radiator; made fragile by direct exposure to sunlight; or pinched and shorted out by the weight of desks, chairs, computers, and other devices.

If you have any doubt about the quality or serviceability of an external cable, try substituting a known-good replacement.

Is the device properly connected to a working telephone jack?

Test a conventional dial-up modem by plugging in a known-good standard telephone to the socket and see if you receive a dial tone. While you're at it, try dialing the number to reach your ISP; you should hear the beeps and squeals of the modem at the other end of the line trying to communicate with your laptop. If the phone line is dead, then you know you've got something to discuss with the telephone company and not a problem with either your modem or your laptop.

If your incoming phone line seems to be dead, you can find out if the problem is within your home or office by locating the phone company's network interface. This is usually a small gray or black box at the point where the phone cable comes in from the pole or an underground vault. Your phone company should be able to assist you in locating it and instructing you on how to open the box and plug a working telephone into the home or office side of the connection; if no signal is there, then you know the problem belongs to the phone company.

On the other hand, if your phone works at the network interface, that tells you something is wrong with the internal wiring of your home or office. That problem belongs to you to fix or to hire someone to troubleshoot. If the problem is on your side, you may be able to save yourself the not-inconsiderable cost of a visit by an electrician or a telephone technician by disconnecting every phone device in your home or office. (Devices include phones, fax machines, answering machines, and possibly burglar, fire, and other types of alarms.)

Connect a simple phone to the jack nearest the interface; if you have a dial tone, bring that same phone to each and every jack to try them. If you find a dead jack, you may have located a problem with that jack or the wiring that leads to it; a short in either could, in certain circumstances, add a hum to the line or bring down the entire system.

If all of the jacks are live, you can then reconnect each of the various devices. Check each one for a dial tone and other functions before moving on to the next. You may find that reconnecting one device may add a hum or shut down the system because of a short in its cable, an internal short, or a failure of an electronic circuit within.

Certain wireless phone systems are susceptible to interference. You might be amazed to find out all of the various sources of radio frequency (RF) energy in a home or office. They include things like microwave ovens, garage door openers, a neighbor's wireless phone system, television sets, and nearby antennae for radio and television stations and government and military installations. You may be able to obtain devices that are more resistant to outside interference or find other places to install your phone systems.

Certain advanced features offered by phone companies can cause dropped connections for dial-up modems. Principal among these is call waiting; some modems are unable to deal with the tone that is sent to indicate another incoming call. More advanced modems can be instructed to ignore momentary breaks in the data stream. (You can also temporarily turn off call waiting; consult your phone company for instructions. You may be able to add one-time disabling each time you initiate use of your dial-up modem.)

Sometimes even what appears to be a properly functioning telephone jack may cause some problems because of *reversed polarity;* a standard telephone may work, but the modem may become confused. If you suspect this, you can purchase an inexpensive telephone polarity tester from Radio Shack or other electronic parts suppliers. If you find reversed polarity, the solution is to remove the phone jack from the wall and swap the connection points of the red and green wires (for line 1) or the yellow and black wires (for line 2).

Is the problem with the port built in to the laptop itself?

There could be an electrical problem, or a conflict of system resources. Using current versions of Windows, the easiest way to check for this is to go to Control Panel⇨System icon⇨System Properties⇨Hardware tab⇨Device Manager. Check the Ports (COM & LPT) and the Universal Serial Bus controllers in search of conflicts and use the troubleshooting tool to attempt to fix them. Ports are used by POTS, DSL, and cable modems, so a failure here can knock out any external communication device.

Troubleshooting an internal dial-up telephone modem

As I've noted, there are three types of internal modems. Each comes with its own trials and tribulations:

- ✔ Built-in to the motherboard or attached directly to it on a mini circuit board. These are the most difficult to get to, requiring the nearly complete disassembly of the laptop case, and they may be impossible to repair or replace. After you have satisfied yourself that this problem is not with a device driver or system resources, work around the failed hardware by attaching an external modem to the USB port or a PC Card slot.

- ✔ Installed into a special access slot on the bottom of the laptop case. This connection is sometimes called a *mini-PCI slot* and should work with any brand of device designed to its specifications. These tiny circuit boards are easy to get at; it usually requires removal of a single small screw to open an access panel. If you are convinced the problem is not due to a problem with a device driver or with system resources, proceed with the assumption that the hardware itself has failed. You can choose to replace the tiny circuit board or work around the problem by attaching an external modem to the USB port or a PC Card slot.

✔ Plugged in to a PC Card slot. These cards are pretty sturdy. If convinced the problem is not caused by a bad device driver or a resource conflict, see if you can borrow a known-good replacement from a friend, acquaintance, or computer store to test your system. If the substitute card works, you know the original device is the problem. Otherwise, you can work around the problem by attaching an external modem to the USB port.

Troubleshooting the software for dial-up telephone modems

Regardless of whether you are using an internal modem or an external device, your telecommunications software must be properly configured to recognize its presence and to agree on a set of protocols for use. Happily, nearly every modern modem comes with a self-installing program on CD or floppy disk, or is set up to work with plug-and-play features of current versions of Microsoft Windows.

For example, if the modem is connected to a USB port but the software is looking for it on COM1 (a standard serial port), you may be unable to bring the two together without adjusting the settings. Use the same procedure I suggested to check the ports (but instead expand the Modems section) to see if the laptop is reporting any problems with the modem itself. This is especially relevant for internal modems, but a Plug and Play modem should also be able to communicate the presence of problems back to the Windows system.

When you visit the modem's properties page, see if Windows is reporting any problems with the device driver; check the modem maker's web site for a more current version of the driver, and download and install it if recommended.

Certain software settings can result in dropped calls; in addition to being unable to deal with call waiting, some modems are impatient about slow negotiation with another device. Examine your modem's software and look for a Properties tab that may offer an option something along this line: "Cancel the call if not connected within *xx* seconds." Add 15 seconds to the number and see if the problem is fixed; you can experiment with a few longer settings or even turn off the cancellation option.

And finally, don't blame me . . . or the modem maker . . . if a supposed 56K device never quite reaches that speed. In a reasonably up-to-date phone system you can hope to communicate somewhere in the range of about 40,000–56,000 bps; in the boondocks (or in a city with antiquated equipment) you may be limited to about 32,000 bps. And even if your local system is state of the art, if calling to a modem in a place that is less up to date, communication speed cannot be any faster than the slowest link in the chain.

You can also ask your local telephone company to test the quality of your line and to report on what it estimates to be its top dial-up speed. But remember that this has nothing to do with the speed of any link that exists on the other side of your local phone company's central office, and you can expect them to attempt to sell you DSL service.

Troubleshooting a cable or DSL modem

If you are using a cable modem, check to see if any attached television is still able to receive the latest poop on Erica, Bianca, and Babe on *All My Children* and can also tune in to *SportsCenter* for updates on the other soap opera I follow, the Boston Red Sox. In other words, if the television is not receiving a useable signal, chances are you're not going to receive an Internet connection.

However, the fact that the video feed is working does not rule out the possibility of problems with the cable company's Internet signal. Your best bet here is to call your cable company (Comcast, Cox, and Cablevision are among the largest providers) and find out if there are any systemwide outages. This raises the problem that comes from putting all of your technological eggs in one basket: If your cable provides Internet, you cannot go to a web site to check on system status, and if your cable also delivers telephone service, you may be unable to use an attached phone to reach customer service.

Just for your information, in my home and office I use cable for Internet and while in the process of writing this book I cut the cord to the telephone company and added VOIP phone service. *But I also maintain a cell phone from a different provider.* So, in theory, I have at least three ways to maintain contact with the outside world: Internet over the cable, telephone over the Internet, and a wireless cell phone.

Although you can experiment with a number of settings under Windows, your best bet is to take advantage of the fact that you are a subscriber to a service. Call your cable company for a cable modem, or your phone company or an independent broadband Internet supplier for a DSL modem. Enlist the assistance of their support staff. In many instances, cable companies and DSL providers provide modems. (They may be included in the service fee or rented on a monthly basis.) If you suspect a hardware failure, you have every right to insist on a replacement.

Soon after my first cable modem was installed I decided that I was dissatisfied with uneven speeds — the download speed seemed to vary minute by minute. After I called to discuss the issue with the cable company, they offered to swap one brand of DOCSIS modem for another; within five minutes of the changeover, it was obvious that the problem had been fixed. I never found out (and it didn't really matter) whether the original modem had been faulty or somehow not fully compatible with the incoming cable signal in my office or my own computer setup.

And now, four years later, as I upgraded my office to include a telephone adapter for voice over Internet phone service, I found decreasing download speeds and experienced some dropouts on the new phone service. I called the cable company, and it brought me a third-generation cable modem, and now I am communicating by keyboard and telephone at top speed. (For the record, as I write this paragraph I am receiving an astounding 3,911 kbps in download speed, something on the order of 100 times faster than a dial-up modem. That's a good thing.)

Chapter 16

Breaking Out of the Box: PC Cards, USB, and FireWire

*T*he beauty of a laptop, of course, lies in its compactness and portability. Here's a case where small is definitely better than large. But as I've already discussed, petite avoirdupois generally comes at the price of limited access to the internals. (In other words, it's difficult to gain access to the inside of a little box.)

Unlike desktop and tower PCs, laptops do not include extra internal bays to hold additional hard drives, CD or DVD drives, or other devices. And although laptop motherboards are similar to those used in desktop machines, they do not offer rows of slots designed to accommodate plug-in adapters or cards to add new features.

Both laptops and desktops share the ability to communicate with external devices that plug in to small ports. The most common of these connections are called *serial* and *parallel ports,* and they are useful for the relatively easy demands of devices such as modems, printers, and pointing devices.

This was the bad news for the first few generations of laptops: what you bought from the manufacturer is what you would have for the life of the machine, with just a few areas for expansion, such as adding more memory. The next step in the evolution of laptops put some storage devices such as hard drives and CD or DVD drives into pockets in the casing of the computer, allowing them to be removed for upgrading. (Almost all of these bays used a proprietary design for the drive hardware, meaning that an assembly for an IBM ThinkPad could not be used on a Dell Inspiron. And this near monopoly also limited the availability of devices and boosted their prices.)

Taking a Detour on a Two-Lane Road

Within the electronic brain of your computer, data moves along from place to place on an 8-, 16-, or 32-lane expressway that is somewhat confusingly called a *bus* (or data path). There's plenty of open roadway, and access is limited to well-managed on- and off ramps.

Information in the computer is made up of words that bring together groups of *bits* (binary digits). The original personal computers used words made of eight bits; a package of data of that size is called a *byte*. Modern PCs and laptops move words made up of 16 bits, or 2 bytes, from point to point on the internal bus. (And just for the record, current versions of Intel and AMD microprocessors juggle words of 32 and even 64 bits internally.)

Let me get back to the automotive metaphor: Think of a 16-bit computer word moving from the microprocessor to the video display adapter as a convoy. On the motherboard, these 16 bits move alongside each other on tiny wires; they depart at the same time and arrive at their destination at the same time (give or take a few millionths of a second here and there). The words move along to the drumbeat of a computer's clock. In computing terms, this is called a *parallel* circuit.

You might think that a parallel circuit would be a very fast and efficient way to move large amounts of data from one place to another, and in most instances you would be right. The first few generations of PCs used thick parallel cables with bundles of 25 or so wires (8 wires for a one-byte word of data outgoing, 8 wires for a one-byte incoming word, plus additional lines for grounding and specialized signals) to communicate with devices like printers.

But when it came to other forms of communication, like using a modem to venture out onto a telephone line to reach the Internet, a parallel pathway would not work because in many ways the phone system of the 21st century is little changed from Thomas Edison's original design: two wires, one in each direction. (Take a look at the connector for the phone on your desk. For a single-line phone there's one red and one green wire; a two-line phone adds a yellow and black pair.)

And so (back to automotive imagery one last time, I promise) the parallel superhighway that exists within a computer has to suddenly squeeze all of its traffic into a single lane in each direction for what is called *serial* communication. The computer's 8- or 16-bit words have to line up one behind the other instead of alongside each other. And slowing things down just a little bit more, the computer has to find a way to mark the beginning and end of each word. It does so by adding a start and a stop bit, and just for good measure most systems also add some form of error checking that allows the computer to reject a word that seems to have a misspelling.

The most rudimentary form of error checking adds a bit that declares that the sum of the bits in a particular word is either even or odd; at the receiving end the word is summed again. This scheme works well enough if one of the bits is garbled along the way. If more than one bit changes from a 0 to a 1, the word's evenness or oddness may not change.

So it would seem obvious that a parallel pathway is much, much faster than a serial road, and that is absolutely true when it comes to short distance commuting from device to device on the motherboard. But as computers have become faster and faster and move larger and larger amounts of data, parallel circuits run into problems of physics.

Remember that I said that the 8- or 16-bit words arrive at their destination *more or less at the same time?* The fact is that over distance and under the pressure of fast clock speeds, tiny imperfections in the wires of a parallel bus or cable cause some of the bits to arrive just a tiny sliver of time behind the others. Engineers call this *skew,* and the more it occurs, the more words are rejected. When a word is rejected, it must be re-sent; this data backup can significantly slow the transmission speed; when there is a problem, a word is sent, checked, rejected, requested again, sent, and checked. There's also the risk of interference between the lines. Either way, the result is a massive bottleneck on westbound I-95 at the tollbooth. (Oops, I snuck one more automotive metaphor into the chapter — couldn't be helped.)

Serial ports don't have the problem of timing arrival of computer words, and interference between two wires is much more easily controlled. For the first decade and a half of the PC, parallel and serial ports coexisted on desktops and laptops; neither was fast enough, but between the two designs you could attach a printer and a modem and get by. (More on modems in Chapter 15.)

But even if you could get a serial port to communicate with an external device (not always as simple as you might like because of various standards for word length, start and stop bits, error checking, and other overhead), there was this major land mine: Each serial port in a computer needed to lay claim to a particular set of interrupts (IRQ), memory (DMA) channels, and memory resources. If you wanted to attach four devices to a computer through serial ports, it was theoretically possible to do so, but the chances of running into a conflict of one sort or another was very high.

Certain devices are much more demanding of system resources than others, sound cards and network cards among them.

Happily, though, while early PC and laptop users tried to sort all of this out by themselves, engineers were hard at work on other means for computers to communicate including broadband (cable and DSL phone connections) and WiFi. And although early computers and laptops could be cajoled into poky

The first solution was the introduction of PC Cards (which when introduced were called by the unmemorable name PCMCIA Cards and then the slightly less forgettable CardBus). *PC Cards* allow extension of the computer's internal bus to a new device; these tightly packed credit card-sized cards plug in to sockets in the side of a laptop.

Today PC Cards are used for communication devices including modems, network interface cards (NICs), and WiFi cards. You can also purchase flash memory cards with capacities of a few gigabytes (see Chapter 7) and tiny hard drives.

But the biggest breakthrough for input and output on modern computers and especially laptops was the development of the *Universal Serial Bus (USB),* which pumped up the old serial concept to amazing speeds and allows use of a wide range of external devices at speeds little different from those connected internally.

Although it has not caught on to the same extent as USB, FireWire is another modern high-speed serial standard. FireWire is more commonly used in the Mac world.

Picking a card, any PC Card

PC Cards attach to 68-pin sockets that branch off a computer's internal PCI bus, mini versions of the slots within a desktop computer.

Modern laptops have one or two PC Card sockets and accept 16- or 32-bit cards; you'll be hard pressed to find any of the slower cards on the market. If you have a choice, don't work with a slower card instead of a faster one. PC

PCMCIAs are wild

When PCMCIA Cards were first introduced they were limited to 16-bit data paths; the later CardBus standard expanded the path to 32 bits. (Think of a bus as a superhighway carrying 0s and 1s of information; a 32-bit path is twice as wide and potentially twice as efficient in delivering data as a 16-bit channel. CardBus devices also run at a faster bus speed. The original PCMCIA was capable of a slow throughput of about 20 MBps at a bus speed of 10 MHz, devouring 5 volts of power in doing so; CardBus devices worked at a bus speed of 33 MHz and deliver about 133 MBps of data, consuming just 3.3 volts.)

Cards also come in several thicknesses, which are meaningful only because a slightly thicker card can hold more circuitry than a thinner one.

The most common card designs follow:

✔ **Type I.** A 3.3mm-thick card, often used for RAM, flash memory, and other simple devices.

✔ **Type II.** A 5mm-thick card, used for more complex devices such as NIC and WiFi cards. You can even buy a tiny hard drive that fits in this slot. Type II slots can also accept thinner Type I cards.

The PC Card specification was also intended to allow for two other forms:

✔ **Type III.** A 10.5mm-thick card originally intended for use with removable hard drives.

✔ **Type IV.** Not widely used, this design could accommodate thicker, more complex, or multipurpose cards with more than one function.

Newer and improved! USB 2.0

Limits don't last long in a hot high-tech market, and one of the most useful barrier busters is the Universal Serial Bus. The USB opened up laptops (and desktops) to almost limitless expansion that works from the outside in.

A modern laptop that includes a USB port (especially one that complies with USB 2.0 or a later version of the standard) can easily work with small external hard drives, CD or DVD drives, modems, network interfaces, wireless adapters, audio cards, specialized video capture and output devices — just about any expansion that can be applied to a PC of any size. USB was introduced in 1996, and the considerably faster 2.0 version arrived in 2001.

Here's the skinny on USB 2.0:

✔ If your laptop has it, use it.

✔ If your laptop doesn't have it, add it.

✔ If your laptop offers the older, slower USB 1.1, upgrade to USB 2.0.

The numbers tell the story: USB 2.0 is capable of moving data at a top speed of 480 Mbps, with a promise of even faster speed in future versions. And it gets better: A laptop (or a desktop) can connect as many as 127 devices in a single *chain.* Best of all, each USB port used a single set of interrupts, *direct memory access (DMA),* and memory resources no matter how many devices are attached. DMA is a way to bypass the microprocessor when it is necessary to transfer data from one location in memory to another.

USB uses a four-wire cable. Two wires handle data transmission, a third carries five volts of power to peripherals, and the fourth is an electrical ground. Data is sent in serial form, but USB is closer in technology to an Ethernet network or the Internet in the way information is gathered into packets; in addition to start and stop bits that identify the computer words, the *packets* include a destination and return address. This is key to the way that an entire chain of devices links to a single USB port.

Under USB, the computer takes an active role in the management of the port. This begins when the system identifies all devices attached at bootup or plugged in later; the computer manages how much of the pipeline it assigns to each device depending on their need for speed. For example, hard drives and CD or DVD drives need a bigger pipe, while keyboards and mice make minimal demands on the system. Every time a device is added to the bus or removed, the computer reconfigures bandwidth allocation and adjusts identification codes used to label packets of data.

USB devices are *hot swappable,* meaning they can be plugged in to a laptop that is already running, or removed without shutting down the system. And the icing on the cake: Support for the USB is fully integrated into current versions of Microsoft Windows (Windows 98SE, 2000, ME, and XP) so that you can *plug and play.* The first time a new device is plugged into a laptop, the system will search for necessary drivers and other software; if it finds what it needs already on the computer, you're good to go. If not, you're asked to direct the laptop to the location of any needed drivers or software — on a CD, a floppy disk, or at an Internet address.

The USB standard provides electrical current along with data channels. The power is sufficient for many devices such as WiFi, modems, and NICs. But you'll likely have to provide power from an AC adapter for devices with motors, including hard drives and CD/DVD players and recorders.

The data side of the USB chain can be split off many times, allowing as many as 127 devices to connect to a single port. However, each of the devices on the chain is also sharing the same low-power electrical feed. I recommend you use a *powered* hub once a port is split into more than four lines. Powered hubs use an AC adapter to boost the electrical amperage to a sufficient level for multiple devices. And, some USB devices require their own power source, especially hard drives and CD/DVD drives with motors.

Although you may not contemplate adding 127 devices to your laptop — after all, the idea is to get smaller and more compact — it is important to understand that USB does allow you to replicate all of the functions of a full-sized computer while at your desk and then take just the core laptop when you are on the road.

Down to the FireWire

The fastest wired communication standards on consumer-grade laptops are FireWire and USB 2.0, which are capable of transmitting data as much as 3,500 to 4,000 times faster than an original standard serial port. The accompanying table shows the comparison.

FireWire versus USB 2.0

Port	Typical Speed	Speed Index
Standard serial port	115 Kbps	1
Standard parallel port	115 KBps	8
USB 1.1	12 Mbps	104
ECP/EPP parallel port	16–24 Mbps	133–200
IEEE 1394/FireWire	400 Mbps	3,478
USB 2.0	480 Mbps	4,174

The arrival of high-speed USB allows laptops to have direct communication with devices including digital cameras, external hard drives, and CD and DVD drives (which are very demanding of bandwidth).

The first iteration of the standard, USB 1.0, is not quite as zippy — only 12 Mbps — but is sufficient for some uses. A USB 1.0 device (or one that follows the slightly improved 1.1 specification) will work in a USB 2.0 port, although it stays at its original speed.

Usbing a USB port

Most laptops offer two USB ports, and devices can be directly plugged in to either. (It doesn't matter which one you use; the computer sorts out all of the details for you.) If you need to attach more USB devices than your laptop has ports for, you can add a *hub* to split the port into additional connectors. A typical hub plugs in to the laptop at one end and offers four ports of its own.

If a USB device does not work or shows erratic performance, it may not be receiving enough power. If it can be operated with an AC adapter, try that. Or try operating it directly from the port on the laptop or from a powered hub.

When USB was first introduced, it was expected that some components, such as external keyboards, would extend the chain with a built-in port; users have not seen many devices with that sort of facility.

Adding a USB 2.0 port to an older laptop

If your laptop is an older model that does not have any USB ports, you should be able to add two or four USB 2.0 ports by making use of a PC Card adapter. You must be running a version of Windows that supports USB (Windows 98SE, ME, 2000, or XP) and the laptop needs to be powered by a Pentium or equivalent processor (including Intel Celeron and AMD CPUs). Installation is very simple; follow the manufacturer's advice in adding necessary drivers and other software.

If your machine is so old that it doesn't have a PC Card slot, you're out of luck; there is no other access to the laptop's motherboard bus and no way to convert a standard serial port to USB.

Upgrading a USB 1.0 port to 2.0

If your laptop comes with USB 1.0 or 1.1 ports, you can use most USB devices at the slower speed of the original specification; this is acceptable for some uses such as modems, printers, NICs, and WiFi adapters. However, the slow speed of the original USB is barely adequate for use with hard drives and probably unacceptable with CD and DVD drives.

But, as with a laptop that does not include any USB ports, you can get around the problem by using a PC Card that adds two or four USB 2.0 ports. (You'll just ignore the built-in, older ports in favor of the newer ones on the card.)

Devices designed for USB 2.0 are *backward compatible* with the earlier USB 1.1 specification, working at the slower speed. Cables designed for USB 1.1 should perform at USB 2.0 speeds with an advanced port; however, you need a USB 2.0 hub in order to extend high-speed communication.

Going Parallel and Serial: Disappearing Acts

A long, long time ago — at least a couple of years in the ancient past — one of the primary means of communication for desktops and laptops was the parallel port. Today, though, parallel ports, old-fashioned serial ports, and floppy disk drives are pieces missing from modern laptops. If you absolutely insist on having one, you've got to add these as external devices.

Listing to port

So, what was a parallel port, and why has it gone missing?

In early designs of computers, engineers found they could transfer data fast and accurately by creating an eight-lane superhighway and spread an 8-bit computer word so that it moves one bit alongside each other down this parallel set of wires. This was deemed a better design than stacking up the computer words so that one bit ran behind the other with the additional overhead of codes to mark the beginning and end of each word.

But as I explored in this chapter, new technologies have allowed engineers to push bits through a two-wire serial connection at extremely fast rates. Parallel communication paths have reached a point where speed is slowed by tiny imperfections in the wires, resulting in parallel words no longer traveling in perfect perpendicularity to each other. In other words, some of the bits may drag behind the others, slowing down the entire highway.

The original design for a PC parallel port was to send information in one direction and for one purpose: from a computer to a printer. That may have been why it was also called the *printer port.* Another name, *LPT1,* reaches all the way back to mainframe printers, which used to be connected to a line printer, a huge clanking machine that assembled a line's worth of text on a row of rotating wheels and then punch it against a ribbon. Line printers are long gone, but deep within the settings of a modern computer you still see references to a device called an LPT (as well as one called COMM, which is a synonym for an old-style serial port).

As computers and devices became more capable, the parallel port's design was modified slightly to allow movement of data and instructions in both directions; enhanced or bidirectional parallel ports could receive an out-of-paper or out-of-ink signal from a printer.

From there, designers began to come up with more uses for the parallel port, including external hard drive, CD-ROM drives, and modems. But it all came to a screeching halt with the introduction of the high-speed USB port; today there are very few new peripherals that don't make use of either a USB or wired or wireless network connection. (You may still find some devices that offer both a USB and parallel port to maintain compatibility with older computers.)

So, what do you do if you need to connect your new parallel port-less laptop to an older printer? The best solution is adapt a USB port to stack up its serially spaced bits and output them as if they were coming from a parallel adapter.

One such device is Keyspan's appropriately named USB Parallel Printer Transfer Cable. One end plugs in to your laptop's USB port and the other end of the cable into the incoming parallel port on a printer. There's nothing more to do: Plug in both devices and you're back to the future. An alternative is Keyspan's Mini Port Replicator, which attaches to a USB port on your laptop and delivers — in a package smaller than a deck of cards — a serial port, a parallel port, and two USB ports for other devices. You can see both adapters in Figure 16-1.

Figure 16-1:
This pair of plug-and-play external commu-nications devices expand on a laptop's facilities. At left is the Keyspan Mini Port Replicator, and at right the Keyspan USB Parallel Printer Transfer Cable.

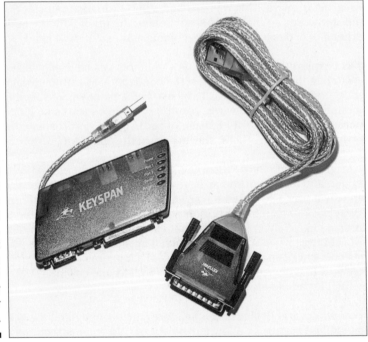

If your machine was delivered without a serial port, or if the built-in port fails, another option is to downshift directly from a USB port to an old-fashioned serial port. An example of a USB Serial Adapter is shown in Figure 16-2. The Keyspan USB Serial Adapter is a plug-and-play device that adds a high-speed serial port — as fast as 230 Kbps (twice the speed of a standard serial port) and a device driver that manages the new hardware.

Figure 16-2:
The Keyspan USB Serial Adapter bridges the gap between a modern laptop with a USB port (or an external hub) and an older peripheral that expects a standard RS-232 serial connection.

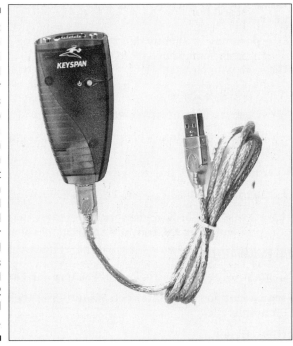

Testing a parallel port

If you are still using a parallel port, or a parallel device that you've managed to connect to a modern laptop, what do you do if the device stops responding? Your first assignment is to determine which of the following is the problem:

✔ The parallel port (or a USB to parallel port converter)

✔ The parallel cable between the computer's port and the printer or other device

✔ The device attached to the parallel cable

If you have an actual parallel port on your laptop, check these things:

1. **Go to the Windows Control Panel.**

   Start by checking within Windows to see if it finds any problem with the hardware or with any device driver associated with it.

2. **Click System icon⇨System Properties⇨Hardware⇨Device Manager.**

3. **Expand the + mark next to Ports (COM & LPT) and then double-click Printer Port Properties.**

   The name of the port may be slightly different depending on its design, and a handful of machines may have more than one port, marked as LPT1 and LPT2.

4. **Check the Device status report.**

   What you hope to see is, "This device is working properly."

5. **Click the Troubleshooting button, which walks you through several test steps.**

6. **Click the Driver tab and check the device driver's health.**

   You may be asked to uninstall and reinstall the printer port driver.

   If Windows reports that the hardware is working properly, make sure that the cause of the problem is not the software application you are using.

7. **Go to Control Panel⇨Printers.**

   On some systems you choose Control Panel⇨Printers and Faxes instead.

8. **You should see an icon for the printer you want to use; click to highlight it and then right-click.**

9. **Click Properties⇨General.**

   There you see a Print Test Page button.

10. **Make sure your printer is plugged in and turned on, and then click the Test button.**

    Watch for any warning lights or messages on the printer. If the printer comes to life and prints a test page, you have established several things:

    • The parallel port is working properly.

    • The cable is okay.

    • The printer is functioning.

    So what else could be wrong? I'd suspect a problem with the software application.

11. **Open your word processor or other program that uses the printer and check all of its settings.**

12. **If you have no success with a test page, turn your attention to the device itself.**

    Does it have any built-in diagnostics? Many printers go through a test routine when they are first turned on, displaying warning lights or a message on a small LCD screen. It is plugged in to a working AC outlet, and the power is turned on, right? The problem could be as simple as a paper jam or lack of paper, ink, or toner.

13. **Try a swap of known-good components.**

    If you have another laptop or a desktop PC with a parallel port, try attaching the suspect printer or other device to it. If it works properly, you have a good indication of a problem with the parallel port on the original machine.

14. **Substitute a known-good cable between the computer and the device.**

    See if normal function returns. If it does, this is an indication that the original cable has failed, possibly because of a crimp in the wiring or a bent pin.

If you are finally convinced that your laptop's parallel port has failed, it probably does not make economic sense to have the motherboard or its connectors repaired. Instead, purchase an inexpensive USB to parallel converter (or a serial to parallel converter) and use either as a workaround.

Where's the FireWire (aka IEEE 1394)?

Although it is all but ubiquitous on laptops, USB is not the only high-speed show in town. A competitive technology is IEEE 1394, also known as FireWire on Apple products and i.Link on some Sony video products. (I call it by its formal techy-spec name, IEEE 1394.)

This specification uses a six-wire cable for computer devices: a pair of wires for data, a second pair for clock signals, and a third pair delivering electrical power. A four-wire version of the cable is for self-powered devices such as camcorders. IEEE 1394 is very close in speed to USB 2.0, delivering 400 Mbps; an advanced specification called 1394b moves data at twice that speed. Future plans call for optical fiber versions at 1,600 and 3,200 Mbps.

You can buy an Apple laptop with FireWire built in, or you can add IEEE 1394 to a Windows machine by plugging in a PC Card that adds a pair of ports. As with USB, you need to be running Windows 98SE or later versions (Windows 2000, ME, and XP).

As with USB, IEEE 1394 breaks up data into packets that include IDs for the sender and receiver. Unlike USB, though, an IEEE 1394 chain is not actively managed by the computer; instead, devices can communicate with each other and divide available bandwidth so that components with high demand can grab a larger segment of the pipe.

Part V
The Software Side of Life

The 5th Wave
By Rich Tennant

"I **AM** pushing, but the 'enter' button seems to be stuck!"

In this part . . .

Without getting too metaphysical here, one of the differences between a human being and a rock is that humans have an operating system. We have some automatic code (breathe in and breathe out, process food to extract energy and necessary chemicals and elements, and strike a regular heartbeat to pump blood to organs). And we have a set of software (genetic predispositions, learned and shared experiences, and formal training). A rock . . . just sits there.

So, too, there is a vast difference between a slab of plastic, silicon, and metal and a box of the same ingredients that is governed by a set of instructions. The spark of "intelligence" given a computer by its human creators begins with an operating system (Microsoft Windows, Linux, or Apple's Macintosh code included) and is extended by specific, repeatable behaviors in the form of software (like a word processor, spreadsheet, or Internet browser).

In this part you look at upgrading your operating system or moving it from one hard drive to another. Then I discuss good software housekeeping, including how to remove unwanted programs and tidy up after them.

Chapter 17

Installing a New Operating System or Migrating Upwards

In This Chapter

▶ Starting anew with Windows XP

▶ Making like a goose and migrating

▶ Recovering nicely

Most of this book is about hardware. Why, it's right there in the title: *Upgrading & Fixing Laptops For Dummies.* Laptops are boxes of hardware, similar to desktops except they are much smaller and fit in a nifty carrying case with zippers and Velcro straps. But as you may have explored already throughout this book, all of that hardware is not of any use without a capable and properly configured operating system and a set of applications that give the hardware things to do.

I need to talk about software in this book about hardware because the operating system and the applications *configure* the hardware to adjust its personality, make *settings* that affect its operation and features, and can even *disable* or *enable* a piece of hardware.

For the purposes of this book, I am going to assume that you are the sort of person who likes to use the latest, greatest, most recently updated versions of operating systems and software. I do this for two reasons: first of all, because you're a with-it, happening kind of guy or gal, and secondly because (with a few exceptions) the most current software and operating systems are *backward compatible.* That means that in addition to offering the new stuff that makes people upgrade, these pieces of programming also retain compatibility with older hardware and applications.

And so, the official operating system of this edition of *Upgrading & Fixing Laptops For Dummies* is Microsoft Windows XP in its similar Home and Professional versions. And just for the record, the core of my software is made up of the various pieces of Microsoft Office (including Word, Excel, Outlook, and PowerPoint), the Microsoft Internet Explorer web browser. My armamentarium of utilities includes Symantec products Norton SystemWorks

(Norton Utilities, Norton AntiVirus, Norton CleanSweep, and Norton Password Manager.) I also make regular use of Diskeeper from Diskeeper Corporation and Dragon Naturally Speaking from Scansoft. I describe most of these in more detail in The Part of Tens later in this book.

But first I'm going to take you through upgrading your Windows operating system on an existing hard drive, or on a new hard drive that is installed internally or externally to your laptop.

 A laptop built to run Microsoft Windows or another PCcentric operating system, such as one of the various flavors of Linux, is very similar to one built to run the Apple Macintosh operating system with the exception of the microprocessor and the chipset on the motherboard. (And Mac owners can even run software like Virtual PC, which runs Microsoft Windows *within* the Macintosh operating system.) Macintosh laptop owners can use this book for all of the hardware side of the equation: hard drives, USB ports, wireless communication, networks, and LCDs. And in 2005, Apple announced it would switch to Intel as the source of its microprocessors beginning in mid-2006, with all models based on Intel CPUs by the end of 2007, which will make interoperability with PC hardware and software even easier.

Seeing a Windows XP Installation

Before you consider installing Microsoft's latest operating system be sure that your laptop is up to the task. Some say latest and greatest, while others have a slight difference of opinion, but like Paul Simon wrote, I'm all right with it in a sort of a limited way for an off night.

Microsoft's official requirements for Windows XP Home Edition follow:

- A PC with at least a 233 MHz processor, although 300 MHz is recommended. The operating system will work with processor in the Intel Pentium and Celeron families as well as AMD's K6, Athlon, and Duron classes.

- A minimum of 64MB of RAM, with at least 128MB recommended. Using just 64MB may result in slowdowns and a loss of some advanced features.

- At least 1.5GB of available space on a hard drive for installation and operation.

- A video adapter capable of displaying Super VGA (800×600) or greater, and an operational LCD or monitor.

- A CD-ROM or DVD drive to load the operating system.

- A functioning keyboard and mouse or other pointing device.

Before you begin upgrading, it is worthwhile to visit the support web site for your laptop manufacturer to look for an available BIOS upgrade intended to support Windows XP. If you install Windows XP and then later update the BIOS, you may have to reinstall the operating system to make use of certain features. Chapter 6 talks about BIOS in depth.

And you should also make certain that any applications you intend to re-install on the new disk will work with Windows XP; not all work properly and some refuse to work at all. Microsoft offers a software download that you can run to gauge your machine's capabilities and check installed applications against an official list of programs known to work properly with XP. To obtain the program, go to www.microsoft.com and search to find the Windows XP Upgrade Advisor. You can also go to another Microsoft web page to search the Windows Catalog for each of the applications you intend to install. Look for the catalog at www.microsoft.com/windowsxp/home/upgrading/compat. mspx or use the search bar at www.microsoft.com.

Making a fresh start or a great migration

My trusty old Gateway Solo 2500 SE laptop's 4GB hard drive had become way too small for its current use. The machine was perfectly acceptable as an extension of my writing desk: Running Windows 98SE and Microsoft's Office suite, I could work in Microsoft Word and Excel and surf the net using Internet Explorer 6.0 at speeds little different from the machine on my desktop. Over the years I had adapted the machine with more RAM and had added a WiFi PC Card and USB Ethernet interface, which permitted me to connect to the Internet in most situations. (More on PC Cards and USB in Chapter 16, if you're interested.)

In addition to the operating system and Microsoft Office applications, I also ran Norton SystemWorks for maintenance and antivirus protection. Also on the drive were Adobe Photoshop and the ACDSee image database system. I kept a copy of AOL 9.0 as a backup Internet access route; it could be asked to use a dial-up modem (installed in a PC Card slot or as a USB device) and could also jump into the fray once a broadband or WiFi connection had been established.

All told, about 1.5GB of my available 4GB was occupied before I added any data to the system. For a quick trip down to a research library or a weekend writing jaunt, that represented more than enough room.

But I also had come to depend on the laptop as the traveling repository for digital photographs taken with my 5MP camera. The basic format for images from that camera, at highest resolution, results in files of about 3.5MB for each picture in the compressed JPEG format and as much as 15MB for pictures shot at highest resolution and stored as a TIFF. If I resize an image for publication or printing at an 8×10-inch format, a single image can demand something like 22,355,878 bytes. For purposes of this book, all you really need to know is this: Digital images at their highest resolution require a great deal of space.

This is, by definition, fuzzy math because file sizes can vary based on resolution, whether they are color or black and white, storage file extension, and the complexity of the image itself (a picture half filled with an unvarying Cerulean blue sky requires a bit less space than a picture of a grandstand full of baseball fans with infinite variations in detail per seat).

Anyhow, at 22,355,878 bytes (which translates into about 21.32MB) I could hold about 120 images on the available 2.5GB of space on my drive. If I chose to use the compressed and compressible JPEG format, I could hold about 700 images. On a three-week extravagant trip to Australia and New Zealand, I started running out of space during the second week. The original hard drive was a Toshiba model with two platters and four data heads and an official capacity of 4.32GB. Built in to the 8.5mm-high drive is a minimal 512KB buffer. The drive's heads were rated at a 13ms average seek time (a minimum of 3ms and maximum of 25ms) and a 33.3MBps data maximum transfer rate.

I worked with BiX Computers (www.bixnet.com) to choose a replacement drive. They recommended installing a new 40GB drive (also from Toshiba) that would boost storage space tenfold, greatly improve the buffer size, and improve overall speed of access and transfer in several areas.

The Toshiba MK4025GAS is able to squeeze an astounding 64.8Gb of data per square inch, allowing 40.007GB of storage on a single double-sided platter. The drive includes an 8MB buffer, about 16 times more capacious than the one it replaced. The drive's heads are rated at a 12ms average seek time (a minimum of 2ms and maximum of 22ms) and is capable — in a state-of-the-art laptop with an ATA-6 interface — of a 100MBps data maximum transfer rate.

If you are installing a new drive to replace a failed and irreparable hard drive, or if you are upgrading a machine and have no need to hold on to any previous work, the cleanest way to do the job is to install the operating system from a distribution disk and reinstall applications. In doing so you do not have to worry about keeping fragments of old or updated programs, bad links, temporary files, and other electronic detritus.

I had two choices. I'll call them The Fresh Start or The Great Migration options.

Techies sometimes call the fresh start a *clean install*. It means that you do not have to deal with any of the leftover pieces of the old system or applications; they come onto the drive after the operating system is in place. A migration process involves *cloning* the old the drive to another location and then copying it back, warts and all, onto a new piece of hardware.

Belts plus suspenders

If you are installing a new hard drive to replace the factory original, you may want to create a Utility partition on the drive before adding the operating system and basic applications. In doing so you replicate the protective measures taken by the manufacturer that permits you to easily revert to the default setup for the machine. In most cases you can accomplish this by using the original system formatting and operating system installation disk supplied with the machine at the time of purchase. It should work with any new compatible drive, even if it is from another hard drive maker or is of a much larger size than the original. You will likely have to activate your installation of the operating system using the Product ID code (found on the installation disk or a sticker attached to the notebook itself).

Starting fresh on an old drive

You begin the Fresh Start upgrade with the old drive still in place:

1. **Make a backup of all data and important settings.**

   You can copy this information over an Ethernet to a hard drive on another machine, copy it to a CD-R, or (if you have no choice) use a stack of floppy drives to offload the information.

   If your machine is connected to a network and at least one of the machines is running Windows XP Home or Professional, you can use a utility that is part of the operating system. The Files and Settings Transfer Wizard collects, just like it seems to promise, files and settings from applications on one machine and stores them in a file that can be retrieved and used by a newly installed version of Windows XP.

2. **Gather your original copies of applications — word processors, spreadsheets, graphics, audio programs, and utilities — and decide on a reinstallation sequence.**

   Be sure to check that each is compatible with Windows XP. In some cases, the programs have to be updated with fresh patches from the manufacturer's web site once installed; in other cases a program that worked perfectly well under Windows 95 or 98 may not do its tricks with the latest operating system.

3. **Disconnect the AC power adapter and remove the battery from the laptop.**

4. **Remove the old drive from the laptop and take it out of its holding case. Set it aside on a soft and nonconductive surface.**

5. **Install the new drive into the holding case, taking care to mate it with any plug adapters and lining it up with the same screws used for the former drive.**

6. **Slide the new drive into place and attach it in its bay.**

7. **Return the battery to its slot and reattach the AC adapter.**

It is not a good idea to perform a major operation like installing an operating system using battery power; if you run out of juice before the install is fully completed, the entire job may fail.

8. **Turn on the laptop and boot the installation program for the new operating system from the CD drive.**

9. **After Windows XP is installed and up and running, reinstall applications to the new drive.**

In most cases you need to do this from the original installation media. If you are very lucky, all of your old applications work properly with Windows XP, although some may need to be patched for the new operating system, and a few might need to be replaced with completely new versions.

10. **Use the Files and Settings Transfer Wizard to collect the, uh, files and settings from their storage place.**

Installing Windows XP on a blank drive

The simplest installation is what is called a clean install, which is either performed on a completely blank new drive, or on an old drive where all data and the previous operating system have been removed. You don't need to manually remove the former data; all that needs be done is to repartition the disk and reformat it. Of course, before you've done that you have backed up all irreplaceable data to an alternate media — a CD, DVD, Zip disk, a location on a different machine connected by a network, or another method.

The process of partitioning (or *repartitioning* a previously used disk) is explained in instruction manuals for your operating system or the hard drive. You can also find full details on the Microsoft Knowledge Base, reachable through www.microsoft.com. Basically, before you can install an operating system you must create a primary partition (a defined "look here first" place) on the first physical hard drive in your system, and then format that partition. *Formatting* creates an indexing system that can be accessed by the machine to store and retrieve data. When it comes to installing an operating system on a new or erased disk, there's a Catch-22: the system needs to boot itself to life even though the drive is blank. The solution lies in the use of an appropriate startup disk. They include the following:

✔ Microsoft Windows XP CD-ROM

✔ Microsoft Windows 98 or 98SE startup disk

✔ Microsoft Windows Millennium startup disk

✔ Microsoft Windows XP boot disk

The simplest route, of course, is to just pop an XP CD-ROM into your laptop, turn on the power, and let the system boot from the CD and install the operating system. In order for that to happen, though, the BIOS of your laptop has to be set up to permit booting from a CD and configured to check the CD drive for the presence of a bootable disk. Consult the instruction manual for your laptop for instructions on how to adjust settings in the BIOS or System Setup Program. Chapter 6 talks more about BIOS.

What you're looking for is the Boot Sequence or Boot Order. A typical laptop might offer the following options:

✔ Floppy disk (sometimes called *diskette*) drive

✔ Hard drive

✔ Secondary or modular bay hard drive

✔ CD or DVD drive, including CD-R, CD-RW, and writeable DVD drives, and Network boot

For most users, the hard drive is the default boot device. But you can permanently or temporarily change the boot sequence for the purposes of loading an operating system or to get around a failed device.

Access to the BIOS or System Setup Program differs slightly from machine to machine. On current Dell laptops, for example, you display the BIOS by restarting the machine and pressing the F2 button immediately after the Dell logo appears on the screen. If you miss the precise moment, you'll have to wait until Windows fully loads, then shut it down and try again.

If you can boot from the CD drive, then you can begin installing Windows XP by starting the system using one of the permitted CDs outlined earlier.

Microsoft sells three types of operating system installations to consumers:

✔ A new installation for a new drive or system, to be set up and configured by the user

✔ An upgrade from a recent previous version of Windows (sold at a discount from the full price for a new installation), to be set up and configured by the user

✔ An additional license permitting use of an existing copy of Windows XP on additional machines you own or use

A fourth means of distribution of Windows is an *OEM* (original equipment manufacturer) copy that comes preinstalled on a new machine. This version can be used to reinstall the operating system on that computer if necessary, but will not properly install or will fail to register properly with Microsoft if used with a different machine.

If you have purchased an upgrade version of Windows XP, you start by booting from the upgrade disk but soon into the process you are asked to remove the Windows XP CD and insert the CD from your previous operating system for validation purposes. Once Microsoft is satisfied that you are, in fact, upgrading from a previous version, you are asked to remove the old CD and replace it with the new one to continue. At the time this book went to press, Microsoft permitted upgrades from the following older versions: Windows 98, Windows 98SE, Windows ME, Windows NT 4.0, and Windows 2000 Professional.

Your first task is to read and accept the *EULA,* which is not an Hawaiian dance step, but legalese for the end-user license agreement. This is not open to negotiation; you have to accept Microsoft's terms as stated or you can use the CD as a shiny coffee coaster.

The first thing to understand is that Microsoft software is not sold; it is licensed to you for use in certain specified situations. (Microsoft is not alone in making this sort of distinction, but it is the one company that almost every computer user has to deal with in one form or another.) The EULA is a contract between you and Microsoft; if you really don't want to accept its terms, you have to take it up with the retailer or online site that sold you the package . . . err, sold you the license. The EULA's Grant of License section prohibits you from attempting to *reverse engineer* the software. (That means take apart the internal code to figure out how it works and make your own version.) It also restricts leasing or renting the software to someone else.

If you purchase a fresh consumer copy of Windows XP for installation on a new hard drive or computer, certain versions may include permission to make a second copy of the operating system for the owner's exclusive use on a laptop. (The well-intentioned reason for this sort of exception was that a single user would not be using his or her desktop machine at the same time as a portable machine, and therefore only one copy of the operating system would be in use at one time.) The original copy has to be on the local hard drive of the desktop machine and not on a network server. Microsoft, though, has been back pedaling away from this sort of additional use in recent years. Be sure to read the EULA carefully. If the license does not include this right, consult the www.microsoft.com web site and search for How to Order Additional Licenses for Windows XP.

If you have received a copy of Windows preinstalled by the OEM, in most cases the EULA is very specific: The copy is attached to the machine and cannot be additionally installed on another machine or transferred to another computer or another user. Even if you remove the software from that computer or decommission it to the landfill, OEM software is usually inextricably linked to the original machine.

If your copy of Windows was supplied to a large business or institution (including some government and educational organizations), the EULA may allow transfer of the operating system to other computers and allow installation or upgrade over a network.

And things reach another level of complexity if you upgrade an older version of Windows to a current edition. Your EULA for the upgrade version specifies that you cannot sell or give away your old operating system disks; the original product and the upgrade product are considered a single unit. I doubt that the secret police are going to come to check the dusty shelves of your closet for old copies of Windows; they are much too busy checking to make sure that scofflaws have not cut the product tags off pillows. However: You may find that someday down the line Microsoft will once again ask you to prove you still own the original disk as part of a future upgrade to your upgrade.

Basic Windows XP installation

In the easiest situations, you can simply insert the Windows XP CD-ROM into your laptop's CD or DVD drive and restart the computer. As I have discussed, the system BIOS or Setup Software should be instructed to check the CD as one of its possible boot devices; if the hard drive is blank and there is no boot disk in the floppy disk drive, the CD is checked for the purpose.

You see a message along these lines: "Press any key to boot from CD." I trust you can figure out what you've got to do at this time. (Hint: Press a key.) At the Welcome to Setup screen, press the Enter key to begin the installation and configuration of Windows XP.

Follow the instructions you see onscreen to select and format a partition for the installation of the operating system (the active partition) and the location for other applications and data (which can be in the same partition or in a separate one).

The installation process for Windows XP can take more than an hour, and you'll be called upon to make a number of decisions and settings, including your local time zone and display options. If your machine is attached to a local area network *(LAN)* or to a broadband Internet connection, you are asked to match the machine to the needs of either or both connection.

Depending on your machine's configuration, you may be asked to reboot your computer once or more during the process. This is especially the case if you are upgrading a previous installation of Windows; the new operating system will spend some time searching out all the existing hardware and software to look for any incompatibilities or needed drivers updates.

Floppy disk or network boot

The option to boot a system from a floppy disk drive dates back to the earliest DOS *(Disk Operating System)* of the PC, but we have probably seen the end of the line. Among the reasons: Nearly all laptops and desktop PCs have a CD drive capable of holding at least 600MB of information. And in any case, the boot information itself has become so large that it will not fit on a single floppy. Finally, laptop makers already sell computers that no longer have floppy disk drives, a move that is in the process of being adopted by desktop makers.

Microsoft has officially announced that it will no longer support booting systems from a floppy disk drive past the current versions of Windows XP Home and XP Professional. However, a number of third-party utility makers, including Symantec and its Norton Utility series, offer ways to create an emergency boot disk as part of their recovery process from system failure. For information on how to obtain Windows XP Setup boot disks from Microsoft, go to the Knowledge Base at www.microsoft.com and search for article number 310994, which is helpfully titled, "How to obtain Windows XP Setup boot disks."

If your computer is attached to an Ethernet and configured with a network interface card, that includes the ability to boot from files stored on a server in the network. (Those boot files have to be for Windows XP. Also, your system has to be set up to allow this sort of remote startup and usually requires a site license for the operating system software; this is an advanced technical process and should involve an MIS department or consultant.)

Employing the great migration strategy

If your goal is merely to find a way to squeeze 4.1 or more gigs of stuff onto a 4GB drive, another solution is to use a cloning process. The trick here is to use a software utility that makes an electronic snapshot of a drive's full contents, including the operating system, applications, settings, and data. Later that snapshot is copied back to a new drive.

The advantages of cloning include:

- ✔ You do not need to reinstall the operating system and find the original installation disks for all of your applications.
- ✔ All updates and patches that you have applied to the drive over time are maintained.
- ✔ The same folder and subfolder names and whatever logic you applied in creating them are kept.
- ✔ All of your data, including backup copies and earlier versions plus temporary and fragmentary files, is retained.

The disadvantages of cloning may or may not be of consequence to you:

✔ Any problems with the existing operating system and its applications, including missing or corrupted elements and incorrect settings will be moved to the new drive.

✔ You lose the opportunity to reorganize the folder and subfolder hierarchy.

✔ All of your data, including temporary and fragmentary files, is maintained.

TIP

You can reduce the chances of suffering some of the disadvantages by doing some housecleaning before the cloning. Start by deleting any data files and data folders you do not need. Use the facilities of Windows or a specialized Uninstall program to remove any applications you don't need to retain.

One such system works: the EZ-Gig II kit, a solution offered by BiX Computers at www.bixnet.com. The package includes a new hard drive and a cable from the external case to a special PC Card that plugs in to the laptop. It also includes a plastic external case that serves as the temporary home of the new drive while cloning is underway; it can be used to house the old drive as an external storage device. The kit to upgrade a laptop computer is shown in Figure 17-1.

Figure 17-1:
A laptop hard drive upgrade kit from BiX Computers includes a new drive (at top) plus a PC Card, cable, and external housing. The original hard drive is removed from its bay on the drive; it's placed in the external housing and connected to the laptop by the cable to allow data transfer.

Cable   PC Card

New hard drive

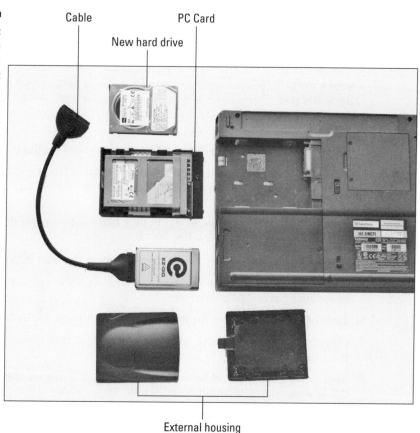

External housing

Here's how the process works:

1. **Begin by cleaning up the old drive.**

   Delete any files that are not needed. Use the Windows uninstaller or the specialized application removal utility that comes with some programs to excise from the disk any programs you don't need to keep.

2. **Run a defragger and the error-checking function in that order.**

   Use the Windows defragmentation utility or one of the better third-party defraggers such as Diskeeper from Executive Software or the Speed Disk utility that is part of Norton Utilities or Norton SystemWorks from Symantec. Then use the Error-checking function that is part of Windows or a third-party product such as the more advanced Norton Disk Doctor from Symantec.

   Use the built-in error-checking or defragmentation utilities of Windows XP or 98 with these steps:

   1. Go to My Computer.

   2. Highlight the drive to be worked on.

   3. Right-click.

   4. Click Properties➪Tools.

   Speed Disk and Disk Doctor are both accessible from Norton Utilities, which is available as a standalone product or as part of Norton SystemWorks. These two utilities remove or block off bad sectors and corrupted files so that some of the sins of the old drive are not visited upon the new one.

3. **Uninstall any virus protection software that exists on the old drive.**

   Modern and capable versions of this sort of protection include prevention of copying or alterations to the boot sector, something you want to accomplish as part of the cloning process.

4. **Install the new hard drive in the plastic external housing that is part of the EZ-Gig II kit.**

5. **Attach the included cable to the connector on the new drive.**

   Examine the keyed notch on the cable to make certain it aligns with the equivalent pin on the connector.

6. **Turn off the AC adapter for the notebook and remove the battery.**

7. **Plug the supplied PC Card, with cable attached, into the laptop. Install the supplied EZ-Gig II CD into the laptop.**

8. **Replace the battery and install the AC adapter. Turn on the power to the laptop.**

   Follow the EZ-Gig software as it guides you through the process of creating an exact bootable clone of your old hard drive on the new drive.

9. After data transfer is complete, shut down the computer.

10. Remove the PC Card. Disconnect the AC adapter and remove the battery.

11. Disconnect the EZ-Gig cable from the new drive and carefully remove the drive from the housing.

    Place it on a soft and nonconductive surface.

12. Carefully remove the old hard drive from the laptop and then remove the plastic holding parts and other components from the housing.

    Place the old drive in a safe place.

13. Install the new drive in the old drive's housing, mating it with any special data and power connector and aligning it with screw holes.

    Carefully slide the housing into the laptop's bay and latch or screw it into position.

14. Reattach the AC adapter and install the battery.

15. Turn on the computer.

    If you've been very good in this or a previous life, the new drive will come to life and look and act just like the one it replaced, except that it may be much larger and faster.

At this point you can decide whether to continue to use the old drive. The EZ-Gig kit allows you to install the old drive into the external housing and connect it to the laptop using the same PC Card you used to make the clone.

Opening a back door to recovery

One generally useful and quick way to configure a new drive is to use the original recovery CD that was supplied with your laptop computer. This disk is intended to restore the machine to exactly the way it was when it arrived from the factory. It partitions the disk, formats it, and reinstalls the operating system and most applications and settings; in the process it erases (or make inaccessible) all previous data on the disk. That's not a problem with using a recovery CD on a new hard drive — there's no data to lose. Read this paragraph one more time and make absolutely certain you understand that the recovery CD will take away access to anything that might be on the disk before you undertake a recovery.

One other feature of many current recovery CDs is that they create a hidden Utility partition that contains diagnostic tests, stores hibernation data, and may include emergency files that can restore the ability of a damaged hard drive to boot once again. The hidden partition is accessed by using the special tools that are part of the utility itself. Isn't technology wonderful?

Be sure to follow all of the instructions exactly as they appear onscreen or in the computer's manual; keep in mind that some procedures may be specific to your laptop model and may differ from other installation procedures you may have performed. (A few such recovery CDs may not work with a new hard drive of different specifications from the original drive, but that sort of unfriendly utility is not all that common.)

If you do choose to use a recovery CD to partition, format, and install an operating system and applications to a new hard drive, once the machine is up and running you should immediately visit the Microsoft Update web site (www.microsoft.com) to install patches to the operating system to bring it up to date. The recovery CD should also provide Windows drivers specific to the devices that were originally installed in your notebook. You should also visit the manufacturer's web site to check for updates to the drivers or applications introduced since the machine was first delivered to you. And don't forget to install a current antivirus program before using the machine. Don't assume that the web sites of application makers are always perfectly safe, either.

During the operating system installation you will likely be asked to activate Windows; the Product ID code is usually located on the CD envelope and sometimes also on a sticker on the bottom of the laptop.

Finally, visit the sites for all applications and update them before you migrate the data to the new hard drive. In some cases, you may need to contact customer service for the application makers to inform them that you have *uninstalled* an application from one drive and are *reinstalling* it on a new drive. They may want to know this as part of their attempt to block software piracy. Your license generally allows you to run your software on one machine only.

Advanced recovery in Windows 2000 and Windows XP

Advanced users can use the somewhat technical but very powerful Recovery Console in Windows 2000 or Windows XP for some specialized surgical procedures. You must have administrative privileges to do so. If you are the sole user on a standalone computer, you are almost certain to be set up as the administrator; if your system is maintained by a central IT office, you may need to enlist the assistance of a computing services technician.

Facilities of the Recovery Console include:

- Repairing a damaged boot sector
- Reading some or all of the data from a drive that is inaccessible to the operating system

✔ Writing data or recovery files or drivers directly to a drive, without using the operating system tools

✔ Formatting and partitioning

You can get to the Recovery Console via two routes:

✔ If you are unable to get the operating system to start on a hard drive, install the Windows XP or Windows 2000 Setup CD in your drive and boot the system from there. Onscreen instructions offer you access to the Recovery Console, and walk you through the process.

✔ Install the Recovery Console utility on your computer. This becomes, in effect, a separate operating system available to you at startup. That is, if the hard drive will start up. If not, use the first option outlined earlier.

Installing Windows 98

Although Windows 98 is no longer the recommended Microsoft operating system, and official support is being withdrawn bit by bit, many older machines and some legacy hardware and software are unable to work with the newer Windows 2000 or XP. And for many users, the final version of Windows 98, called 98SE (second edition) is capable enough for laptop tasks. (For the record, Windows XP is more *stable* than any of its predecessors — less likely to crash or freeze — but it is also considerably larger and more demanding of processor power and RAM. If you have a laptop running Windows 98SE, you may not need to upgrade to XP and probably shouldn't unless you have a specific reason to do so.)

If your machine is still running the original Windows 98, or one of the dinosaur operating systems like Windows 95 or Windows ME, you should consider going to Windows 98SE at the very least. This allows access to useful facilities including Plug and Play, USB, and WiFi communication.

Here are the minimum requirements for use of Windows 98SE:

✔ Intel 486DX 66 MHz or faster processor. A Pentium or later processor is recommended.

✔ At least 16MB of RAM, with 24MB recommended.

✔ 195MB of available space on your hard drive. The actual required space may vary between 120–295MB, depending on the hardware in your machine and optional software components.

✔ A CD-ROM or DVD-ROM drive and a 3.5-inch high-density floppy disk drive.

✔ A video adapter and monitor that supports VGA or higher resolution.

✔ A mouse or other pointing device.

If your hard drive uses *overlay* software to enable support of larger disk sizes than older operating systems permitted, the drive overlay software must be installed before Windows 98 is installed. Consult the instructions provided by the hard drive manufacturer or utility maker for details.

Skipping to 98 disks

Microsoft sells or makes available through computer manufacturers three versions of Windows 98 installation disks.

Recovery disk supplied with laptop

This recovery disk is intended for recovery or reinstallation of a failed operating system or hard drive. You should also be able to use this disk to install Windows 98 onto a new hard drive that you install to replace the original storage system; you need to enter the product key that is attached to the CD envelope or on a tag on the laptop itself.

On some of these recovery disks, you need to reinstall the entire software suite that first came with the machine as delivered by the manufacturer. That may be a pain or a waste of time, but you can always go back and remove unnecessary programs and utilities later.

Be sure to read the original instructions that came with your restore or recovery CD; if you can't find the manual, check the manufacturer's web site for advice. Keep in mind that the recovery disk will likely delete or make inaccessible any existing software and data on the drive.

Note, too, that the recovery disk for your machine may be so old that it installs Windows 98 and not the later 98SE version. In that case, you must purchase a Windows 98SE upgrade to obtain the new features.

Microsoft Windows 98 for PCs without Windows package

As its name suggests, this CD-ROM version is intended for use on a hard drive that does not have an existing operating system. Just pop the CD into your laptop's CD or DVD drive and follow the instructions for installation. The package comes with its own product key that should be entered at the requested moment.

Microsoft Windows 98 Upgrade package

Offered at a discounted price, this CD-ROM requires that you prove that you own a copy of the previous version of Windows. If the previous version is already installed on the hard drive, the installation should proceed automatically. If you have removed the older operating system or are seeking to install the new version on a new replacement hard drive, you can prove to Microsoft

The Windows 98 CD trap

How can you load the operating system from a CD when the drivers for the CD are part of the operating system? That's the confusing double bind that many Windows 98 users face. The solution is mostly solved through the availability of a set of generic CD-ROM drivers that work with most CD-ROM drives. These drivers should allow a laptop's BIOS to bring to life most ATAPI and less-common SCSI drives and permit the Windows 98 Startup disk to go to work. If the supplied drivers do not work with your CD-ROM drive, contact the maker of your computer or CD drive for assistance. You can find several versions of all-purpose CD drivers by doing an Internet search for "generic CD driver."

that the upgrade is permissible by inserting the original installation CD from the older version of Windows when asked to do so. The installation CD notes the previous version and then returns to upgrading.

Once the new operating system is installed, visit the Microsoft Update web page to obtain all of the available system updates and device drivers. It may require several visits and machine restarts before all of the requisite pieces are in place.

Finally, install a capable antivirus program such as Norton Antivirus or similar products from manufacturers including McAfee. Be sure to scan your drive for any existing problems, and connect to the home pages of the antivirus makers for daily updates.

Preparing for a fresh install

As with other operating systems, before you install Windows 98 on an empty hard drive, the drive has to be partitioned and formatted. As I've explored, many hard drive manufacturers provide an automated utility to take away some of the pain. Windows 98 supports the FAT16 and the more advanced FAT32 file systems; it does not support NTFS, which was introduced with Windows NT and Windows XT. You've no reason to choose FAT16 unless you need to maintain compatibility with older hardware.

As a reminder, FAT16 can deal with no more than 2GB for each allocated space or drive letter. As an example, a 10GB hard drive could be set up with 5 drive letters (usually beginning with C and running through G), each with 2GB of allocated space. Or, you could make each of the virtual drives a different size, as long as none of them exceed 2GB.

FAT32 all but makes drive size irrelevant, supporting drives up to 2TB — but not smaller than 512MB. It is also more efficient in storing data, resulting in less wasted overhead.

If you will be using Microsoft's facilities to partition and format the drive, use the FDISK and FORMAT utilities. Here are the steps. Note that the process can take an hour or more.

1. **Insert the Windows 98 Startup disk in the floppy disk drive and restart your computer.**

   The startup disk displays a menu of options.

2. **Choose Start Computer Without CD-ROM Support and press the Enter key.**

   You are taken to the DOS command prompt, which is hidden beneath Windows 98.

3. **Type FDISK and press Enter.**

   If the hard drive is larger than 512MB, you are asked if you want to enable large disk support, which opens the door to disks with larger real or virtual drives. If you enable large disk support, the drive you partition and format will be inaccessible from Windows 95 and some other earlier and different versions of Windows.

4. **At this stage, the most important option on the Fdisk menu is Create DOS partition or Logical DOS Drive. Select it and press Enter.**

5. **Press 1 to select Create Primary DOS Partition and then press Enter.**

   You are asked if you want to use the maximum available size for the primary DOS partition; the primary partition holds the operating system.

   If you choose the FAT32 file system, you can have the entire hard drive partitioned and formatted as a single unit, or you can divide it. If you choose (or are forced to choose) FAT16, you have to divide the disk into even or uneven slices no larger than 2GB each.

   For a machine running Windows 98, Microsoft recommends that the primary partition be at least 500MB to hold the operating system plus temporary files. If you have defined more than one partition, make one of them the active partition. Although more than one partition can contain boot information for one or more operating systems, only one of them can be active at a time — and that partition boots the operating system at startup. You can change a partition's status to active or inactive at any time.

6. **Select the Create Extended DOS Partition option and press Enter.**

   Now's when you assign drive letters to the additional space on the hard drive. You can adjust the size of the partition or you can use the default size. The Create Logical DOS Drive(s) in the Extended DOS Partition menu allows you to assign remaining hard drive space to additional drive letters and assign space to each logical drive in MB or as a percentage of available remaining disk space.

7. **Keep dividing until the system tells you that all available space in the Extended DOS Partition has been assigned.**

8. **Press Esc until you quit FDISK and return to the command prompt.**

   The next manual task is to format the drive.

9. **Restart the laptop with the Windows 98 Startup disk in the floppy drive.**

10. **From the Start menu, choose Start Computer Without CD-ROM Support.**

11. **When a command prompt is displayed, type** FORMAT C: **and press Enter.**

    I'm assuming the new drive is called C. Nearly all laptops have only one internal hard drive, and it is almost always labeled as C. If for some reason you want to format a drive of a different label, change the command. Be sure to include the colon after the drive letter.

    You're going to see a threatening message something (or exactly) like this:

    ```
    WARNING, ALL DATA ON NON-REMOVABLE DISK DRIVE C: WILL BE
            LOST! Proceed with Format (Y/N)?
    ```

12. **If you're sure of what you're doing, press the Y key and then Enter to begin the format.**

    Once formatting is completed, you are asked to give the volume a name:

    ```
    Volume label (11 characters, ENTER for none)?
    ```

    You don't have to give your hard drive a name, but sometimes it helps you quickly recognize the drive on a network. You can use any name of as many as 11 characters. Don't use symbols or spaces in the name.

13. **Repeat the formatting and labeling process for any additional drive letters you created.**

    Once the drive is partitioned, formatted, and labeled, you can install Windows 98.

14. **Insert the Startup disk in the floppy drive and restart the computer.**

15. **This time, choose Start Computer with CD-ROM Support.**

    From this point on, the CD installation disk for Windows 98 should take over. Answer the questions posed on screen and proceed through installation.

Chapter 18

Adding or Removing Software, for Better or for Worse

In This Chapter

▶ Adding software you want

▶ Uninstalling software you don't want

▶ Cleaning up programs running in the background

▶ Rooting out spyware and adware that sneak onto your machine

Sometimes software applications are like the guests who come to dinner and just won't leave. They take up valuable space, they use your limited resources, and they long ago stopped being entertaining or useful. And sometimes a piece of software is a totally uninvited guest that stubbornly refuses to leave no matter how many hints you drop.

Before you go any further, stop and consider the various ways in which software applications, utilities, and bad-acting *malware* (including spy programs, viruses, and thieves) get on your machine:

✔ When you first install the operating system (or enable the O/S put in place by the manufacturer of your laptop), you are adding a whole bunch of programs to your system. These are *probably* the safest programs on your system since they are aimed at setting up the basic working platform for your machine or are developed or adapted by the original equipment manufacturer specifically for your model laptop.

A default installation of Microsoft Windows XP puts in place the operating system (which includes a Control Panel for configuration and a library of common device drivers for various pieces of hardware that attach to the innards or external ports of the laptop). Some entry-level programs include a pair of very basic word processors (WordPad), a simple drawing program called Paint, and a rudimentary audio and video playback program. The operating system adds utilities including a disk defragmenter (more about that later) and some security features including a firewall. An installation of Microsoft Windows also ordinarily includes a communications manager and the Internet Explorer web browser.

Be sure to keep your copy of the operating system current with updates provided by Microsoft. For example, most of the latest security features including an improved software firewall are delivered as part of Windows XP's Service Pack 2.

If you are installing the operating system to a blank hard drive, you can choose a custom set of features that excludes some of these programs and utilities. If Windows has already been put in place, you can go in and remove some of the features. I discuss how a bit later in this chapter.

✔ You may have installed a full-featured application or suite of programs to augment the basics. For example, you may have added Microsoft Office or Microsoft Works to give you more functions. Almost all installation processes allow you to pick and choose whether you want to add some advanced or arcane functions; you can always put them in place later if you suddenly discover that you really do need a Swedish thesaurus.

✔ Your system may have gained a piece of software and a device driver or two when you added hardware to your system. Once again, you may have had options about how much of the software or utilities you wanted to install.

✔ You may have given permission to a web site to download some active content (to allow you to interact with a web page or view some special effects). Among this sort of downloaded code are Java applications.

✔ Someone may have *pushed* some software onto your computer without your permission or knowledge. This can be accomplished by tricking you into opening the door over the Internet or by just going ahead and forcing it into place.

✔ An evildoer may have snuck something onto your computer by attaching it to a piece of e-mail.

Pleading the Fifth

I am not going to get into a debate about whether Microsoft — the maker of Microsoft Windows and many of the other market-dominant software programs — is perfect, good, bad, or evil. All that is needed to be said is this: Microsoft is by far the most dominant maker of operating systems and basic office suites. You can use another maker's operating system, one of the flavors of Linux, for example, or another brand of office software, like WordPerfect. You're just not going to find a lot of suggestions at the office water cooler when you ask for technical help. Devotees of Linux, WordPerfect, and the like tend to gather in electronic support groups to trade tips, tricks, and fixes.

Your first line of defense is your dedication to safe computing. Stop and think before installing any program on your machine: Do you know what company is responsible for the product? Does it come on an original CD or other media and not someone's bootlegged, hand-labeled copy? Is the web site you are visiting legitimate, and does the company behind it present a digital certificate of authenticity? (A digital certificate, provided by a recognized authority, is supposed to guarantee that the software or web site you are dealing with comes from the company you expect and not from a fraudulent or malicious source.) Most importantly, do you really need this additional code on your system? Your second line of defense is a fully updated and capable set of security hardware and software devices and utilities: a *firewall* to protect against unwanted intrusions and an antivirus program to stop sneak attacks before they do damage.

Installing an Application

In the old, old days of computing — back before Windows was born and years before your laptop was a twinkle in the eye of its designer — many programs were self-contained files. A word processor was a single program called something like word.exe. (exe is computer-speak for *executable,* meaning it is a file that does something when it is invoked, as opposed to a data file that contains information.)

Putting a new application on your computer was often as simple as copying the executable file to your system and creating a shortcut (called batch files in early DOS) to invoke the pieces when they were needed. Alas, the installation of programs has become much more complex even as Windows has made their use so much simpler.

In a nutshell, a modern program that is installed into Windows is often made up of dozens or even hundreds of little pieces distributed all over your hard drive. Some are placed in a subdirectory that holds the main executable program and can be spotted by using Windows Explorer and going to the folder for Program Files. (For example, you may see a subdirectory called Microsoft Office or Norton SystemWorks.)

However, it does not end there. Not by a long shot. Applications running under Windows use all sorts of shared functions and libraries of icons, fonts, and commands. (Among these are the *DLLs,* or dynamic link libraries, which are part of the mechanism that allows any software company to make its product nearly identical in appearance and command structure to any other.) As part of the installation, pieces are put every which where. And most programs installed under Windows also make changes to the Windows Registry, which is a special file of instructions that the operating system consults at startup and at other times.

How do you install an application? By following the instructions that come with the program. Follow these general tips *unless the instructions advise otherwise:*

✔ I'm assuming you are installing a commercially written program and using an original disc as provided by the maker. If for some reason you are using something other than the original disc (or a downloaded version from a source other than the official site of the manufacturer), you have three concerns:

- Are you legally permitted to install this program?

- Will the program run once installed and be properly activated over the Internet if the manufacturer requires such action?

- Does the homemade disc or the downloaded file contain a virus or spyware?

✔ If you are running Windows XP Pro or Windows NT, make sure you are logged in as a user with Administrator privileges; most individual users of these operating systems make no distinction between users and administrators. However, if your machine is under the management of an *IT* (information technology) department, it may have set up the operating system to limit your ability to install new programs or significantly change the operating system.

✔ Make sure that no other programs are running. Go to the programs and choose Close or shut them down with these steps:

1. Press Ctrl+Alt+Del to go to the Windows Task Manager.

2. Choose the Applications tab.

3. Highlight each task that is running and click End Task.

✔ Shut down your antivirus program. (If you insist on trying to install an unofficial copy of a program despite the concerns I laid out a bit earlier, be sure to thoroughly scan the disk or file before beginning the installation process.)

You are asked to shut down your antivirus program to prevent it from sounding an alarm or stopping the installation process because it has detected actions that might otherwise be considered threatening: making changes to the Windows Registry and other settings of the computer among them. Be sure to reenable your antivirus program after the installation is completed.

✔ Run your laptop from an AC power source if possible, or at the very least, make sure you have a fully charged battery; you don't want the machine to shut down in mid-installation.

Ditching an Application

In those very early years of personal computing, you could remove a program by deleting its executable file or the subdirectory that contained a set of executables. Today, though, the simplicity and uniform environment that is at the heart of Microsoft Windows comes at the price of some very deep complexity when putting in and taking off programs.

Under Windows, you cannot simply delete whatever executable files you find and expect to be rid of a program. At best you will disable the program while leaving bits and pieces of it scattered all over the disk; at worst, you may end up disabling a whole set of programs or some of their functions because you have inadvertently removed some shared components or left instructions in the Registry that refer to an absent program.

One other benefit: The shorter and better managed Windows Registry in your laptop, the faster it starts and the more stable its operation.

Although Microsoft would prefer otherwise, not all programmers follow their rules and suggestions exactly. One example you may find is in the Add/Remove Software utility; you can see an example of the main screen of that utility in Figure 18-1. Some programs may offer a button called Change/Remove, which leads to a choice between making adjustments to the program (including adding or removing individual functions) and completely removing the software. Others offer separate Change and Remove buttons, while yet another possibility is simply a Remove button.

Note that this utility is called Add/Remove Software. However, most modern software includes its own installation programs, and this is usually the most efficient and effective means to add an application. Use the Windows utility only if required.

And so, you have three proper ways to uninstall a program:

- ✔ The application may have put into place an *uninstall* program that searches out and destroys all of the components wherever they are. Look for an uninstall program in the same subdirectory where the program itself is located.

- ✔ The application may have made use of the built-in Add/Remove Software utility that is part of Microsoft Windows.

  1. Go to the Control Panel and click Add/Remove Software. Give your laptop a few seconds to give you a list of programs it is able to remove.

2. Click the object of your lack of desire and then click Remove.

✔ You may have installed a specialized disk cleanup program that is capable of hunting down all of the pieces of a program and removing them.

If the removal or installation process makes significant changes to the Windows Registry or important settings to the operating system, you may be asked to reboot your computer. In general you should follow this instruction and do so immediately when requested by the installation or removal utility. In some cases you can continue using the laptop, but changes made to the Registry will not take effect until the computer is rebooted.

Figure 18-1:
This is the
Add/Remove
Software
Utility from
Microsoft
Windows
XP. Most
current
software
will link
its own
installation
process to
this screen,
allowing
proper
installa-
tion and
removal.

Dealing with Background Applications

Not every program that runs on your computer automatically occupies space on your screen; some run in the background. They are there — and they do use some of your important system resources, including memory and a slice of the microprocessor's attention — but they are wither minimized onscreen or barely noticeable as an icon on the taskbar or system tray. You may also see some background applications in the small notification area that usually sits on the lower-right corner of the screen and includes the clock.

Examples include utilities such as antivirus programs, instant message managers, calendars, and system monitors. And — this is important — some Windows XP components themselves run in the background; for that reason you need to understand what is running, its purpose, and whether it can be safely removed or disabled.

Here's how to find out what is running in the background:

1. **Go to the Task Manager.** You can do so in several ways:

   - Bring the cursor down to the taskbar (usually on the bottom and sometimes on the side of the Windows screen, even when a foreground application is running) and right-click. From the submenu, select Task Manager.

   - Press the Ctrl+Alt+Del key combination. This directly opens the Task Manager.

2. **Click the Processes tab.**

   Here you see a list of programs running in the foreground. Most of them should be recognizable. For example, as I am writing this section on my laptop, I've got Microsoft Word running, and in the background is Microsoft Office OneNote, a productivity utility. You can see the Task Manager display in Figure 18-2.

Figure 18-2:
Microsoft
Windows
Task
Manager
shows
applications
currently
running on a
laptop. A
machine
connected
to the
Internet
usually has
a number of
additional
utilities
running.

If you see something running that shouldn't, or that you no longer need to have open, close the program. You can do that two ways:

✔ Switch to the program. You can do this by clicking it in the task bar or pressing the Alt+Tab key combination until the program is highlighted. Close the program by using the standard shutdown process — usually by clicking File➪Close.

You can also shut down most programs by clicking the Alt+F4 key combination.

✔ If the Task Manager is still displayed onscreen, you can use the Switch To button to go to any open program. Highlight the program you want to close, and then click the End Task button.

To examine programs and utilities running in the background, click the Processes tab. Here you find some full programs as well as pieces of foreground applications and Windows XP elements. An example of the Task Manager Processes tab is shown in Figure 18-3.

Figure 18-3:
The Processes tab shows the jobs vying for the processor's attention. CPU usage can drop to 0 percent or so when the computer is idle; if usage is near 100 percent or the Commit Charge ratio is near 1:1, you may be overtaxing the micro-processor.

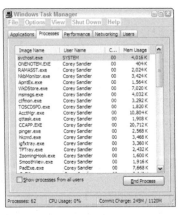

The screen shows you the Image Name (the name of the executable file), the User Name (which tells you who "owns" the process; it can be the system itself or the logged-on user), the CPU usage (a report on the percentage of time a particular process used the CPU since the last update) and the Mem Usage (the amount of system RAM taken by the background process).

Some of the processes may be recognizable, but others may not; you may be able find the meaning of some of the jobs by using a search engine on the Internet. One interesting web site is at www.answersthatwork.com. Click the Task List button to look up descriptions of many tasks; you'll find that most, if not all, are quite legitimate, but you may also find some malware mixed in with the helpful products.

At the bottom of the Processes screen are a trio of important summaries: the number of processes running, the total amount of CPU usage they represent, and the total commit charge. That last measure tells you the ratio of memory used by all of the current processes in relation to total available (called *peak*) memory. Note that peak memory may be a larger number than the actual physical memory in the system; the computer also uses *virtual memory* — space located on the system's hard drive and used to "page" blocks of information between the slower but more capacious hard drive and the faster RAM. You can highlight any of the running processes and then click End Process to shut it down.

Shutting down background tasks

The direct way to shut down a background task is to maximize it from the system tray or notification area. But as you've no doubt noticed when you took a look at the Processes tab, not all background tasks are evident.

First, explore how to shut down the background tasks that are minimized on the Windows screen.

✔ Double-clicking most icons will perform the assigned task for that program or open a window with a set of menu choices. For example, double-clicking the icon for your antivirus program (which is usually running in the background all the time) allows you to run a manual scan of a particular program or disk or to update the virus definitions. Another example of a background program is the controller for USB or PC Card devices; double-clicking allows you to safely shut down and remove the device.

✔ You may be able to bring forth a shortcut menu for a background application by right-clicking the icon. For most programs, you can close or disable a background application from this shortcut menu. However, the program is probably set up to automatically load the next time you reboot the computer.

Which background programs should you close?

The answer: only the unnecessary ones. The problem: determining which ones go and which ones stay. The solution: work cautiously and make notes on what proves essential and what is demonstrably superfluous.

Among your goals are to find and remove adware, spyware, and other assorted junk. You can also hunt for leftover pieces of programs you thought you had uninstalled using proper removal utilities.

You can prune some of the programs that automatically load into the background each time you start your machine by going to the Startup submenu. Click Start⇨All Programs⇨Startup; move your pointer into the list of programs and right-click to remove each one you no longer want to have loaded. What you see here are not the programs themselves but shortcuts that cause them to load; when you remove a program from the Startup menu you are not uninstalling it from the hard drive, merely stopping its automatic load.

Some of the junk arrives in a more or less legitimate manner: When you install a piece of software it may scatter all sorts of extra little features everywhere. For example, a calendar program may install an alarm clock that runs in the background, and a personal finance program may place an automatic reminder to pay bills on a particular date. The best way to reduce the chances of such junk being installed is to choose the custom installation option when you add a program, and then carefully examine all of the options for features. You can always add the feature later if you decide that it actually is of value to you.

Your laptop maker may have added utilities it considers useful, and you may find junk: a utility to help connect to a broadband link or a troubleshooting utility (generally a good thing), a direct link to its tech support system (maybe helpful), or a direct link to its online store (probably less valuable). Another source of junk are web sites offering free utilities or programs to enhance your computing experience. Maybe yes or maybe no: If such an offer pops up on my screen unsolicited, I always do one of two things — either decline the offer or stop and research the program. A quick Internet search should tell you if other users are using the program.

And then there are programs that you simply don't want to see on your machine, including adware, spyware, and viruses. If given a choice, just say "No way." Unfortunately, many of the pushers of this sort of junk don't bother to ask your permission.

Some web portals, including shopping pages and certain search engines, sneakily install adware that pushes advertisements onto your system. Even worse is *spyware,* which can range from harmless but invasive programs that report information about your Internet activities back to a central site; this sort of spyware is used to learn about your interests and proclivities so that advertisers can target their pitches directly to you. The evil twin to spyware is a program that tracks all of your keystrokes and mouse clicks with the aim of discovering — and misusing — your passwords, credit card numbers, and banking information.

If you can spot junk, adware, or spyware in the system tray or the Task Manager's Processes tab, you should be able to remove them using the methods I've already outlined in this chapter: using the Control Panel's Add or Remove Programs utility or right-clicking the icon and choosing Remove or Uninstall from the submenu.

Many background applications allow you to shut down or exit the program by right-clicking them, but this does not stop the program from reappearing the next time you start the computer. Even more annoying: You may be able to tell the program not to display, but it is still there, doing its thing. You have to remove the program to truly be rid of it.

Searching and Destroying Spyware and Adware

Thus far I've been talking about ways to deal with programs that are well behaved and follow the rules. I wish I could stop right here. It would save a lot of headaches and trouble. Alas, though, there are two types of pain in the electronic neck:

✔ Overly zealous salespeople and tracking companies constantly seeking ways to put their messages onto your screen and to find ways to customize their intrusions. If they can discover that you are a male between the ages of 25 and 40 and interested in fast cars and rock music, they can sell that information to an advertiser who is looking to target you. If they can determine that your laptop's primary user is a young woman who religiously shops for shoes and self-help books, they can customize a different set of annoying pop-up messages. This class of program is called *adware.*

✔ More malicious and possibly dangerous to your privacy and finances: pieces of code that spy on your activities. The spyware also sometimes attempt to poke around on your hard drive in search of account numbers, passwords, and other personal information.

Adware can be intrusive; spyware can take all of the fun out of being online. The first line of defense against both is to be very careful with the information you disclose to online sites. Why are they asking your age and income level? If you are visiting a site to buy books, why do they want to know what kind of car you drive? Give out as little information as possible, and pay special attention to the little checkbox that most legitimate web sites present on the information screen. It reads something like this: Check here to receive valuable offers from our third-party partners. (Sometimes the checkbox language is phrased in a very sneaky negative option: Check here so that you don't receive offers from our third-party partners.)

Laws on the books make it illegal for a web site to resell your e-mail address or to place a program or a *cookie* that identifies your personal information without your permission. That doesn't mean that some companies won't go ahead and do so anyway. And when it comes to spyware, this sort of program is illegal from the get go.

Even if you take great care in denying permission to outsiders to place adware or spyware on your machine, it can still end up your hard drive. And you'll rarely find these programs identified on your startup tray or in the list of programs that you can remove through the Control Panel. Instead, adware and spyware can be concealed under phony names or hidden from view.

The solution here is to use a capable and regularly updated spyware/adware removal tool. Several of these programs are available for free or as *shareware*. (Shareware is free, but the developer will ask with varying degrees of intensity for a contribution if you decide to keep and use the software.)

Among the best free tools are Spybot and Ad-Aware; you can find either by going an Internet search for their home pages. Several commercial antivirus and system utilities have expanded their products to include the ability to hunt down and destroy unwanted guests. On my system I run Lavasoft's Ad-Aware SE; you can obtain a free copy for personal use by searching online. In Figure 18-4 you can see an example of the report of 67,590 objects scanned on my laptop.

These programs work by searching for known adware and spyware programs, and by looking for new ones that contain particular types of information or instructions. When they find a suspect program most will offer you the option of quarantining the programs in a special subdirectory or deleting them immediately. I recommend you use the quarantine option, at least until you are certain that the removal program is doing its job properly. If you quarantine a program that you later determine is important, you can bring it back into action. Some especially well-hidden programs may require several passes by the removal software, including reboots.

Figure 18-4:
Ad-Aware
found 56
running
processes
and 1,897
process
modules
(including
15 new
objects that
somehow
made their
way onto
my machine
since the
last time
I ran the
utility).

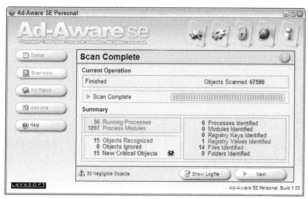

Be sure to update the adware/spyware software regularly to keep a step ahead of new or changed programs. I recommend running the removal program at least once a week, and more often if your machine suddenly seems to have slowed to a crawl.

Choose a time when you expect to regularly be away from your machine and set an automatic adware/spyware scan, an antivirus scan, and a defragmentation operation. On my machines, this all happens on Fridays at 5:30 P.M., a time when I am usually willing to turn away from my computer and clean my desk or file some paper or just kick back and think for a while. If the scans start and you are not ready for them to run, you can always cancel or reschedule the processes.

Chapter 19

Essential Utilities for Laptop Users

. . . .

In This Chapter

▶ Undeleting files that went oopsy-daisy into the Recycle Bin

▶ Putting fragmented files back together

▶ Scanning your machine for hidden corruption, malfeasance, and disruption

▶ Repairing a fuzzy photo

▶ Fixing an imperfect audio file

. . . .

*1*n baseball, a utility infielder is a generalist, a player who can take any position on the basepaths: first, second, short, or third. That's a valuable skill, because a manager never knows when a regular position player is going to pull up lame or otherwise leave the game. In personal computing, a utility program is just the opposite: a specialist that can do only thing but does it very well.

On my laptop team roster, I need both generalists and specialists. You probably already have your own copies of the all-around players: Windows XP, Microsoft Office Suite, and depending on the sort of work you do, Adobe Photoshop or another graphics program. These products are all Swiss Army Knife products: jam-packed with more features than you are ever likely to use. Some people find that kind of comforting, while others are overwhelmed at the sheer number of bells, whistles, and adjustments that can be made to a basic word processor, spreadsheet, or Internet browser.

Starting at the Beginning

When Microsoft introduced DOS (the Disk Operating System that made it possible to instruct the PC to load a program, format a disk, and display a directory, along with a few dozen other essential basic tasks) there were more than a few holes in the infield. Principal among them were solutions to problems that not many early computer users realized they had:

✔ A need to "undelete" a file that had accidentally been deleted.

✔ A need to defragment a hard drive that had become hopelessly chopped up (in an electromagnetic sort of way).

The issue of undeleting a file was a pretty important one: In the original versions of DOS, it was very easy to make a mistake typing a command or entering a filename and erasing your only copy of the Great American Novel. Poof: gone!

And defragmentation, if left untreated, can become a serious problem on a computer, causing the operating system (or Windows) and programs and files to open slower and slower and s-l-o-w-e-r to the point where the machine is almost unusable. I explain the not-all-that-complex concept of fragmentation and undeleting in the "Cracking fragmentation" sidebar.

A secondary value of defragmentation (and sometimes a primary one) is that contiguous files are easier to recover in case of corruption to the file attribute table — the index of filenames and locations maintained by the operating system. Data recovery programs can find the single file without having to look for its broken pieces.

TECHNICAL STUFF

Cracking fragmentation

What is fragmentation? Start by considering the fact that not every file is the same length. You may write a short note to yourself, and the computer will store it in a space of, say, 64 KB of space. (The actual minimum size for a file depends on the size of the disk, the operating system, and the file management system used to format the drive.) The next file you store might be a digitized photo or a song that occupies 3MB (a space 50 times larger than your note). What happens if you later reopen that short note and add a few more pages to it? One possibility is that the note will be split into two pieces and placed wherever there is a hole. Another possibility is that first small file will be "deleted" and a longer, single file will be placed somewhere else on the disk.

So that brings me to "deleting" a file. You might think this means the file is physically erased from the surface of the drive, but to do so would waste a relatively huge amount of time. Remember that computers are all about speed. Instead of erasing the file, the hard drive controller changes the first letter of the filename to a nonstandard character (such as an %; actually, it uses the hexadecimal value E5) that the file indexing system doesn't recognize. The file is still there, but the index no longer sees it.

And so the two solutions: A defragmenter searches the drive for all of the file or program pieces and then locates an open space to recopy the pieces into a contiguous stream of digital information. The first defraggers did simply that, but later versions used more sophisticated programming to place more commonly used files in locations where the read/write heads can more quickly find them.

And the first "undelete" program was basically as simple as this: It searched the hard drive for files that began with hexadecimal E5 and then presented a list of those files. When you found the one you wanted to save, you instructed the program to change that nonstandard character to one that would make the entire file visible to the operating system. (From such a relatively simple utility was born the substantial fortune of Peter Norton, a good-hearted friend of mine from the early days of the PC.)

It took many years before Microsoft added its own undelete and defragmentation (defragger) utilities to DOS and then to Windows (which still has something very much like DOS at its very lowest level). You can catch a glimpse of a command-driven interface that emulates the old DOS by going to the Command Prompt from within Windows. Click Start➪All Programs➪ Accessories➪Command Prompt. There you see a sight that warms the hearts of some of us old propeller heads: the C:\ prompt.

Try this: Display the prompt, type DIR, and press the Enter key. You see the directory for the current subdirectory in use. See Figure 19-1 for a subdirectory as seen by the operating system beneath Windows XP.

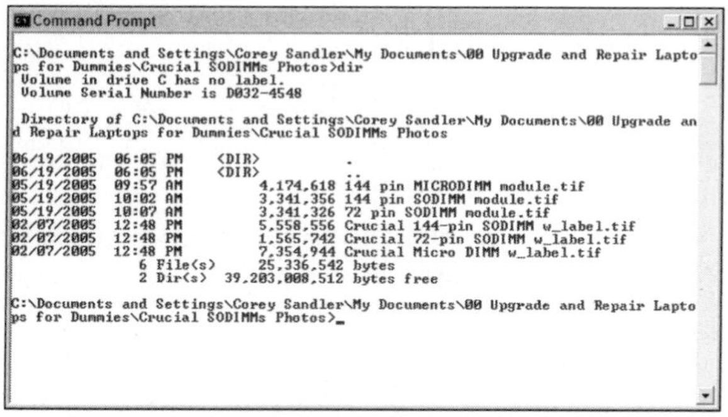

Figure 19-1:
A display of the directory of files from a subdirectory of the operating system that underlies Windows XP. Windows users think of directories and subdirectories as folders.

If you want to be adventurous, try a few old DOS commands. At the C:\ prompt, type VER and press the Enter key. You find out which version of the DOS-like command-driven interface is available from within Windows. You can also type HELP and press the Enter key to display a list of permissible commands. And you can enter a command and follow it with the /? switch to obtain a list of subcommands. For example, at the C:\ prompt enter DIR /? to see all of the various ways you can display the directory.

When you're done playing, type EXIT and press Enter to return to the wonderful world of Windows.

Microsoft Steps In

Over the years the friendly folks at Microsoft have seen the various utilities and add-ons sold by other companies and have said, "Why not have it all?" Step by step, DOS and then Windows were expanded to include versions of nearly all the enhancements made by outsiders. Today, Windows XP includes the ability to undelete files from the trash can (a bit of Norton and a bite of Apple to some people's eyes). It also includes a defragger utility and system restore utility, each of which echoes in one way or another offerings by third parties.

The Microsoft utilities of Windows have nothing particularly wrong with them. They do the job and come with an official promise of some level of support and compatibility with other Microsoft products. That is not quite the same as a guarantee that they are the best at what they do, or that they are without any flaws. (On the other side of the coin, when you purchase and use a non-Microsoft product you run some level of risk — decreasing over time as market share increases and as the federal and international court systems ratchet up the pressure on Microsoft to come as close as possible to an open system — that changes in the operating system will make the utilities obsolete or unusable.

All these minor warnings aside, I recommend laptop users install some important utilities from companies other than Microsoft on their machines. Those utilities are either faster, more efficient, or more capable than the versions that have been grafted onto Windows.

Denying the past with Undelete

The two best undelete programs for my money (and yours) are:

- ✔ The Norton Protected Recycle Bin, which is a component of Norton Utilities and also included in the larger system tune-up and repair package Norton SystemWorks.
- ✔ Undelete from Diskeeper Corporation.

Norton Utilities expands on the capacity, ease of use, and user controls of the basic Windows Recycle Bin. Once installed (and fine-tuned to meet your patterns of use and the amount of available space on your hard drive), it just sits there as what techies would call a LIFO garbage can. *LIFO* means "last in, first out." In other words, once the can becomes full, the space occupied by the oldest file in the can is released to the operating system to hold new information. Depending on how heavily you use your machine and how large a drive you have, the enhanced recycle bin may hold files that are weeks and even months old.

If you commit an "oops" and delete a file you meant to keep, or if you want to try to find an earlier version of a file that had been overwritten, you go to the desktop and right-click the Recycle Bin. The ghost of Peter Norton (he sold his company to Symantec in 1990, though his picture and name still appear on many of its products) searches the drive and presents all of the files that can be restored. Click them and you're back to the future. For information, consult www.symantec.com.

Undelete from Diskeeper works in a similar manner, replacing the Windows Recycle Bin with its own Recovery Bin. This product offers the same sort of protection as does Norton, but it goes a bit further in providing automatic file version protection for Microsoft Office files. If you accidentally save over a still-valuable Office file, this program can help you recover. If you're wondering how you might save over a file, consider this scenario: You open a Word document or an Excel spreadsheet to use as a template for a new file and then choose Save instead of Save As.

Undelete also is capable of holding on to files that the Windows Recycle Bin declares too large to hold. And version 5.0 of Undelete adds Emergency Undelete, which can recover files deleted before Undelete was installed on your system. . .provided they have not been overwritten by other data. For information, consult www.diskeeper.com.

Nagging about defraggers

The defragmenter utility included with Windows works . . . in a relatively slow and clumsy way. If that's all you've got, make sure to apply it to your hard disks at least once a month — more often if your machine is heavily used and especially if you work with large files (graphics, music, speech) that increase the chances of fragmentation. You can get to the built-in utility by going to My Computer and then right-clicking the icon for your hard drive. Click Properties⇨Tools. You'll find a Defragmentation tool on that page. Chapter 2 talks more about this topic.

In my opinion, two better choices are available, and they are sold by the same two companies that make the best undelete programs:

  ✔ Diskeeper is, in my experience, the fastest and most efficient defrag utility. It can be run on a scheduled basis or set up to run in the background, eliminating fragmentation while you use your computer.

  ✔ Norton's Speed Disk is part of Norton Utilities and in addition to reassembling fragmented files it can reorder their location on the disk so that the more heavily used programs and data files are easier for the computer to locate.

Diskeeper is an example of a company that has decided to specialize in just a few products and do them especially well. I have no knock whatsoever against the way its program works, although I prefer to do my defragmentation on a scheduled basis rather than add another program running in the background while I work on other tasks. That said, the sophisticated programming in version 9.0 and later gives other applications priority access to the hard drive while it is running. Other features include the ability to defragment critical system files as recommended by Microsoft. For information consult www.diskeeper.com. In Figure 19-2 you can see a Diskeeper analysis of the status of a hard drive before work is performed.

Norton Speed Disk is nearly as fast and capable of many of the same advanced features as Diskeeper. For most users it is a worthy upgrade from Microsoft's built-in defragger with the bonus that it comes as part of the larger Norton Utilities or Norton SystemWorks. For information consult www.symantec.com. In Figure 19-3 you can see Norton Speed Disk at work moving pieces of files on a heavily fragmented drive.

Figure 19-2:
Diskeeper reports that the hard drive is slightly defragmented, with an estimate of a 5-percent improvement in read time when work is completed. You're likely to notice a real drag on performance with more than 10-percent fragmentation.

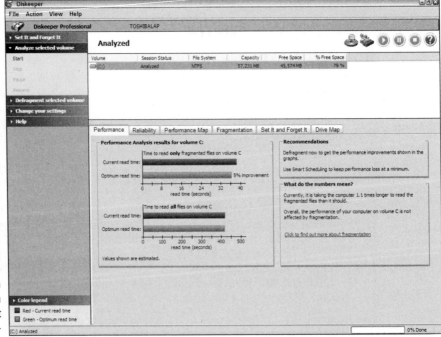

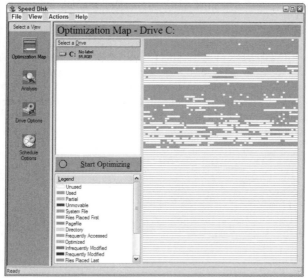

Figure 19-3: Norton Speed Disk at work: The legend in the lower left shows the types of files being moved and demarks those that should not be relocated because of system require- ments.

Doing a full cavity search

The third essential utility is some form of system tune-up. Like it or not, your computer software is under regular assault from any or all of these sources:

- ✔ Viruses sent your way by e-mail or over the Internet

- ✔ Malware or adware that forces its way onto your machine from the Internet

- ✔ Corruption caused by electrical surges or a mechanically failing hard drive

- ✔ Improperly written or poorly behaving software that may change the operating system's setup and driver files

- ✔ Crashes that cause an improper or incomplete system shutdown

Any of these problems and others can cause errors in the Windows Registry (a collection of instructions and settings that sets much of the personality of a system). These problems can also damage program files, file attribute tables, and other indexes necessary for proper operation.

The solution is to use — on a regular basis — a system utility that examines the Windows Registry and repairs or restores it to a previous properly config- ured state. By this point in this chapter, you should guess that I recommend use of Norton SystemWorks from Symantec, a suite of utilities that includes Norton Utilities (to discover and repair many Windows and drive problems and encompassing the Speed Disk defragger and the Norton Protected Recycle Bin), Norton AntiVirus, CheckIt Diagnostics, and more.

Every Friday at 5:30 p.m. I usually devote an hour or so to clearing my desk and preparing for the next week. At precisely that time (because I asked it to do so) Norton SystemWorks pops up on my screen and runs a One Button Checkup on my machine; it examines the Windows Registry, checks for the integrity of programs, looks for corruption or other damage, queries Norton AntiVirus to see when last the machine was scanned for viruses, searches for orphaned shortcuts to programs or data that has been deleted or moved, and cleans out assorted garbage, including temporary files. You can see the results of one such checkup in Figure 19-4.

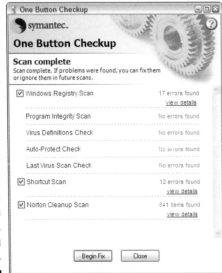

Figure 19-4: Norton System Works' One Button Checkup is the opening salvo of my weekly health scan for each of the computers in my office, including my laptop.

One Button Checkup takes about 10 minutes to complete on a modern machine. At 6 p.m. my machine automatically initiates a Norton AntiVirus scan; that process on a well-populated 40GB hard drive can take one to two hours to complete, and I leave it to process by itself. (If I'm going to leave the office I turn off the monitor and leave the computer to run by itself.)

Finally, I have Diskeeper run a defragmentation session on Sunday at 4 p.m., which is usually a time when I make a point to explore the world outside of my office. If defragging is done weekly, the process usually takes less than an hour on a large drive; if the system has been left to its own for a month or more, or if there is a relatively small amount of available working space, defragging can take several hours to complete.

Another utility suite with similar features is System Mechanic Pro. In its version 5.0 and later it includes similar system maintenance facilities, antivirus protection, and undeleted functions. This product's major shortcoming is its small market share; the ubiquitous Norton/Symantec suites have better and quicker reactions to new virus outbreaks.

Try to get in the habit of shutting off any background programs and disconnecting from the Internet before running a defragger. In certain conditions, if your system checks for e-mail or updates a Web page in the middle of a defragmentation session it will cause the utility to start the process over again.

Can you see me now?

If you travel with a digital camera or prepare PowerPoint or other presentations using images, your laptop travel kit should include graphic database and editing tools.

From my point of view, the reigning database champion here is ACDSee, which allows you to organize, convert format, and quickly find images stored on your machine. For information on this product, consult www.acdsystems.com. Some digital cameras provide similar software as one of the software utilities. (As an example, Nikon offers Picture Project.) Any database is better than just dumping your pictures into a single folder, but I prefer the tools offered by ACDSee.

When it comes to editing your photos, line art, and screen captures for presentations or printing, the market offers a number of products. But the longtime champion, still unsurpassed, is Adobe Photoshop, which is available in a full-featured professional version that includes image manipulation and restoration as well as bitmap drawing facilities (Adobe Photoshop CS2) and an extremely capable but smaller and less expensive version aimed at photo and image manipulation (Adobe Photoshop Elements). You can find information about both products at www.adobe.com.

Can you hear me now?

For many of you road warriors, laptops also serve as sound studios. In my case I often conduct interviews using a microcassette recorder or a digital recorder, and I sometimes use those audio files in PowerPoint presentations or to upload audio to my office for transcription. The source can be a microphone, a line input from an external device such as a tape recorder or receiver, or a downloaded WAV, MP3, or other digital file received over the Internet.

What can possibly go wrong? Well, just as an example, I use an external microphone that I clip onto the collar of people I interview. In the best case, the person I am interviewing is wearing clothing that allows the mike to sit a few inches away from the body, the subject speaks clearly, and there is no significant background noise. In the worst case, the microphone is muffled by clothing, the speaker has a weak voice, and the wind is howling or a fan is running or some sort of buzz, hiss, or repetitive noise in the background makes the file either difficult to understand or unusable in a presentation.

One of the best solutions I know of is Sound Forge software from Sony. This product is available in a full professional version that has more bells and whistles than the Space Shuttle and is a simplified but still highly capable (and less expensive) product intended for home and less demanding business uses. Both Sound Forge 8.0 and the simpler Sound Forge Audio Studio are available at retailers and direct from www.sony.com/mediasoftware. This product is miles beyond the simple sound recorder and editor usually supplied with sound cards installed in laptops and desktops.

Although you can (and should) use Sound Forge as a first-class digital recording software utility, for me the heart of its facilities are on the repair side: three different types of extremely flexible and capable equalization tools that allow you to emphasize or deemphasize as many as 20 distinct frequencies in a file or an infinitely adjustable graphic equalizer; an Audio Restoration tool that permits you to sample a particular noise and then subtract it from the sound file, and normalization and volume controls that can repair many sins caused by weak recordings. In Figure 19-5 you can see a digitized waveform from an analog recording, along with some of the options in the Audio Restoration plug-in.

Figure 19-5:
Sony's
Sound
Forge 8.0
includes a
full suite of
repair and
enhance-
ment tools
for audio
files, an
extremely
useful tool
for road
warriors
who need
to edit
sound files
for use in
presenta-
tions or as
a source
for tran-
scriptions.

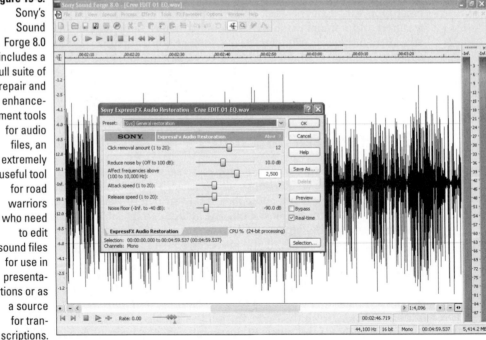

Part VI
The Part of Tens

The 5th Wave — By Rich Tennant

"I tell him many times — get lighter laptop. But him think he know better. Him have big ego. Him say, 'Me Tarzan, you not!' That when vine break."

In this part . . .

Ten, count 'em, ten quick solutions to big problems. Ten essential dos and don'ts for laptop users. And ten of my favorite things for the road and desktop.

Yes, you've reached the Part of Tens. This is a distillation of hundreds of pages and tens of thousands of words in this book, and millions of words and hundreds of thousands of miles traveled (lugging a transportable computer, then a portable computer, then a laptop) for more than 30 years as a journalist.

As you've explored in this book, you can upgrade or repair a laptop many more than ten ways, but these are some of the best.

Chapter 20

Ten Quick Solutions

Arthur Dent and his buddy Ford Prefect lived through strange adversity by adhering to the advice of *The Hitchhiker's Guide to the Galaxy* in Douglas Adam's wondrous book of the same name: "Don't panic." As hitchhikers with laptops, those should be your watchwords, too. Don't panic if your computer crashes to the ground, if you spill a cuppa Joe on the keyboard, or any other unhappy accident befalls it. Take a deep breath, think about the situation, and then try to save the day.

In this section I start you on the way to recovery from 10 possible disasters. Please forgive me if I begin each lesson with a small guilt trip; I'm merely trying to stop problems *before* they happen.

Your Computer Falls Off the Table

Now why'd you go and do that? Always make sure your laptop is on a firm footing on a sturdy table. Except, of course, if you are working on the seat-back tray table on airliner — one of the more common locations for laptops and one of the most dangerous.

Anyhow, the computer has fallen. Don't panic.

Laptops are pretty sturdy, and most will survive a tumble of a few feet to the ground. . .with a few exceptions. The biggest risk comes if the laptop's LCD screen was open at the time of the crash; if the front or side of the screen hits the ground first, it can be cracked or completely broken off its hinges. If that happens, you're not going to find a solution in this book; you're going to need to take or send it to a repair facility — and you'll have to decide if the cost of repair exceeds the value of the machine.

But you should be able to retrieve the information that is stored on the hard drive. The first thing to do is hook up the laptop to an external monitor or television and enable output to that screen. (Consult the instruction manual for your laptop to learn the keystroke combination or switch.) If you see an image on the monitor or screen, your motherboard, hard drive, and keyboard are not damaged. See Chapter 12 for more details.

Don't panic if you don't see an image: Consider whether now is the time to offload any essential data, pictures, and music to another computer. You can use the CD-R or DVD-R to burn a disc to hold a great deal of data, or you can connect the machine to an Ethernet by cable or WiFi and grab the data in that way. Another alternative is to use the WiFi system or a dial-up modem and send the files to your own e-mail account.

If you are unable to communicate with your laptop, another way to get the data off the hard drive is to remove it from the machine and install it in a working laptop or in an external enclosure and attach it to a desktop or laptop to offload the data. See Chapter 7 for full details on this process.

Finally, there's this: Was the hard drive writing data when it fell? Although the tiny hard drives used in modern laptops are pretty sturdy devices, one of the worst-case scenarios is for the laptop to tumble at the exact fraction of a second when the read/write heads are recording information to the drive. If the jolt is hard enough, one of two things can happen: First, the data can be corrupted, with the head bouncing around instead of hovering over its assigned location. Or, the jolt could be hard enough to cause the read/write head to make contact with the surface of the disk. Though the head is extremely light, the disk's high speed can make the collision seem like a Hollywood remake of "The Day the Earth Caught Fire." (Great movie, by the way. . .an overlooked sci-fi classic.)

A corrupted hard drive can sometimes be partially or fully repaired using basic tools like those included in Norton SystemWorks or in System Mechanic. (See Chapter 19 for details.) Or you may have to remove the hard drive from the laptop and ship it to a professional data recovery company; these guys are capable of stripping information off a drive and rerecording it on a new drive or onto a CD or DVD.

You Spill a Cup of Coffee/Soda/ Water on Your Keyboard

Didn't your mother teach you how to keep your room clean? Haven't I warned you sufficiently? (Okay, even I sometimes bring a can of soda into my office; but I keep it on a side table three feet away from anything and everything electronic.)

But now you've kicked the can, tumbled the coffee, or unbottled the water onto your laptop's keyboard. Don't panic. The first thing to do is to turn off the power, because water and electricity are an unpleasant combination. If the machine is running off the battery, you can safely depower using Windows shutdown procedures or by pressing and holding the on/off switch (on most laptops). But if the laptop is running off an AC adapter, be sure that the adapter and the wiring that runs to the wall outlet are not wet. If they're even damp, don't touch them and instead turn off the power at the circuit breaker.

With the power turned off, disconnect and remove the battery. Then you can begin to clear the spill by blotting it up with absorbent towels. If we're talking about a small spill, that may be all you have to do. But if we're talking about 16 ounces of Jolt or a mocha grande with whipped cream, the cleanup (and the potential for damage) is greater.

The good news is that most laptops have a plastic or rubber-like membrane beneath the keycaps, and your assignment may be removal of the keys and a careful cleaning. If somehow the liquid has gotten into the laptop's innards — the hard drive, the motherboard, or other parts — the extent of damage may depend on what was spilled. Water will dry without leaving a residue; if nothing shorted out at the time of the spill, the machine may be ready to return to service in a day or so once it has fully dried. (Do not use a hair dryer or other heated source to dry the machine; you can use a gentle flow of air from a fan.) Coffee or soda, though, both dry as sticky, corrosive gunk, and you may have to send the machine to a professional shop to be disassembled and cleaned. See Chapter 3 for more details.

If the AC adapter became totally soaked, consider purchasing a replacement; substitute chargers are available from the maker of your laptop as well as from third parties. Do not attempt to open it yourself and make repairs.

You Smell Something Burning

This is not good news, but it may not be fatal. Don't panic. Quickly shut down the computer.

Here are some possible causes for an unpleasant electronic odor:

✔ Insufficient or blocked cooling vents.

✔ A failing or overloaded AC adapter.

✔ A short-circuited or failing internal circuit within the case.

Once you have turned off the computer, allow it to cool for half an hour or so. In the meantime make a survey of the exterior: Use your nose to determine if you can isolate the source of the odor, use your fingertips (carefully) to try to find any hot spots, and use your eyes to see if you can find any blockages to the cooling vents.

If you can see that the vents are blocked by an accumulation of dust, dirt, or a melted chocolate bar, you can assume that this is the problem. Carefully clean off the vent; the best tool is a vacuum hose. Don't use a can of compressed air, since this will push crud *into* the body of the laptop, which is exactly the opposite of what you want to accomplish. Another way in which the vents may be blocked is if you place the laptop on a soft surface, like a blanket on a bed. The machine is designed to stand off a solid surface so that air can circulate underneath.

All AC adapters will generate a bit of heat, but not enough to toast bread. If the adapter is extremely hot, two possibilities may be causing it. First of all, it may be failing and need to be replaced. A second cause for generation of heat may be related to the voltage it is receiving from the wall outlet. Most modern adapters can work with incoming voltage in the range from 100–240 volts; that covers most every electrical standard in the world. (Utilities in the United States and Canada generally supply alternating current between 110 and 120 volts cycling back and forth at 60 Hz — 60 times per second, with cycles measured in Hertz, named after physicist Heinrich Hertz.)

Whatever the input, the AC adapter converts the power to a level and type required by the laptop and its battery. My current Toshiba laptop demands 19 volts of DC (direct current); machines from other manufacturers may require as little as 12 volts or as many as 24 volts. If the incoming voltage is at one of the extremes of the adapter's range, especially at the high end, it has to work harder to drop the voltage down and convert it to DC. One byproduct of the conversion is heat. I would be very wary of any adapter that became extremely hot.

The third possibility is that something has gone wrong within the laptop case. Don't panic. Consult the instruction manual, web site (on a different machine), or support desk to determine whether the laptop's design includes a fan that runs anytime the machine is running, or a fan that is switched on anytime the interior reaches a certain temperature.

After the laptop has had at least half an hour to cool off, turn it back on. If the fan is supposed to come on immediately, feel for a gentle rush of air coming out of the vents; if the fan is supposed to switch on at a certain temperature, use the machine for a while, checking for the fan. If the fan never comes on and the heat builds, you'll have to send the machine to a repair facility to have the fan replaced — if that makes economic sense.

As a short-term solution — and I mean only about 30 minutes at a time — you can run an exterior fan that blows beneath the laptop and assists venting. That should allow you to offload any essential files to another machine or to a CD-R; it may require several cycles.

You Receive a Threatening Note from the Computer

Don't take it personally . . . and don't panic. Find a piece of paper and write down the message, including any code numbers. And then write down as much as you remember about what you were doing just before the message appeared. Had you just loaded a program? Had you just executed a particular command? How many programs were running at the moment?

Look for an indication of the source of the message. Do you see the name of a particular piece of software or software maker in the note? Is the note merely informational? (Your antivirus definitions need updating, for example.)

Users of Microsoft Windows XP will see some error messages that offer assistance in repairing the problem; if your machine is connected to the Internet, clicking the button takes you to a web page that offers some suggestions for fixing the problem.

Does the note tell you that the machine has stopped? One tipoff is the dreaded "fatal error" message. You may be able to restart the machine by clicking a button within the message or you may have to force a power-off or a restart by hitting the classic Ctrl+Alt+Del key combination and then selecting Shut Down. If that doesn't work, as a last resort turn off the power to the machine. (Some laptops will shut off if you press and hold the power button for a few seconds; other machines may have a small reset button that is activated by the high-tech method of inserting a straightened paper clip.)

If the machine restarts and the problem is nowhere to be seen, you can hope it was a very rare hiccup. If the computer works for a while and then the message reappears, consult your notes and see if this was a recurrence of the same sequence of events that caused the failure before.

Sign on to the Internet — on the laptop if it will allow, or on another machine if necessary — and seek assistance. If you believe the source of the message was Windows, go to the Microsoft Knowledge Base at www.microsoft.com and type in the title of the error message.

If the source of the message is a product from another company, go to the support section of that manufacturer's web site and look for a solution there. Or call the maker and read the message to a cheerful, helpful customer service engineer . . . or to a sullen, barely comprehensible drone. . .and seek assistance.

If you can narrow down the cause of the problem to a particular program, consider uninstalling the program. Reboot the machine and see if it is performing properly. Run a system check using Norton SystemWorks, System Mechanic, or a similar utility. If all seems well, reinstall the software. In the process, check to see if the web site has an updated version of the program or a new device driver.

Your Ports Set Sail

On many machines, the weakest links are the places where data and power enter and exit the machine. Just imagine a laptop falling or bouncing even just a few inches with a power cable plugged into the rear, an Ethernet cable or a phone cord attached to the side, and an external mouse connected to another port. Snap, crackle, and pop!

As I explore in Chapter 4, some laptops are sturdier than others when it comes to the ports. The better design has connectors separated from the motherboard by a cable to allow a bit of flex if strain is placed on the port. Unfortunately, many laptops have connectors directly attached to the motherboard; if they break off, they damage the board. In a tiny fraction of such situations a technician can resolder the broken connector to the motherboard.

But don't panic. With the exception of the connector that provides power from the AC adapter — essential for both powering the machine and charging the battery — there are workarounds for nearly every other situation. They key is to make use of the USB port on the laptop, which is relatively robust and extremely versatile.

The USB port can be used for network interface cards for Ethernet, external pointing devices, serial and parallel port adapters, and even as connectors to external monitors and televisions. If your laptop has only one USB port, it can be expanded through the use of a hub. Another workaround for some of the same devices is the PC Card slot.

Your Machine Won't Start

You press the on button and look away for a moment to organize your workspace; it always takes at least 10 seconds (and sometimes more) for the machine to come to life, and not many people enjoy staring at a blank screen even for just that short period of time. But then you look back and the screen is still black.

Don't panic. A laptop might not come to life for many reasons, and most of them are easy to fix. Let me work through the most common causes.

The battery isn't providing power

Check to see that the battery has not been accidentally disconnected from the laptop. Most machines place the battery in a bay or a slot on the underside of the machine with a latch to hold it in place; that latch can become dislodged during travel.

The battery may also be completely discharged. Usually, though, a laptop shuts down when battery power declines to about 5 percent of full capacity; that's usually enough to allow the machine to begin to come to life the next time you try to start it but not sufficient to permit operation.

Batteries do not last forever. They usually have a period of slow decline during which they hold their charge for a shorter period of time, or the number of hours they power the laptop decline. The final stage for some batteries is essentially a short: They will not accept a charge at all.

The best way to determine if the battery is not working properly is to check to see if the machine works properly when connected to an AC adapter. Most laptops can be run from a wall current without a battery present.

The AC adapter isn't providing power

Begin with this: Is it plugged in to a working wall outlet? Some outlets are turned on or off by a switch, and some outlets may be disabled by a blown circuit breaker. Test the outlet by plugging a radio or desk lamp into it.

If you are sure the wall outlet is delivering electricity, move on to examine the adapter. Look for obvious signs of damage: Burn marks are a bad sign, as are any cuts in the AC cable coming in or the DC cable going out. If you see this sort of problem, I suggest you retire the adapter and purchase a replacement unit from the original manufacturer or from a third-party parts supplier.

Now check that the adapter is properly connected. In most designs, the adapter is a rectangular box that sits between two cables. The plug at the end of one cable must be connected to a wall outlet and the other end to the adapter. (This cable can usually be disconnected from the adapter to allow use of cables with different types of plugs — a polarized two-prong plug like those used in the United States, Canada, Japan, and many other parts of the world, a two- or three-prong round pin connector like those used in some parts of Europe, or a three-spade angled connector used in other areas.)

On some adapters, the connector that runs from the adapter to the laptop is also detachable. This is of no benefit to the user, but it does allow the manufacturer to use a single adapter with a number of different laptops. Make certain that both cables are properly connected to the adapter, that the AC end is plugged in to a working wall outlet, and that the DC end is connected properly to the power input on the laptop.

If the machine works properly with the AC adapter in place but the battery will not accept and hold a charge, the most likely source of the problem is the battery. That can easily be fixed by purchasing a replacement from the manufacturer or from a third-party source such as www.igo.com.

Your Hard Drive Imitates a Pancake

If the computer comes to life (you see LEDs flash and hear the hard drive spin) but Windows does not load, try shutting off the machine and restarting it. Sometimes I even throw in a gentle wake-up call: With the laptop sitting on a sturdy surface, lift the front or back of the machine and let it come back to the tabletop in a controlled fall — about the way you might casually let a pen drop onto the surface of your desk.

Why would I do that? Because hard drives, optical drives, and fans are the principal *mechanical* parts of an electronic computer. Like a creaky screen door they sometimes need a bit of an extra push, especially at times of high humidity or after an extended period without use.

Don't panic. The next thing to do is see that the hard drive is properly connected to the laptop. Most modern portable computers install the hard drive in a bay or similar opening, much like the way the battery is attached.

Disconnect the AC adapter and remove the battery to remove the chances of an electrical surge. Make certain the computer is sitting on a sturdy table. Ground yourself, and then open the latch that holds the drive in place and gently slide the drive out. Look for any signs of corrosion, dirt, or damage to the connectors. If all seems in order, slide the drive back into its holder and make sure it clicks into place. Reinstall the battery and then the AC adapter.

If the hard drive comes back to life after a momentary death (Do hard disks see a flash of blinding light at the end?) you may want to consider this a warning that a real ending is near. Make sure that you make backups of all critical data files.

You may go weeks or months between intermittent failures, which you may find tolerable. But if the stoppages begin to come more frequently, I advise you to invest in a replacement hard drive and install it yourself; prices are so low that there is little excuse not to have a machine that is ready to roll any time you need it. (If your machine is still under warranty, you may have a hard time convincing the manufacturer to replace the hard drive because of an intermittent problem; keep at it, though, and insist on your right to compute.)

Another type of hard drive problem is the result of system boot track corruption. This can be caused by a momentary electrical problem or a computer virus. Your hard drive will start to spin, your LCD will display the ordinary System Setup information, and then you will see an onscreen message such as this all-time favorite: "BOOT DISK FAILURE. Please insert a system disk and reboot."

Once again, the first thing to do is shut down the machine and then restart it to see if this was a one-in-a-million error. If the computer comes to life and Windows starts, the first thing you should do is run a system check utility such as Norton SystemWorks or System Mechanic. If either of these programs gives your machine a clean bill of health, the next step is to conduct a full antivirus scan. Once that is completed, you can proceed with work; I suggest updating your backups of essential data files.

You can use the original distribution disk for Windows (as supplied by the maker of your laptop or as purchased from Microsoft) or a special system restore disk you created using a program such as Norton Utilities to boot the system from the CD drive.

Once Windows has been started in this way you should be able to go to My Computer and open the folder that contains the hard drive. Check that the data files are intact. See if you can launch programs from the drive. If the machine does not load Windows, the next step is to use an alternate means to boot the system and then explore the hard drive system tracks. Windows XP includes a capable System Restore system, which may be solution here *if the system can read the hard drive.*

Start by trying to boot using the "Last Known Good Configuration." While the machine attempts to boot, press the F8 function key. Select the option that offers the LKGC option I just spelled out. That choice lets you go back in time to the settings and configurations in use the last time everything seemed well with the world. If it works, go immediately to the Control Panel and check the health of devices there and then run a System Check utility. Run a diagnostics program that checks for the disk's hardware and software integrity.

If you are unable to boot in this manner, your next best step is to try restarting Windows in Safe Mode, one of the other options available from F8. If this works, go to the Control Panel and look for problems among devices and run a System Check utility. Run a diagnostics program that checks for the disk's hardware and software integrity.

If neither of the F8 options delivers you to back up and running safely, the final step is to reinstall Windows. Do so with a careful hand. If you've lived a good life, helping little old ladies cross the street and volunteering at a homeless shelter, and are lucky, reinstalling the operating system may solve your problems and not delete any data files on your disk. The Catch-22 is that Microsoft says that it does not recommend reinstalling Windows as a solution to a hard drive that is experiencing mechanical problems. But if you have no choice, then you have no choice.

You may have to go to the system BIOS to enable your computer to boot from the CD. Here's how to reinstall Windows XP by starting your computer from the Windows XP CD:

1. **Restart your computer with the Windows XP disc in the CD-ROM or DVD-ROM drive.**

   Watch for an onscreen message that reads, "Press any key to boot from CD." You will, I'm sure, realize that you need to press any key.

   You will see a screen that offers you the option to setup Windows XP by pressing the Enter key.

2. **That's what you want, so press Enter.**

3. **Press F8 to agree to the Windows XP Licensing Agreement.**

   You've got to agree, so don't fight it.

4. **The system should be able to detect a current installation of Windows XP; make sure it is highlighted and selected in the box onscreen and then press R to repair it.**

5. **Follow the succeeding instructions to reinstall Windows XP.**

   When the task is complete you may have to reactivate your copy of the operating system by contacting Microsoft online and providing the Product Key.

Your Wireless Network Has a Failure to Communicate

WiFi rules, except when the conversation is strictly one way. Hello? Hello? Is anyone out there? Wireless communication can be as simple as turn on and tune in, but it can also be very frustrating if the conditions are not right or the settings are improper. I go over many of the details in Chapter 13.

So what to do if your WiFi does not work? Don't panic. Go back a paragraph and consider those two essentials:

✔ Turn on. Nearly every laptop with WiFi capabilities has a physical switch on the case or a soft switch in software that enables or disables the transmitter/receiver. This is important for several reasons: The device uses power and you've no reason to devote battery resources when it is not needed. Some locations may require you to turn off any wireless device, including airliners in flight, hospitals, and some government or military sites.

  If your WiFi does not work, the first thing to do is check to see if it turned on. Consult the instruction manual or support desk for assistance if necessary.

✔ Tune in. Just because you have a WiFi card doesn't mean you'll find a signal everywhere you go. And just because you find a signal doesn't mean that the transmitter owner will allow anyone to sign on and share the bandwidth.

  You find three types of WiFi networks:

  • A **private network** such as one set up within a home or business and restricted to a particular set of users. The router associated with the WiFi transceiver has a list of the unique identification number assigned to WiFi cards permitted to use the system and any other machine is not given access.

- A **subscription-only network.** Providers ranging from major cell phone companies, other utilities, and local companies offer hot spots in communities, airports, and other public areas. In most cases you can sign on to a welcome page, which sometimes includes advertisements for local companies and basic information, and then purchase access (by the hour, day, or for longer periods of time). As an example, the T-Mobile cell phone company has hot spots for its customers in places including many Starbucks coffee shops and FedEx Kinko's stores.

- A **free public network.** Many libraries, some community organizations, and some commercial operations such as Panera sandwich shops offer free wireless Internet access. All you need to do is show up with a properly equipped machine and grab a seat. (They may expect you to buy a sandwich or a cup of coffee.)

You may also find that some private network owners do not restrict access to their personal wireless routers. In fact, that may be the most common setting for a wireless network in someone's home; you may be able to troll for networks by aimless wandering. Although I live deep in the country, I find that from time to time a neighbor's wireless router pops up on my list of available networks; weather conditions seem to make the signal stronger at some times. Be sure you ask your neighbor, however; some users don't know that they need to restrict access and might not appreciate your tagging along and possibly slowing down their operations a bit.

No matter what kind of wireless network you are using, there is always the risk that someone is eavesdropping. I suggest that you avoid conducting banking and other financial matters over a public network; if you absolutely must do so, change your password regularly and keep a close eye on your accounts in search of any unusual activity and notify banks and credit card companies immediately if you see anything out of the ordinary. Make certain you have an antivirus program in place and scan your machine regularly.

What happens if you're a subscriber or an authorized user of a private network or are attempting to sign on to a public network and have no success? Check to make sure that the WiFi adapter is switched on. Then check to see if the Device Manager under Windows shows a hardware failure or fails to note the presence of a wireless adapter. Many laptop manufacturers also provide a specialized WiFi control utility that may include a troubleshooting utility.

If you determine that your WiFi system has failed, you may be able to replace the module. However, some manufacturers require that this repair be done at an authorized repair facility to comply with Federal Communications Commission rules to shield against unintended interference. One way around this expensive solution is to use a PC Card WiFi system as a workaround; those require nothing more than plugging in to the slot.

The LCD Won't Display

The LEDs flash, you hear the hard drive spin, and you feel the gentle, reassuring rush of air coming out of the cooling vent. But your LCD does not display. . .or at least doesn't display what you expected to see. I guess you can see by now that I'm going to advise: Don't panic. You can take several steps to determine whether your LCD is dead, demised, and bereft of life (or merely sleeping).

Shut off the machine and leave it be for 10 seconds. While you are waiting, make certain that it is properly attached to its AC adapter, which is in turn plugged in to a functioning wall outlet. Turn the machine back on and watch the screen carefully. Depending on your machine's design, you should see bits of text or images onscreen before Windows loads; the clue to the nature of your problem may lay here.

The first thing you should see is an indication that the system BIOS is loading. On some machines you see a few lines of simple text, white on black, that identify the BIOS manufacturer and version; you may also see a message that tells you the key that opens the BIOS screen before the operating system is loaded. (You may be asked to press the Esc key or one of the function keys.)

On my current laptop, the manufacturer chooses to use the opening screen as an advertisement for itself (as if I don't already know the maker of the machine that is beneath my fingers). And so I see the name of the manufacturer in big red letters and a slogan telling me how wonderful these folks really are; there's also an advertisement from those marvelous folks who made the microprocessor inside the case. Down at the bottom of the screen is a line of text that instructs me how to open the system BIOS.

If you see nothing at all

You've got a problem with the LCD itself, the connection between the display device and the motherboard, or the display adapter on the motherboard. Turn off the laptop and attach an alternate display to the machine — either a standard computer monitor plugged in to a video output connector or a television screen attached to a TV output. Consult the instruction manual for your laptop (or study the key caps carefully) to determine how to change the output from the laptop to an external monitor or television.

Now start your machine and shift the video output to the alternate display. If you see an image, try pressing the key to display the system BIOS. Go to the section that deals with video output and see if it is properly set up to work with an LCD screen. In some situations, the BIOS can become corrupted by a power anomaly, a magnetic field, or even a virus. Try selecting the option to reset the BIOS to its default settings. Be sure to save your changes to the BIOS.

Turn off the computer, let it rest for a few seconds, and then restart. If the LCD still does not display properly, this tells you that the likely problem is with the LCD or its connection to the motherboard. Alas, this is a job for an expert technician, and should only be done if it makes economic sense.

The good news here is that you can use the alternate monitor or television to view the contents of your hard drive as you offload important files to a recordable CD or over a network to another machine.

If you see the opening splash screen

This tells you that the LCD, its connection to the motherboard, and the display adapter are working. Press the key to display the system BIOS and go to the section that deals with video output; reset the BIOS to its default settings. Save the changes to the BIOS.

Restart the computer and see if it proceeds through to Windows. If not, you may have a problem with the system tracks on the hard drive. See the suggestions in the disaster earlier in this section, "Your Hard Drive Imitates a Pancake."

Something Wicked Comes Your Way

Files are missing. Your hard drive is clicking away at times when it should be quiet. The machine runs painfully slow and keeps crashing. You are receiving angry notes and angrier phone calls from friends and business associates accusing you of sending them a virus-infected e-mail. And every once in a while a truly strange message appears on your laptop's screen: "Kilroy Was Here" or something a bit more profane.

If these are the things you see, you just might be infected by a virus, whether you are a redneck or not. But (say it with me, class) don't panic.

First of all, you should have been running a fully capable and current antivirus program on your laptop. The best of the programs include Norton AntiVirus, McAfee VirusScan, and PC-cillin. Any of these should detect a virus when it arrives on your machine, and they should detect and warn you if your machine starts to perform actions worthy of suspicion: changes to the system tracks, alterations to file indexes, and mass e-mailings with recipients randomly selected from your address book.

If you receive a message warning you of this sort of activity, stop whatever you are doing. Shut down any programs that are running, including your Web browser and e-mail. Physically disconnect the cable to your broadband Internet router or shut off your wireless router. And then follow the instructions of your antivirus program to quarantine or remove the virus. After the virus has been isolated, you should run a full antivirus scan in search of any other viruses or malware.

How can a virus get onto a machine even if you have an antivirus program installed? The answer is that new works of nastiness are introduced on an almost-daily basis, and you just might be so unlucky as to receive a virus in the relatively short time between its release and the receipt of an update to your antivirus program. The best of the antivirus companies react within hours to reports of a new virus; it's up to you to regularly update the virus definitions on your machine. (Make sure that your program is set up to automatically communicate with its manufacturer anytime you connect to the Internet.)

What do you do if you suspect a virus and for some reason you do not have an antivirus program running on your laptop? You should almost panic . . . and immediately shut down your machine and disconnect it from the Internet. Then run or walk — the machine is not going to do anything while it is turned off — to a computer store and purchase the best antivirus software you can find.

If you have a virus on your machine — or suspect that you do — most antivirus makers instruct users not to install their programs (and allow the existing virus to do more damage) but instead that you boot the machine from the antivirus software CD and scan the system from that disc. You may have to change your system BIOS setup options so the CD drive is the first place the system searches for bootup tracks. Once the antivirus program has cleaned up your disk, you can install it on the hard drive and enable automatic, regular updates.

Chapter 21

Ten Essential Dos and Don'ts

As songwriter Jim Croce once warned us, you don't tug on Superman's cape, you don't spit into the wind. . .and if I might add, you don't mess around with your laptop when you're miles away from home. That's just one of my top-10 don'ts to protect your computer's health. The point being you should take care of your machine at all times at home and on the road, and only perform major changes or maintenance when you are near the tools, backups, and support from those you know and love. It's a jungle out there!

Living Long and Prospering

No computer should ever be turned on and then ignored for the rest of its useful life. The machine needs to be kept clean inside and out, its parts need to be tested regularly, its storage system needs to be inspected and reorganized from time to time, and it needs to be protected against unauthorized intrusion. All of these tasks are even more important when it comes to a laptop; because of its miniaturization it's more subject to damage from dirt, heat buildup, and the bad news that follows a fall to the floor.

No smoking, please

Smoke is bad for you, your coworkers, your family, and your laptop. Smoke carries contaminants, dust, and sticky stuff that can clog filters on the cooling system and breathing holes on internal drives. (If you have any doubt about this, find someone who does indulge and ask him or her to exhale a lung full of smoke through a clean handkerchief.) So, don't smoke in and around your laptop and don't use your machine in a smoky bar or office.

Taking care of the environment

Dirty and dusty environments might include workshops, basements, dorm rooms, and your kid's bedroom.

Keeping a steady hand

Don't drop, shake, vibrate, or otherwise do anything to dislodge the innards or misalign the moving parts. This is bad anytime, and this is really bad if it happens when the machine is running. It could cause the hard drive read/write head to bounce onto and damage the spinning disk beneath.

Being careful out there

Avoid packing your laptop in luggage that you will not carry onboard an airplane yourself. If you don't know why, just peek out the window of the plane as ramp workers load or unload baggage — most are tossed onto a moving belt or into a cart. And bags can get wet in the process and suffer extremes of temperature while in flight.

Keeping the exits clear

Don't block the laptop's air vents, but do occasionally gently vacuum out any dust caught on the exterior filter or screen. Don't run the laptop while it's inside its carrying case, because its padding and sides block the flow of air.

Maintaining your cool

Pay attention to the indoor or outdoor temperature. Cold below about 40°F can reduce battery life, make plastic parts brittle, and damage the LCD. Heat above about 100°F can warp plastic and damage the LCD; if the outside air is anywhere near that temperature, the internal fans aren't going to do much to cool the hot microprocessor and memory.

If the humidity level is very high, internal parts can become wet, which is not a good thing for electronic parts; high humidity can also cause floppy disks or CDs to become stuck in their holders. Of course, if the atmosphere is extremely dry, the chances of electrostatic buildup and discharge are increased; in that situation ground yourself before touching your laptop, especially after you have walked across a carpeted floor.

At great extremes of altitude, above 7,500 feet or so, the cooling system can also be compromised, and the hard drive read/write heads may not be able to properly float above the disk surface like they are supposed to. (In case you were wondering, commercial airliners are pressurized so that the air density is equivalent to a few thousand feet even while the plane is flying as much as 25,000 to 30,000 feet above the ground.)

That's not to say you can't run your laptop in any environment other than a 68° clean room. But if your laptop has spent the last few hours in the cold trunk of a car, the best practice is to give the laptop a few hours to warm up to room temperature before turning it on. This avoids condensation buildup on internal parts and allows mechanical parts to feel comfortable before they are asked to move. The more extreme the temperature differential, the more time you should allow the system to come to room temperature before powering it up.

Being unattractive

Keep the laptop away from strong magnetic fields that could cause problems with storage systems and other pieces of electronics. Sources of magnetism include any large motors (refrigerators, shredders, winches), television sets, and unshielded audio speakers.

Don't be a receiver

Stay away from radio transmitters, including commercial sites. Smaller radios, including cell phones, are not likely to threaten your data but it's still not a good idea to place an active transmitter of any size directly on or near your laptop.

If you suspect radio frequency interference from electrical devices, the first step should be to move the laptop away from the source. Some external devices can be shielded from interference through the use of a *toroidal coil* (a small iron circle) that surrounds the connecting cable; the device may come equipped with one, or you can purchase a coil from an electronics shop.

Staying light

Don't place heavy objects on top of the cover that holds the LCD, and don't squeeze the laptop into a carrier so tight that it places pressure on the case.

Caring for your LCD

Avoid touching the LCD with anything other than a soft, lintless cloth. Be careful not to leave a pen or other object on the keyboard when you close the laptop's cover; it can scratch or even puncture the LCD. Never lift the laptop by the LCD display.

Special Tips for Road Warriors

The previous warnings notwithstanding, a laptop's internal parts are pretty well insulated from damage (although you do need to take care of the little bits). One of the most common points of failure on a modern laptop are the various external points of connection — the little plug for the AC adapter, the ports for an Ethernet or telephone cable, and the exposed pieces of a PC Card, like a wireless antenna or a connector for an add-on cable. Be very careful plugging devices into your laptop and take extra care to assure that external devices are disconnected and out of the way when the machine is ready to be moved.

When you travel, make sure that the system is turned off and the cover properly latched. All openings should be properly closed, with no PC Cards, USB devices, or cables attached. If the machine is going to be left unused for weeks at a time, consult the instruction manual to see if the maker suggests you remove the battery and store it separately from the machine; if you leave the battery in place, make sure it is properly locked in place.

At the airport, your laptop is certain to receive special attention from the security screeners. An ordinary X-ray machine should not damage the contents of your laptop, but you should pay attention to how it is run through the machine. Make sure the laptop is placed in a plastic basket right-side up, and that it doesn't tumble off the end of the conveyor belt.

Frankly, I am less concerned about the effect of the X-ray machine at the airport than I am about the chance that someone at the other end will run away with my laptop while my shoes are being inspected. To deal with that worry, here's what I do: I put my carry-on suitcase, coat, shoes, keys, cell phone, and everything else through the machine first and my laptop last. Then I go through the metal detector keeping an eye on the progress of my laptop and grab it as soon as I am cleared.

Never make changes to the operating system and installed software on the road. And avoid adding new software if at all possible. Your laptop should be clean and ready to work when you go out the door; leave major maintenance and changes for when you are back home at your desk with all of your backup copies of software, tools, and friends nearby.

If you expect to have to use someone else's printer while on the road, you might want to consider obtaining a copy of the device driver software for that printer ahead of time; get the manufacturer name, model name, and model number and visit the company's web site to obtain the software. You can either install the driver before leaving or take it with you to have ready for installation when needed.

As an alternative, you should be able to send any document that needs to be printed as an attachment in an e-mail and then download and print it on a computer at your destination. This allows you to avoid having to make changes to your laptop's configuration for a one-time use.

Which brings me to my final set of tips for travelers:

1. Take the time the day before you head out on a trip to run your laptop through a full set of diagnostics.

2. Run a system check, if you have this sort of utility installed, to fix any problems with the Windows registry, shortcuts, and other operating system elements.

3. Run a full antivirus scan.

4. Test any applications you expect to use on your trip, including your word processor, date book, Internet browser, and e-mail.

5. Clean out the Recycle Bin.

6. Defragment your disk using the Windows utility if that's the best you have, or with a faster and more efficient third-party utility.

7. Make a backup copy of any unique files that are resident on your laptop.

   You can upload the files to a desktop machine on your network or copy them to a CD-R or other removable media.

8. Transfer a copy of any work in progress or presentations you need to make from your desktop PC to your laptop; you may also want to move a

copy of the date book or calendar program you keep current on your desktop. Use an Ethernet cable, WiFi connection, or sneakernet. (A USB memory key or a CD-R are the modern ways of transferring a set of files when there is not a network in place.) You can create a folder on the laptop for the work, or use the Windows briefcase function to hold copies that will later be synchronized to the desktop.

9. Check the integrity of the data files you transferred.

10. Test your applications one more time to make sure they work properly after defragmentation.

11. Check the contents of your computer kit bag to make sure it is properly stocked with anything you can envision using on your trip. See Chapter 23 for my kit contents.

Chapter 22

Ten of My Favorite Things

*T*he theory is, you know, that a laptop computer gives you everything you want in one small package. Designers pride themselves on squeezing 10 pounds of wizardry into a 5-pound package.

To some extent that's what they've accomplished. I only wish that I were capable of traveling with just the slim, lightweight laptop. (I am leaving aside the necessary AC power supply — a device that has undergone its own slimdown program over the years.)

Before I proceed, let me brag abou t. . . I mean describe . . . some of the strange and wonderful places I have lugged my laptops in the past decade as a journalist.

✔ In a former monastery in the literally breathtaking city of Cusco, Peru, at 11,203 above sea level where we paused for a breath of oxygen before traveling deeper into the Andes to visit the cloud castles of the sacred city of Machu Picchu. My laptop ran a bit hot in the thin air, but then I was dragging a bit myself.

✔ Onboard a train on a one-track line 100 miles past the last stretch of road in northern Ontario en route to the subarctic.

✔ By ship from Auckland, New Zealand, to Sydney, Australia, across the wild Tasman Sea with one hand on the keyboard and the other holding the computer down on the desktop.

✔ On more seatback tray tables than I could possibly remember, flying east, west, north, and south.

✔ Out the door of my office and into my bedroom to review a file or surf the Internet using a WiFi connection within my house (or hitchhiking onto a signal in the ether from a neighbor's system).

And so as I've intimated, when I pack my bag to head out on a trip I carry a whole bunch of extensions, add-ons, and useful doodads that were not delivered to me with the laptop. I'm talking hardware here: things that sit under, plug in to, or adapt a machine.

They also, alas, take up space and add a bit of weight. I pick and choose them carefully, adding some devices for certain trips and subtracting others when I think (or hope) I won't need them.

Here, then, are 10 of my favorite things.

Power, Power, Almost Anywhere

My current work laptop will work off battery power for three to four hours, depending on the sort of work I am doing and the settings I have made for power usage. For example, using the CD/DVD drive burns up a great deal of power; giving full brightness to the LCD will also shorten a day's battery life.

The maker of my machine provides a small AC adapter that can be used to recharge the battery in my office, at home, and in hotels. And like many road warriors, when I am changing planes on a long flight the first thing I do when I get to the gate at the airport is look for an electrical outlet so that I can recharge the battery at least partially. (Look under seats and along posts near the check-in desks; another likely source is near vending machines. Sometimes the agent at the podium will know the location of an outlet.)

But why should I be limited to ordinary sources of power like an AC wall outlet? How about automobile power outlets (we used to refer to them as *cigarette lighter outlets*)? And some airlines now offer electrical outlets near some or all of the seats in their planes. Finally, why do I need to carry one AC adapter for my laptop, another for my cell phone, a third one for the battery charger of my digital camera, and a fourth for my PDA?

One great solution is the iGo EverywherePower 7500, which can draw power from wall sockets, automobile outlets, and airline wiring. And with the use of interchangeable plugs (cutely called iGo iTips) and an included secondary adapter, I can power and charge two devices at once. The package includes a pair of power cords, one for wall outlets and another for power outlets in airline seats or cars. It all folds up into a neat little case, and weighs a reasonable 13 ounces — a bit less than a pound. You can see an iGo adapter with a selection of iTips in Figure 22-1.

Figure 22-1:
The flexible
Everywhere
Power 7500
from iGo
can attach
to a wall
outlet or an
airplane or
automobile
DC source
to power
almost any
electronic
device.

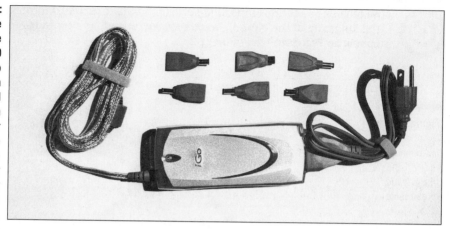

A Thingie to Hold My Laptop

I have found that the thinner and smaller a modern laptop gets, the less likely it becomes that the machine will sit at a comfortable angle for long periods of use. Some early laptop models came with a set of tiny legs that could be rotated into position at the back of computer; over time these useful but breakable little pieces have been taken away.

One solution is the ErgoStand from Mobility Electronics, sold by iGo.com and retailers. Similar stands are sold by other companies. ErgoStand is a few ounces of plastic that can be placed to raise or lower the keyboard by about 5 degrees, depending in which direction you place it. In some situations I find it valuable to raise the angle of the display when I am using it on an airplane's seatback tray table; in doing so the angle of the keyboard is lowered a bit, which puts less strain on my hands. The larger rubber feet on the stand also help prevent the laptop from sliding around on the tray.

A second problem involves heat buildup from the high-speed microprocessor within the case. If the laptop sits flush against a desktop or (even worse) flush against a soft surface like a sofa or a blanket in a hotel room, the proper cooling airflow may be blocked and the laptop's built-in cooling fan will have to work harder.

TIP

The ErgoStand improves the flow of air beneath the laptop by raising it half an inch or so off the supporting surface. A cooler-running laptop increases the longevity of the battery, boosts system speed, and extends processor life. I show an ErgoStand in Figure 22-2.

Figure 22-2:
Low tech but high design, the ErgoStand can raise the front or back of your laptop to make it easier to use, improving the flow of air beneath the machine as well.

Noise, Noise Go Away

Sound is an important part of the laptop work experience. You may be wanting to block out noisy neighbors, extraneous sound from televisions, or the drone of an airliner in flight. Or you may want to hear the audio from a DVD movie or a video game while you travel.

Noise Stop! Pro-Luxe noise-canceling stereo headphones can help erase background noise by generating a gentle whoosh of their own. They can also be plugged in to your laptop to listen to a movie or a music CD, or in to an airplane seat connection to deliver the audio from the movie that you never wanted to see in the theater. (Two tips that work with most airline seat connections are provided.) According to the maker, the neutral sound that is generated by the single AAA battery within is about -12 dB at 300Hz. *dB* stands for decibels, a measurement of sound level; a change of 10 dB down or up represents a decrease to one-tenth the level or an increase by tenfold.

The headphones themselves are much more substantial and comfortable to wear than the cheap devices given out (or sold) by airlines, but they fold in on themselves to fit into a case about the size of a can of soda. You can find Noise Stop! Headphones at retailers or through iGo.com. In Figure 22-3 you can see a set in its original packaging.

Figure 22-3: Headphones add a quiet low-frequency hiss that masks many intrusive sounds.

A Tiny Ethernet Cable and a Phone Cord

Although my laptop has a built-in WiFi transceiver, I nevertheless am always prepared in case I need to communicate in that ancient traditional method of wired connection.

I carry a small self-rolling Ethernet cable to allow me to plug in to an office network if necessary. The unit I have rolls a flat cable from top and bottom, like a double-ended tape measure. You can also just purchase an Ethernet cable with an RJ-45 connector at each end and toss it in your suitcase. A five-foot length should be sufficient; you can always move your laptop to be close to the office network outlet.

I also carry my own telephone connection cord just in case I need to reach way back in time and use the built-in modem of my laptop to communicate. Many telephones in hotel rooms now offer a place to plug your computer into the system. Using the phone system, of course, is generally the least preferred means of communication these days — much slower than a WiFi connection and much, much slower than a wired Ethernet link.

Although you *may* find an Ethernet cable and a phone cord waiting for you at your hotel or temporary office, you can't count on that. And there is no guarantee that the cables will be undamaged. The well-prepared laptop traveler brings his or her own.

A USB Memory Key

A *memory key* is a small block of flash memory attached to a USB connector. The first designs envisioned these devices as key rings holding tens of megabytes of data while some more current designs include smart pens, pointers, and assorted geegaws.

Flash memory is a near-permanent form of RAM; data written to it does not require a constant application of power. I say *near-permanent* for two reasons: First of all it can be erased and rewritten by a computer or other electronic device, and second because it *could* — with an emphasis on the *maybe* — be accidentally erased or corrupted by a strong magnetic or electrical field. That said, I have found them to be extremely robust and reliable.

When these devices first came out I thought of them as great solutions in search of a problem. Why would I need a little plug-in key that could store a relatively tiny 64MB or 256MB of data when I could connect by WiFi, wired Ethernet, or by one of half a dozen other physical media?

But in recent years I have lost track of the number of times I have found great utility in one of these little guys. The principle use: as a durable and convenient modern version of the sneakernet. (In the early days of the personal computer, the easiest way to transfer a file from one machine to another was to copy it to a floppy disk and then walk it over to the other machine — geeks wore sneakers — and copy the file.)

Allow me to explain with a few examples of how I have used a memory key:

✔ I had a file I had written on my laptop that I wanted to send by e-mail from an Internet cafe. There was no WiFi in the room, and there was no provision in the cafe for me to connect my laptop to the wired Ethernet.

(And from my point of view, I had no interest in exposing my laptop to whatever viruses, spyware, and malware there might be circulating on the public access machines.) The solution: I copied the file from my laptop to a memory key and then plugged the key into an open USB connection on the Internet cafe machine. The key became an extra hard drive on the system, and I was able to easily attach a file to an outgoing e-mail. I erased the key, reformatted it, and scanned it for viruses before I used it again on my laptop.

✔ I needed to print a file from my laptop to make a presentation, and the only available printer in the office I was visiting was a standalone machine. No Ethernet and no WiFi. It did have a floppy disk drive, but my new laptop didn't. One thing both machines had in common was a USB port. I copied the file to the key, then moved it to the other machine and printed the file from the word processor installed there. (As a side benefit, my file never resided on the hard drive of the borrowed machine, and so I did not have to worry about the confidentiality of the information I was printing; it has semi-permanent residence only on the key.)

✔ In a similar situation, I arrived with an Excel spreadsheet on my PC-based laptop and found that (horrors!) the office standard was Apple Macintosh machines. No problem: Copy the file to the USB key, move it over to the Mac, and upload it with the software on that foreign machine.

✔ And finally, there is this: Suppose you need to transfer some data from your desktop or laptop and have no other reason to lug a computer from one place to another and do not have any details about the machine you will use when you arrive at your destination. (This is a fairly common situation when I travel to remote corners of the world. I cannot be certain that a machine will be connected to the Internet or that the speed will be sufficient to allow me to download a file I send to myself — which is one solution to this kind of problem.) An easy solution, though, is to copy the file to a USB key and carry its two or three ounces of weight in my pocket instead of several pounds on my shoulder.

Need I Point out the Need for a Presentation Tool?

One common use of a laptop for business travelers is to deliver a presentation — in a customer's office, the board room, or a large forum to accompany a speech. Specialized software like PowerPoint helps you point with pride and view with alarm a presentation that would impress Steven Spielberg and make The Donald say, "You're hired."

You can create a PowerPoint presentation on your laptop or on a desktop before you head out on the road, but the problems come when it's time to share:

- ✔ If it's just you and a client (or your boss), you can sit alongside each other and let the show go on. You may need to wedge yourself in close enough to reach the pointing device or an attached mouse in order to pause the presentation or back up to review a page.

- ✔ If you've got a small crowd, you may be able to gather them around the laptop, but the wider the group, the more likely that some of the people in the room will be at or beyond the useable viewing angle of the LCD screen on your laptop. And you've still got to find a way to get your finger in there somewhere if you want to exercise manual control of the show.

- ✔ If the crowd is more than a few or the room is large, you may be able to output the presentation from your laptop to a large monitor (using a VGA output) or use an LCD projector to put the show up on the big screen in a boardroom or an auditorium. So far, so good, but until you make other arrangements you're still stuck within an arm's length of the laptop to control the show.

My favorite solution, and a regular addition to my kit bag any time I need to make a presentation, is a wireless remote control. Among the best is Keyspan's Presentation Remote. (Consult www.keyspan.com for details.) This little device, about half the size of your basic television remote control, communicates by radio frequency signal to a small receiver that plugs in to a USB port on the laptop. The remote control includes all the functions of a two-button mouse; it comes ready to use for PowerPoint, but you can also download a free software utility from the Keyspan web site that allows you to program the remote for use with any application.

The remote works from anywhere within 40 feet of your laptop, allowing you to wander the room like a television talk show host. And even niftier, the small remote also includes a laser pointer that allows you to emphasize your words and pictures.

Keyspan also sells another device that would be of value to road warriors who make presentations based on DVDs, CDs, MP3s, and can also be programmed for use with PowerPoint. The Keyspan Digital Media Remote uses an infrared transmitter with a full set of VCR-like buttons and a receiver that attaches to a USB port.

Surge Protector and Power Strip

For some reason, even the most business-friendly hotels in the world still have not done the math: Almost invariably, when I turn up with a laptop, a cell phone, a digital camera battery charge, a PDA, and a portable MP3 player I find no more than one or two available electrical outlets. (It's even worse if you travel to a country that uses a different electrical voltage and plug design than those we have at home in the United States and Canada. And worse still on most cruise ships.)

Most laptops and many other modern electronic devices are able to switch down from 240 volts to 120 or 115 volts, but you need to bring the proper plug adapter. Or you can purchase a voltage converter that will step down the power to its more familiar level. But that's not what I'm talking about. In most circumstances I'm more concerned with finding enough standard electrical outlets to do my work in the hotel room and recharge my devices overnight.

And so I bring along a small power strip that expands a single standard electrical outlet into four. It also includes a power surge protector, which is a great thing to have anywhere, but especially on cruise ships or in foreign countries where the power may not be as regular as you'll find at home.

From time to time the security guards at an airport X-ray machine get a bit exorcised when they see the outline of a power strip; I've got to admit it does look a bit threatening. For that reason, and because this is a device that I usually don't need until I am unpacking at the end of the day, my power strip usually travels in my suitcase and not my computer bag.

Bluetooth Adapter

It's so small, why not? A Bluetooth adapter adds one more avenue of communication to a laptop that already features WiFi, Ethernet, infrared, and a modem. Bluetooth devices are not yet even close to the near-ubiquity of WiFi, but I'm beginning to see more and more cell phones and PDAs offering this means of short- to mid-range radio communication. Plugging the tiny Keyspan USB Bluetooth Adapter into my laptop allows me to quickly synchronize my cell phone's address book with the one on my PDA, which is also stored on my laptop.

A Package of CD-Rs

My modern laptop includes a combination CD/CD-R/DVD device. As you've already explored in this book, this means there are four things this particular unit can do:

✔ Play music from a standard audio CD.

✔ Hold as much as 700MB of data from my desktop machine without demanding that much space on the hard drive within my laptop.

✔ Display a few hours of the latest Hollywood blockbuster or clinker, sometimes a reasonable use of my battery (or a connection to an airliner power source) on a long flight at the end of the day.

✔ Serve as a removable backup storage medium while I am on the road.

It's that last facility that gives me the most comfort when I am thousands of miles away from home and I have created some spectacular words of wisdom for my next book or some irreplaceable digital photos that will one day hang on the wall of my office to remind me of places I've been.

Fact is that laptops can be stolen, can fall to the floor, or be fried by an unfriendly power surge. But if I've followed my own time-polished rules I will have made a backup of any new data on my machine at least every other day; if it's been an especially busy trip, I make a backup to a CD-R every night.

And then I store the CD-Rs in a place other than my computer bag. You figured that one out, right? What use is it to have backups in the same bag that might be stolen for the laptop itself. I keep the backups in a carry-on bag, or in an inside pocket of my jacket, or even put them in the mail and send them back home to await my arrival.

With the price of a CD-R somewhere around 25 cents there's no excuse not to practice what I preach. Think of it as the cheapest data insurance policy you could possibly find.

A Set of Emergency Disks

Well okay, this does not quite fall under the category of *favorite* things, but it sure does qualify as an essential. My computer kit bag goes nowhere without a thin plastic carrier that contains two CD-Rs created in my office *and fully tested on my laptop.*

Here are my two CDs:

✔ A legal backup copy of the Windows XP installation disk, labeled with the Product Key. I use Disk Copier, which is part of Roxio Easy Media Creator, to make the equivalent of a photocopy of a program disk including any hidden and system files. Note that I am using this disk for these purposes only: in case I need to boot my laptop from the CD because of a problem with the boot tracks of my hard drive, or in case I need to install a Microsoft utility that is on the disk but not on the hard drive. (I keep the original disk on the bookshelf in my office as a backup to my backup.)

✔ My personal emergency kit, storing files that I'd like to have with me for convenience but are not worthy of occupying permanent space on my hard drive. These include PDF files of instruction manuals for my laptop, my digital camera, and other devices I carry; Adobe Acrobat Reader is already installed on my laptop. Also on the disk is a folder of drivers for various add-ons to my machine, including a connection between the laptop and my cell phone and the latest download of updates to my professional DSLR camera.

To those emergency disks I sometimes add a third:

✔ A copy of all of the files of whatever major project I am currently working on, plus a copy of the data file from Palm Desktop, which holds my working calendar (going back several years and forward as far as I have entered data) and my list of contacts. Although I've copied each of these sets of files onto the laptop as the final step before I close my computer kit bag, I also bring the electronic equivalent of a "hard copy" of the material with me in case of a true catastrophe — the loss or theft of my laptop or its failure — that forces me to do my work on a borrowed (or new) machine.

When you live as much of your life on the road and do as much of your work on a laptop as I do, it's perfectly reasonable to operate in a combined belt-and-suspenders mode. Neither rain, nor snow, nor any other contingency is going to keep me from my appointed rounds if I can possibly help it.

Index

• E •

• F •

• T •

• X •

• Y •

• Z •